D0915435

THE ECONOMICS
OF
IMPERFECT COMPETITION

THE ECONOMICS

OF

IMPERFECT COMPETITION

JOAN ROBINSON

SECOND EDITION

ST. MARTIN'S PRESS

First Edition 1933
Reprinted 1934, 1936, 1938, 1942, 1945, 1946, 1948
1950, 1954, 1959
Second Edition 1969
Reprinted 1972, 1976

Published by
THE MACMILLAN PRESS LTD
London and Basingstoke
Associated companies in New York Dublin
Melbourne Johannesburg and Madras

SBN 333 08362 8 (hardcover)
SBN 333 10289 4 (paperback)

Printed in Great Britain by
LEWIS REPRINTS LTD
member of Brown Knight & Truscott Group
London and Tonbridge

PREFACE TO THE SECOND EDITION

IMPERFECT COMPETITION, THEN AND NOW

MARSHALL'S view of competition was not very precise. An unforeseen rise in the demand for a particular commodity would lead to a rise of output, higher marginal cost being accompanied by a higher price. When demand was low, "fear of spoiling the market" would prevent prices from being cut. As time goes by, firms grow in size and enjoy economies of scale. Economies internal to the firm reduce average cost of production (which includes profits at the normal rate on the capital invested) and the benefit is passed on to the public in lower prices. To meet the objection that the firm which first begins to grow can undersell the rest and gradually establish a monopoly, Marshall fell back on the analogy of trees in the forest. A firm is identified with a family. The sons of the founder are enervated by being brought up in the comfort that his money provides so that the expansion of the firm that he began will peter out. It is true that a joint-stock company is not bound to the life of a family but, says Marshall, joint-stock companies stagnate.[1]

Pigou transformed all this into a neat, logical system. Perfect competition means that the individual producer can sell as much or as little as he likes at the ruling price. Each firm continuously produces the amount of output of which the marginal cost is equal to price. There are internal economies of scale only up to a certain size, at which average cost (including a normal profit) is at a minimum. When demand is such as to call forth output beyond this size from a particular firm, marginal cost, and therefore price, exceeds average cost. Super-normal profits call in fresh competition which brings down the market price and pushes back the output of the firm. When price is below average cost, some firms are driven out of business, and those

---

[1] *Principles of Economics* (seventh edition), p. 316.

that remain expand. Thus the optimum size of firm, with minimum average cost, is always tending to be established.

Here we were, in 1930, in a deep slump, and this is what we were being asked to believe.

The first point in Pigou's scheme was patently absurd. Under perfect competition, any plant that was working at all must be working up to capacity. (Some, for which prime cost exceeded price, might be put out of operation altogether.) Imperfect competition came in to explain the fact, in the world around us, that more or less all plants were working part time.

The notion that every firm is facing a falling demand curve for its own product and that profits are maximised at the output for which marginal revenue is equal to marginal cost, provided an explanation for a situation in which firms could work their plants at less than full capacity and still earn a profit.

This notion was already in the air, but ideas at that time were in a very primitive state. I remember the moment when it was an exciting discovery (made by R. F. Kahn) that where two average curves are tangential, the corresponding marginal curves cut at the same abscissa. The apparatus which we worked out took on a kind of fascination for its own sake (though by modern standards it is childishly simple) and I set about to apply it to the rest of Pigou's system. This reached its culmination in the analysis of price discrimination. I think that this is still useful and that it is worthwhile to master the apparatus for its sake. But to apply the analysis to the so-called theory of the firm, I had to make a number of limitations and simplifications which led the argument astray.

The first was a shameless fudge. I postulated that a firm could find out the conditions of demand for its product by trial and error—that is, I treated the conditions of demand as being unchanged for an indefinitely long period and I assumed that experiments with prices would leave no traces in market conditions. The whole analysis, which in reality consists of comparisons of static equilibrium positions, is dressed up to appear to represent a process going on through time.

To put the argument into a dynamic setting, it is necessary to distinguish between the short-period aspect of competition, which is concerned with price policy and the utilisation of productive capacity already in existence, and the long-period aspect, which is concerned with investment.

In manufacturing industry, the producer sets a price and sells as much as the market will take; he therefore has to have a price policy. (Marshall, with his usual instinctive cunning, took the example of a commodity which was sent to market and sold for what it would fetch; in his story of the supply and demand for fish he had no need to bring price policy into the argument.) A perfectly competitive price policy would be continuously to follow the variations of demand so as always to be selling full capacity output (except when price fell below prime cost). This is clearly absurd. By this standard, competition is never perfect. Prices are formed by setting a gross margin, in terms of a percentage on prime costs, to cover overheads, amortisation and net profit. To calculate the appropriate margin, it is necessary to estimate the expected sales from given plant and to take a view of what net profit may be hoped for. In the controversies which arose over imperfect competition, a policy of this kind was described as "full-cost pricing" but that is even more misleading than the formulation in terms of marginal revenue; the producer may know his total overhead costs for a period, but he cannot know what his average cost is going to be until he knows his rate of sales. Moreover the net profit that he hopes to make cannot be derived from costs alone, without any consideration of "what the traffic will bear".

It is true enough that businessmen cannot be expected to draw my curves for themselves; when we know the level of gross margins, it is pointless to try to deduce from it the value of $e/(e-1)$ (e being the producer's subjective estimate of the elasticity of demand for his output) but it is perfectly sensible to say that the "degree of monopoly" is higher,[1] or price policy less competitive, when the producer, in setting his margin, calculates upon a lower level of utilisation of plant and upon a higher rate of profit on capital.

The concept of perfect competition is totally inapplicable to manufacturing industry (it is doubtful whether nowadays it applies even to fish). The prices of manufactures in the nature

---

[1] Kalecki has been criticised for taking the ratio of margins to prime costs as the definition of the degree of monopoly instead of as a symptom of it. See *The Theory of Economic Fluctuations*, Section 1.

of the case are administered prices. With short-period fluctuations in demand, prices vary very little as long as money costs are constant. Output rises and falls with demand, and (as the overhead per unit of output falls and rises) the share of net profit rises and falls still more. Even in a seller's market when output is up to the limit set by capacity, firms usually prefer to lengthen delivery dates or ration customers, rather than to choke off demand by raising prices today for fear that it might be permanently lost. Movements of demand affect profits strongly, but prices hardly at all.

As for the question of what determines the rate of profit on capital, neither my critics nor my supporters had anything much to say about it.

The Keynesian theory of prices, that money-wage rates are the main determinant of prime costs and that the general level of prices moves more or less proportionately to the level of wage rates, has been made familiar by painful experience. This is sometimes connected with imperfect competition. It is argued that producers can "pass on to the consumer" a rise of costs because they are not competitive; but obviously if there were such a thing as perfect competition, with prices equal to marginal costs, the movement would be automatic. A rise in money-wage rates would shift all the marginal costs curves proportionately upwards. With imperfect competition there is an element of judgement in price policy. Prices move sometimes more, and sometimes less, than in proportion to prime costs according to the general atmosphere of the times.

It was Michal Kalecki rather than I who brought imperfect competition into touch with the theory of employment. He showed that a rise in profit margins, such as may come about by defensive monopolistic agreements in a slump, reduces real wages and so tends to increase unemployment. He also established the very striking proposition that a rise in margins increases the share of profit in the value of output only by reducing the share of wages. The total of profit over a period of time is not likely to be increased by it. Overall expenditure is not raised immediately, so that the main effect of raising prices is to sell less goods for more or less the same total receipts.[1]

---

[1] *Op. cit.*, Section 3.

All this is concerned with the short-period aspect of competition. To behave monopolistically in the long-period sense, means to pursue a cautious investment policy, restraining the growth of capacity relatively to demand. A monopolistic investment policy will generally be associated with a monopolistic price policy, but the converse is by no means generally true. This explains—what for the old theory was a paradox—that the firms which make the most monopolistic profits are often those which grow fastest. Galbraith points out that, in the United States, growth and competition are not generally associated. There are some competitive industries which conform to the orthodox ideal:

> Yet almost no one would select them as a showpiece of American industrial achievement. The showpieces are, with rare exceptions, the industries which are dominated by a handful of large firms. The foreign visitor, brought to the United States by the Economic Co-operation Administration, visits the same firms as do attorneys of the Department of Justice in their search for monopoly.[1]

Marshall's contradiction between internal economies and competition cannot be resolved by Pigou's optimum size of firm, still less by the prediction that joint-stock companies will fail to grow. Rather it is resolved by recognising that there is no need to resolve it. Competition is always in course of bringing itself to an end. At any moment, in prosperous modern industries, the number of firms is tending to fall and competition is becoming more oligopolistic. My old-fashioned comparison between monopoly and competition may still have some application to old-fashioned restrictive rings but it cannot comprehend the great octopuses of modern industry.

Besides the static approach, there were some other serious limitations on my argument. I did not attempt to tackle duopoly and oligopoly and, concentrating on price as the vehicle for competition, I said very little about non-price competition, such as artificial product-differentiation, advertising and sales promotion, which in fact accounts for the greatest part of the wastefulness of imperfect markets. (The twin to my book, Chamberlin's *Monopolistic Competition*, opened up these subjects, but in the subsequent controversies Chamberlin appeared

---

[1] J. K. Galbraith, *American Capitalism*, p. 96.

to be more concerned to defend the market system than to expose its drawbacks.)

To get my simple analysis on to its feet, I had to assume that each firm was selling a single commodity. This has the effect of making the treatment of "industries" misleading. When I revisited Imperfect Competition after twenty years I pointed this out.[1]

> The assumption that each firm produces a single commodity conceals the distinction between the output of an *industry*—that is, a group of firms engaged in production of commodities alike in their methods of manufacture, and the supply to a *market*—that is, the demand for a group of commodities which are close substitutes for each other. In ordinary language when we speak of the cotton industry, the iron-founding industry, the boot-and-shoe industry (leather) we are thinking of a group of firms engaged in a certain type of production, governed by the kinds of object produced and the materials of which they are made. Sometimes a single firm produces very diverse objects which are complements to each other, and therefore sold together (pens and blotting-paper, low-power electric motors and artificial teeth) and sometimes quite unrelated objects are bound together in production because they are bound together in selling by conventional shopping habits (hair-brushes and medicines). Many of the products of a single industry are extremely remote substitutes for each other. There is no overlap, for instance, between the markets for men's and children's shoes or for drain-pipes and stoves. On the other hand, products of totally different industries may be quite close substitutes—rubber and leather shoes; asbestos and cast-iron drain-pipes.
>
> The concept of an industry, though amorphous and impossible to demarcate sharply at the edges, is of importance for the theory of competition. It represents the area within which a firm finds it relatively easy to expand as it grows. There are often certain basic processes required for the production of the most diverse commodities (tennis balls, motor tyres, and mattresses) and economies in the utilization of by-products under one roof. The know-how and trade connections established for one range of products make it easier to add different commodities of the same technical nature to a firm's output than it is to add mutually substitutable commodities made of different materials, or made or marketed by radically different methods. Moreover, the members of an industry

---

[1] *Economic Journal*, September 1953, and *Collected Economic Papers*, vol. i.

have common interests and a common language, and feel a kind of patriotism which links them together, even when they are in competition with each other. It is much easier to organize control over one industry serving many markets than one market served by the products of several industries.

The degree of concentration in an industry, measured by the proportion of its output produced by, say, the three largest firms, or the degree of monopoly in the sense of the closeness of the organization binding the firms, may have little relation to the degree of monopoly in the markets which it serves, in the sense of power to control prices. An unconcentrated and unorganized industry may contain a number of very strong small monopolies over particular commodities, while another, highly concentrated or tightly organized, may be meeting competition in some or all of its markets from the products of rival industries which are substitutes for its own.

Nowadays the definition of an industry is breaking down in another way. More and more, the great firms have a foot not only in many markets but in many industries, in several continents, the connections between their various activities being neither in know-how nor in marketing but merely in financial power.

Since this book has long been used as a text for students, some of its weaknesses have been frozen into orthodox teaching but its strong points, I think, have had very little influence. The strong points are negative. They should have cleared away a lot of rubbish. Of course, nothing can be proved about the nature of reality by a purely *a priori* argument, but the analysis opened up some lines of thought which are still important, and still neglected, today.

First of all, by showing that perfect competition cannot obtain in manufacturing industry, it undermines the complex of ideas erected on the slogan of "price equals marginal cost". In the short period, prices equal to marginal cost would mean that small variations in demand produce violent changes in prices, as can be seen where competition reigns, that is, in the markets for primary products. What it would mean in the long period, with "normal profits", orthodox text-books have never made clear.

Another moral that the argument suggests is that consumer's

sovereignty can never be established as long as the initiative lies with the producer. For the general run of consumer goods, the buyer is necessarily an amateur while the seller is a professional. To make industry genuinely serve the needs of the public, as it is supposed to do in the text-books, would require a monopsony of consumers, equipped with their own experts. Some slight efforts are being made nowadays to protect the consumer interest, but they cannot make much head against the power of advertisement. The great chain-stores exercise some monopsonistic influence in imposing a kind of synthetic perfect market on small-scale producers, but they cannot offer a counterweight to the great oligopolists. Besides, though they serve the consumer interest against the producer, they also have some interests of their own.

Finally, what for me was the main point, I succeeded in proving within the framework of the orthodox theory, that it is not true that wages are normally equal to the value of the marginal product of labour.

All this had no effect. Perfect competition, supply and demand, consumer's sovereignty and marginal products still reign supreme in orthodox teaching. Let us hope that a new generation of students, after forty years, will find in this book what I intended to mean by it.

JOAN ROBINSON

CAMBRIDGE
January 1969

FOREWORD

BESIDES a restatement of current ideas on economic theory, this book contains some matter which I believe to be new. Of not all the new ideas, however, can I definitely say that "this is my own invention". In particular I have had the constant assistance of Mr. R. F. Kahn. The whole technical apparatus was built up with his aid, and many of the major problems— notably the problems of Price Discrimination and of Exploitation—were solved as much by him as by me. He has also contributed a number of mathematical proofs which I should have been incapable of finding for myself. In general I have endeavoured to build on the foundations laid by Marshall and by Professor Pigou. This is a debt which all economists owe, and which may be taken for granted. I have for the most part referred to their works only where I believe that I have detected them in errors of detail.

Of more recent work, my chief debt is to Mr. Piero Sraffa's article in the *Economic Journal* of December 1926, to Mr. E. A. G. Robinson's *Structure of Competitive Industry*, and to Mr. G. F. Shove's articles in the *Economic Journal* of June 1928 and March 1930. Mr. Sraffa's article must be regarded as the fount from which my work flows, for the chief aim of this book is to attempt to carry out his pregnant suggestion that the whole theory of value should be treated in terms of monopoly analysis. Mr. Robinson's work on the optimum size of firms is the foundation of my treatment of competitive equilibrium, and plays an important part in the Appendix on Increasing and Diminishing Returns. Mr. Shove's articles form the basis of my treatment of rent and of the four cost curves. But a reader who is

xiii

acquainted only with those articles would very much underestimate my debt to him, for his teaching in Cambridge for
many years past has influenced directly and indirectly the
whole approach to many problems of economic analysis.   The
more specific points that I have derived from Mr. Shove are
acknowledged as they occur, but my indebtedness to him must
not be regarded as being confined to those points.

A moment has been reached in the development of economic
theory when certain definite problems require to be solved, and
many writers are at work upon them independently. There are
many occasions, therefore, when several explorers are surprised,
and somewhat pained, on meeting each other at the Pole. Of
such an occasion the history of the "marginal revenue curve"
presents a striking example. This piece of apparatus plays a
great part in my work, and my book arose out of the attempt
to apply it to various problems, but I was not myself one of the
many explorers who arrived in rapid succession at this particular
Pole. I first learnt of it from Mr. C. H. P. Gifford, of Magdalene
College, who was then reading for the Economics Tripos.
Shortly afterwards Mr. P. A. Sloan, of Clare College, showed
me an unpublished essay in which it occurred. Next it was published by Mr. R. F. Harrod in the *Economic Journal* of June
1930, in an article which must have been written almost
simultaneously with Mr. Sloan's paper. In a later article
(*Economic Journal*, December 1931) Mr. Harrod set out in an
analytical form some of the relations between marginal and
average curves which I had discovered by geometry. At this
Pole I can claim to have arrived by a route of my own, but his
analytical formulation of the fundamental relation between
average and marginal value has been of very great service to
me since it appeared. Meanwhile a number of explorers were
added to the rapidly growing crowd at the Marginal Revenue
Pole. Professor T. O. Yntema (who also anticipated Mr. Harrod's
formula for the relation of average to marginal value) had,

unknown to me, arrived there long before (*Journal of Political Economy*, December 1928). Dr. E. Schneider, Dr. H. v. Stackelberg, and Professor Mehta, amongst many others, appear to have discovered it independently. Even the naming of this concept presented a minor coincidence. I was dissatisfied with Mr. Gifford's and Mr. Harrod's titles for it, and it was christened for me by Mr. Robinson as "marginal revenue" some time before Professor Viner published an article (in the *Zeitschrift für Nationalökonomie*, September 1931) in which he refers to it by the same name.

The conception of "elasticity of substitution" provides another example of this kind of coincidence, for Mr. J. R. Hicks published his formulation of it in his *Theory of Wages* some time after I had first made use of it. When Mr. Hicks's book appeared my work on the analysis of wages was almost completed, but a study of one of his results led me to remove an error from my argument. In this part of the field my chief debt is to Mr. D. H. Robertson's illuminating article on "Wage Grumbles" (*Economic Fragments*).

A number of writers have recently been evolving methods for dealing with monopoly problems which are at some points similar to my own. Dr. Schneider and Dr. v. Stackelberg have published one or two items which occur in my tool-box. But in my opinion their work is marred by the use of unnecessarily complicated mathematical analysis where simple geometrical methods would serve. I am, however, indebted to Dr. Zeuthen's book on *Problems of Monopoly*. He makes use only of Marshall's "areas" technique, but I discovered at least one important proposition in the course of restating some of his results in "marginal" terms. Professor Chamberlin's *Theory of Monopolistic Competition* provides a plentiful crop of coincidences, but it appeared too late for me to notice them in detail.

There are probably other explorers in the field with whose progress I am unacquainted. If my results are anywhere found to be the same as those of some other writer to whom no reference is made, it must be understood either that my fellow-explorer is unknown to me, or that his work was published when mine was already completed. But wherever possible I have mentioned the names of the explorers whom I found already at the Pole when I arrived there.

Mr. C. W. Guillebaud was kind enough to read my manuscript and made many helpful suggestions. Finally, in addition to his constructive suggestions, I have had the benefit of Mr. Kahn's criticism at every stage of the work from its inception. For this the reader, as well as myself, must be grateful to him, for he has weeded innumerable errors from my pages.

Some passages in Chapter 7 are taken (with a few alterations) from an article in the *Economic Journal*, December 1932, and are here used with the permission of the Editor.

JOAN ROBINSON

CAMBRIDGE
October 1932

CONTENTS

BOOK IV

THE COMPARISON OF MONOPOLY AND COMPETITIVE OUTPUT

BOOK V

PRICE DISCRIMINATION

BOOK VI

MONOPSONY

CHAPTER 17

BOOK VII

THE DEMAND FOR A FACTOR OF PRODUCTION

CHAPTER 20

BOOK VIII

THE COMPARISON OF MONOPOLY AND COMPETITIVE DEMAND FOR LABOUR

CHAPTER 23

BOOK IX

EXPLOITATION

CHAPTER 25

BOOK X

A WORLD OF MONOPOLIES

CHAPTER 27

APPENDIX

INTRODUCTION

"AMONG persons interested in economic analysis, there are tool-makers and tool-users."[1] This book is presented to the analytical economist as a box of tools. It is an essay in the technique of economic analysis, and can make only an indirect contribution to our knowledge of the actual world. It is only by using their tools upon observed facts that economists can build up that working model of the actual world which it is their aim to construct. To tinker with the tool-box is merely a preliminary to the main attack, and, to those who are in haste for results, it may appear an idle occupation far inferior to the fruitful work of the tool-users. The gap between the tool-makers and the tool-users is a distressingly wide one, and no economist can fail to have sympathy with the impatience of the politician, the business man, and the statistical investigator, who complain of the extremely poor, arid, or even misleading information with which the analytical economists provide him. If a government is anxious to know whether in an actual case it should allow a railway the right to charge discriminating prices, it is poor comfort to be told that it will depend upon the relative concavities of the demand curves for transport of various types of goods whether the railway will carry a greater number of tons if it is allowed to discriminate than if it is not. If a rationalisation scheme is being put through, and the public are anxious to know whether the concentration of output upon a few firms is likely to raise prices, it will not help them much to be told that if the marginal cost curves are parallel to the demand curves for the products of the individual firms the price will remain unchanged. It is natural enough for the practical man to complain that he asks for bread and the economist gives him a stone. But the answer of the analytical economist to such complaints should

---

[1] Pigou, "The Function of Economic Analysis", Sidney Ball Lecture, 1929, reprinted in *Economic Essays and Addresses*, p. 3.

not be to fling away his tools and plunge into the tangled problems of the real world, armed only with his naked hands. It should be rather to set about to elaborate his analysis so much that it can begin to be useful. A simple analysis can only be made upon simple assumptions, and the more complicated the analysis, the more complicated the assumptions upon which it will work, and the nearer the assumptions can be to the complicated conditions of the real world. The practical man must be asked to have patience, and meanwhile the economist must perfect his tools in the hope of being able sooner or later to meet the practical man's requirements.

Such an ideal is still far distant, and meanwhile the best that the economist can do is to use what implements he has with the greatest care and precision, and when he does give an answer to some general question to take the utmost pains to make clear what assumptions about the nature of the problem are implicit in his answer. If those assumptions are near enough to the actual conditions to make the answer serviceable the practical man can accept it, but if the assumptions are very abstract the economist will only bring the practical man into confusion and himself into disrepute by allowing him to suppose that the question which is being answered is the same as the question which is being asked.

But the fact that economists often fail to state their assumptions with the necessary precision must not be attributed to duplicity, but to a mistaken modesty. The analytical economist (although his manners usually conceal the fact) is conscious, in the presence of the practical man, of an agonising sense of shame. And when he tries to work on some fresh problem, and sets about to write out the assumptions which are necessary to make it soluble, he cannot help imagining what the mocking comments of the practical man would be if his eye happened to fall on that list of assumptions. He is subject then to a strong temptation either to include in his list assumptions which bring the problem close to the real problems, but which make it quite insoluble by the technique at his command, or to confine the problem within the limits which make it soluble but to hide the assumptions which bound it (if he is too honest to omit them altogether) in a dusty corner of the footnotes where he hopes that no one will notice them.

Such conduct, though it springs from an admirable humility, is a scandalous breach of faith with the practical man. It would be far better that the economist should take a sardonic pleasure in shocking the practical man by the brutal frankness with which he sets out his assumptions—consoling himself for the disgust that this conduct will inspire by his own conviction, which he cannot expect the practical man to share, that he is approaching the problem that has been set to him by the only route along which there is even a chance of finding the answer.

My book attempts to live up to this standard, and if anywhere a necessary assumption is missing from the list, it must be taken to show that I have fallen into the third trap which besets the path of the economist: the danger that he does not himself quite know what his own assumptions are.

In the older text-books it was customary to set out upon the analysis of value from the point of view of perfect competition. The whole scheme appeared almost homogeneous and it had some aesthetic charm. But somewhere, in an isolated chapter, the analysis of monopoly had to be introduced. This presented a hard, indigestible lump which the competitive analysis could never swallow. To quote Mr. Sraffa's comment:[1] "Of course, when we are supplied with theories in respect to the two extreme cases of monopoly and competition as part of the equipment required in order to undertake the study of the actual conditions in the different industries, we are warned that these generally do not fit exactly one or other of the categories, but will be found scattered along the intermediate zone, and that the nature of an industry will approximate more closely to the monopolist or the competitive system according to its particular circumstances". But the books never contained any very clear guidance as to how these intermediate cases should be treated; as a picture of the real world the theory was unconvincing, and as a pure analytical construction it had a somewhat uncomfortable air.

Moreover, the relations between the real world and the competitive analysis of value were marred by frequent misunderstandings. The economists, misled by the logical priority of perfect competition in their scheme, were somehow trapped into

[1] "The Laws of Returns under Competitive Conditions", *Economic Journal*, December 1926, p. 542.

thinking that it must be of equal importance in the real world. When they found in the real world some phenomenon, such as "economies internal to the firm", which is inconsistent with the assumptions of perfect competition, they were inclined to look for some complicated explanation of it, before the simple explanation occurred to them that the real world did not fulfil the assumptions of perfect competition. Or they were tempted to introduce into the theoretical scheme elements which, at a superficial glance, appeared to account for the phenomena of the real world, but which completely destroyed the logical self-consistency of the theoretical scheme.

It was at such a moment of confusion that Mr. Sraffa declared: "It is necessary, therefore, to abandon the path of free competition and turn in the opposite direction, namely, towards monopoly".[1]

Now no sooner had Mr. Sraffa released the analysis of monopoly from its uncomfortable pen in a chapter in the middle of the book than it immediately swallowed up the competitive analysis without the smallest effort. The whole scheme of analysis, composed of just the same elements as before, could now be arranged in a perfectly uniform manner, with no awkward cleavage in the middle of the book. Two simple examples will show this process at work.

First consider the problem of defining a monopoly. It was tempting, under the old scheme, to arrange actual cases in a series of which pure monopoly would be the limit at one end and pure competition at the other, but a definition of pure monopoly which would correspond to the definition of pure competition was extremely hard to find. At first sight it seems easy enough to say that competition exists when the demand for a commodity in a certain market is met by a number of producers, and that monopoly exists when it is met by only one. But what is a commodity? Must we group together as a single commodity all articles which compete against each other to satisfy a single demand? In that case, since every article must have some rivals, and since in the last resort every article represents a use of money which is rival to every other, we should be compelled to say that no such thing as complete monopoly exists at all. Or must we define as a single commodity only a

---

[1] *Loc. cit.*

group of articles which is perfectly homogeneous? Then the slightest degree of difference, from the point of view of their customers, between rival producers even of one sufficiently homogeneous commodity, must be taken as a sign that we are dealing not with one commodity but with several. For if the individual buyer has any reason to prefer one producer to another, the articles which they sell are not perfectly interchangeable from the point of view of the buyer, and we are reduced to regarding the output of each producer as a separate commodity. Thus any attempt at a logical definition of a monopolist drives either monopoly or competition quite out of the field. It is easy enough to find the limiting case at the competitive end of the scale. The limiting case occurs when the demand for the product of an individual producer is perfectly elastic. But what is the limiting case at the other end? The case in which the demand for the product of the individual is the same as the total demand for the commodity? Then we are back at the original problem of how to define a commodity. We know what we mean by "selling in a perfect market", but what is a perfectly imperfect market?

Now as soon as we abandon the attempt to confine monopoly in a pen by itself the whole of this difficulty disappears. Every individual producer has the monopoly of his own output—that is sufficiently obvious—and if a large number of them are selling in a perfect market the state of affairs exists which we are accustomed to describe as perfect competition. We have only to take the word monopoly in its literal sense, a single seller, and the analysis of monopoly immediately swallows up the analysis of competition.

The reader may object that there is clearly some sense in which Messrs. Coats have got a monopoly of sewing cotton, and in which a Bedfordshire market gardener has not got a monopoly of brussels-sprouts. But this objection is easily answered. All that "monopoly" means, in this old-fashioned sense, is that the output of the individual producer happens to be bounded on all sides by a marked gap in the chain of substitutes. Such a gap in nature provides us with a rough-and-ready definition of a single commodity—sewing cotton or brussels-sprouts—which is congenial to common sense and causes no trouble. When a single producer controls the whole output of such a commodity the plain man's notion of a monopolist and the logical definition of a monopolist as a single seller coincide, and the difficulty disappears.

A second example of the manner in which monopoly analysis engulfs competitive analysis can be illustrated from the technique of analysis itself. When Mr. Sraffa declared that the time had come to re-write the theory of value, starting from the conception of the firm as a monopolist, he suggested that the familiar tool, "maximum monopoly net revenue", was ready to hand and that the job could begin at once. But that tool is at best a clumsy one and is inappropriate to many of the operations which are required of it. In its place the "marginal" technique must be borrowed from the competitive chapters of the old textbooks, and adapted to new purposes.

Whilst many pieces of technical apparatus have no intrinsic merit, and are used merely for convenience, the use of marginal curves for the analysis of monopoly output contains within itself the heart of the whole matter. The single assumption which it is necessary to make in order to set that piece of apparatus at work is the assumption that the individual firm will always arrange its affairs in such a way as to make the largest profits that can be made in the particular situation in which it finds itself. Now it is this assumption that makes the analysis of value possible. If individuals act in an erratic way only statistical methods will serve to discover the laws of economics, and if individuals act in a predictable way, but from a large number of complicated motives, the economist must resign his task to the psychologist. It is the assumption that any individual, in his economic life, will never undertake an action that adds more to his losses than to his gains, and will always undertake an action which adds more to his gains than to his losses, which makes the analysis of value possible. And it is this assumption that underlies the device of drawing marginal curves. With bricks of this one simple pattern the whole structure of analysis is built up.

The main theme of this book is the analysis of value. It is not easy to explain what the analysis of value is, without making it appear extremely mysterious and extremely foolish. The point may be put like this: You see two men, one of whom is giving a banana to the other, and is taking a penny from him. You ask, How is it that a banana costs a penny rather than any other

sum? The most obvious line of attack on this question is to break
it up into two fresh questions: How does it happen that the one
man will take a penny for a banana? and: How does it happen
that the other man will give a penny for a banana? In short, the
natural thing is to divide up the problem under two heads:
Supply and Demand.

Under the first head the question is: How does it come about
that an individual seller sells his commodity for the price at
which he does sell it, rather than any other price? Now the price
at which he sells is determined on the one side by what he can
get for it, and on the other side by what it costs him to make it.
Here we come once more upon the dichotomy between demand
and supply. But in this context the conditions of demand are
regarded objectively, from the point of view of the seller, and
form part of the general circumstances which determine what
he will decide to do. Next it is obvious that when a number of
sellers each acting upon sensible and predictable motives, but
each acting independently, are trying to sell the same commodity, their decisions may set up some complicated interactions which must be carefully examined. And when this has
been done the analysis of value has not very much more to say
about Supply.

Then, turning to the second heading under the main question,
the analyst examines price from the point of view of the individual buyer. In this context the conditions of supply are looked
at objectively, as part of the general circumstances which will
determine what the buyer decides to do. And, after that, there
is not much more to be said about Demand. Perhaps this
account of the process of the analysis of value removes the
mystery only too thoroughly, but now it appears more foolish
than ever. "I thought that at least you were going to tell me",
the reader protests, "why, in some fundamental sense, a banana
costs a penny. All you have done is to provide a complicated
filing system for a few perfectly obvious ideas with which I have
always been quite familiar." But this filing system is an essential part of the equipment of the analytical economist, whose
ultimate aim is to find answers to the practical questions presented to him by the real world, and it is in the hope of assisting
him in his task that I have fitted out my tool-box.

This book divides into two parts: Monopoly, the principles of selling; and Monopsony, the principles of buying. But this dichotomy between supply and demand is not quite the same as the dichotomy in the problem of the banana. As soon as the economist steps over to the second half of that problem, and asks, How does it come about that the buyer buys at this price? he enters a region in which he has very little to say. It is a region bristling with important questions, but they are questions in psychology rather than questions in economics. But if the commodity is not required, like a banana, for its own sake, but is required in order to help the buyer to earn money, then the economist comes into his own again. Consequently, the part of this book which deals with buying is mainly devoted to the principles of buying, not commodities, but productive instruments and services. In short, it gives the application of the analysis of value to the problem of the prices of particular factors of production.

The scheme of this book may be tabulated as follows:

Book I. THE TECHNIQUE: Chapter 1, The Assumptions; Chapter 2, The Geometry.

In the first of these two chapters certain necessary definitions are given, and the assumptions which establish the level of abstraction at which our discussion must be carried on are set out in all their naked unreality. In the second, the elements of the technique are displayed.

Book II. MONOPOLY EQUILIBRIUM: Chapter 3, Monopoly Equilibrium; Chapter 4, Changes in Demand; Chapter 5, Changes in Cost.

These chapters provide the analysis of the simple problem of what determines the price charged by a single producer for his commodity, given the producer and given the conditions of demand and of cost.

Book III. COMPETITIVE EQUILIBRIUM: Chapter 6, The Supply Curve; Chapter 7, Competitive Equilibrium; Chapter 8, A Digression on Rent; Chapter 9, The Supply Curve under Perfect Competition.

In Chapter 6 the problem of the supply curve of a commodity is considered in the light of the results obtained in the last Book. In Chapter 7 a fresh element is introduced into the problem. The reaction of monopoly profit on the number of producers selling any one commodity is here considered for the first time. The titles of Chapters 7 and 9 were' chosen for their brevity and not for their logic. What these two chapters (with the digression which lies between them) actually describe is the effect upon demand, for the individual seller, of a change in the output of the industry, assuming that there is no effect on his costs; and the effect upon his costs, when the simplest kind of change in his demand is assumed to occur. Thus the two sides of the problem of the effect of a change in the output of an industry upon the price of the commodity produced are each treated separately. By combining them it is possible to analyse the supply curve of a commodity, in any given conditions, at the level of abstraction which is maintained in this book.

BOOK IV. THE COMPARISON OF MONOPOLY AND COMPETITIVE OUTPUT: Chapter 10, A Digression on the Four Cost Curves; Chapter 11, Comparisons of Monopoly and Competitive Output; Chapter 12, Commentary on the Comparisons; Chapter 13, The Control of Monopoly Price; Chapter 14, Objections to the Comparisons.

The subject-matter of Book IV. is an analysis of the effect upon the output of a perfectly competitive industry when the number of independent producers in it is reduced to one, everything else remaining the same. It is described as the comparison between monopoly and competitive output. This title for it is sanctioned by custom, and though it is verbally inconsistent with the conception of monopoly on which this book is based, it would have been pedantic to avoid the use of it.

Chapter 10 is a digression to acquire the technique necessary for the comparisons. In Chapters 11 and 12 the comparisons are made. In Chapter 13 a corollary is drawn from them. In Chapter 14 they are shown to be not only extremely unrealistic, but actually to contain a logical inconsistency. It may appear frivolous to spend so much time upon comparisons which turn out to be idle. But there are two answers to this objection. First, these comparisons occupy a place in every text-book on economics, and they can be more conveniently made by the marginal technique than by the technique usually adopted. Certain errors which often creep into the text-book comparisons can be avoided when this technique is used. But if this were the only answer it might still be considered frivolous to occupy so much space with a mere class-room exercise, however much it may be hallowed by tradition. The second answer is that these comparisons, which are here made only for perfect competition, prepare the way for the analysis of one of the most important practical questions of the present age: the effect of the combination of firms, selling against each other in imperfect competition, into a single unit of control.

BOOK V. PRICE DISCRIMINATION: Chapter 15, Price Discrimination; Chapter 16, The Moral of Price Discrimination.

This Book deals with the case of a single firm selling the same commodity at different prices. It belongs logically to Book II., and stands here in isolation. Chapter 16 contains a lapse from the strict path of analysis, and suggests some reflections on the question of whether price discrimination is desirable or not.

BOOK VI. MONOPSONY: Chapter 17, A Digression on the Buyer; Chapter 18, Monopsony; Chapter 19, Relations of Monopoly and Monopsony to Perfect Competition.

Book VI. introduces the analysis of price from the point of view of an individual buyer. Chapter 17 contains some definitions additional to those in Chapter 1. Chapter 19 is a brief survey of the edifice which has now been built up with two bricks: the individual buyer and the individual seller.

BOOK VII. THE DEMAND FOR A FACTOR OF PRODUCTION: Chapter 20, A Digression on Marginal Productivity; Chapter 21, The Demand for Labour of the Individual Employer; Chapter 22, The Demand for Labour of an Industry.

This Book deals with the demand curve for a factor of production, the factor being called Labour for the sake of convenience. Chapter 20 contains some necessary additional items in the technical equipment. Chapters 21 and 22 analyse the demand

curve for a factor in a manner symmetrical with the analysis,
given in Books II. and III., of the supply curve of a commodity. The analysis is not so fully given, and only the cases
of a single firm, on the one hand, and a perfectly competitive
industry, on the other, are set out.

BOOK VIII. THE COMPARISON OF MONOPOLY AND COMPETITIVE
DEMAND FOR LABOUR: Chapter 23, Comparisons of Mono-
poly and Competitive Demand for Labour; Chapter 24,
Correction of the Comparisons.

These comparisons are in every way symmetrical with the
former comparisons, and are subject to the same objections and
to the same justification. This Book completes the analysis of
buying.

BOOK IX. EXPLOITATION: Chapter 25, Monopolistic Exploitation of Labour; Chapter 26, Monopsonistic Exploitation
of Labour.

In this Book the prices of the factors of production are looked
at, not from the point of view of the employer, but from the
point of view of the owners of the factors. The word Labour in
the titles of the chapters ceases to stand for any factor of production; it stands now for a factor belonging to the general category of factors called labour. In this section perfect competition
ceases to occupy the position of an interesting special case, and
is adopted as a standard of comparison. The temptation to
stray from the path of analysis and to offer reflections of a moral
character is here too strong to be resisted.

BOOK X. A WORLD OF MONOPOLIES: Chapter 27, A World
of Monopolies.

In this Book we are no longer occupied with the Theory of
Value, and have stepped over into the province of the Economics
of Welfare.
    Chapter 27 represents a primitive and tentative attempt to
show how the monopoly analysis of value may be linked up with
the work of Professor Pigou on the Economics of Welfare. We
are here no longer called upon to resist the temptation to make

moral reflections, and although the character of this Book is no less arid than that of the sections which give the analysis of value and the analysis of distribution, its theme is of an ethical nature.

The reader who is resolved to pursue his way through the following pages will quickly find himself in a mountainous and inhospitable territory. I have tried to alleviate his situation by providing a guide-book. At the foot of the first page of certain chapters a note, marked with an asterisk, suggests sections in the chapter which may conveniently be omitted at a first reading and permanently omitted by any reader who is not interested in purely technical questions, and indicates passages which, in the language of the guide-books, are *"nur für Schwindelfreie"*. But the non-mathematical reader must not take fright at these warnings. Such readers are often intimidated by the mathematical apparatus which theoretical economists employ. But I am myself almost entirely innocent of mathematics, and though I called in the assistance of a mathematician to provide certain proofs, they were always required to give precision to some conclusion of which the general drift was discovered by unsophisticated methods. I hope to have demonstrated in this book that theoretical analysis can be carried to a considerable distance by purely economic reasoning, combined with a knowledge of the conception of "elasticity" and of one or two theorems from the book on triangles in a school geometry.

BOOK I
THE TECHNIQUE

CHAPTER 1

1

THE purpose of this book is to demonstrate that the analysis of the output and price of a single commodity can be conducted by a technique based upon the study of individual decisions.

The fundamental assumption is that each individual acts in a sensible manner, in the circumstances in which he finds himself, from the point of view of his own economic interests. A technique which would study the economic effects of neuroses and confused thinking would be considerably more complicated than the technique here set out.

When the fundamental assumption is made, every economic tendency can be analysed by a series of questions. What would a sensible man do in such a case? Thus *a priori* analysis can be made to advance the study of economic phenomena some way towards a position in which the effects of economic tendencies in the real world can be checked by statistical investigations.

The technique is based upon the separation of the elements in the situation which influence the decisions of the individual into two parts, which are assumed to be independent of each other. The two parts of the situation are represented by two curve..

Thus, when we are considering the decision of an individual producer as to how much of his commodity to sell, the conditions of demand, which (abstracting from advertisement and other marketing costs) lie entirely outside his control, are represented by a demand curve; and the costs of producing various outputs are represented by a cost curve. By considering the conditions of demand represented by the demand curve and his own costs of production, the seller can decide what output to place upon the market. He is assumed always to choose the output which will maximise his net receipts. Or, when we are considering the amount of a factor of production employed, the two elements in the situation are, on the one side, the supply curve of the factor of production and, on the other side, the conditions of demand for the commodity, the supply curves of the other factors and the technical conditions of production, all of which are represented in the demand curve for the factor. By considering these two sets of influences the producer can decide how much of each factor to employ. He is assumed always to make his choice in such a way that the cost of producing a given output is at a minimum. Similarly a buyer is conceived to choose the amount of a commodity that he will buy by considering on the one side the advantage to himself of buying it, and on the other the supply price of various amounts of it.

The study of human decisions involves a study of human psychology, but the background of psychology which economics requires is a purely behaviourist psychology. When the technique of economic analysis is sufficiently advanced to analyse the results of neuroses and confused thinking, it will study them only in so far as they produce statistically measurable effects.

The technique set out in this book is a technique for studying equilibrium positions. No reference is made to the effects of the passage of time. Short-period and long-period equilibria are introduced into the argument to illustrate various technical devices, but no study is made of the process of moving from one position of equilibrium to another, and it is with long-period equilibrium that we shall be mainly concerned.

The main topic of this book was said to be the analysis of value. But the Theory of Value (at least among English economists) is merely a traditional misnomer for the analysis of the output of a single commodity, considered separately.[1] It requires the condition that the single commodities considered are, each separately, a negligibly small proportion of total output,

[1] This point is illustrated by Marshall's famous analogy: "We might as reasonably dispute whether it is the upper or the under blade of a pair of scissors that cuts a piece of paper, as whether value is governed by utility or cost of production" (*Principles*, p. 348). But if costs are constant, *price* is determined, as Marshall himself admits, solely by costs. It remains true that *output* is determined by both blades of the scissors, and this is always true except in the unusual cases of perfectly inelastic demand or perfectly inelastic supply, when output is determined solely by demand or solely by supply.

so that any reactions set up by a change in the output of one commodity upon the costs of production of the output of all industry and consequently on the demand for the commodity can legitimately be ignored.

2

Some elementary definitions are set out in this chapter.[1] Others are introduced as the argument proceeds.

A *commodity* is a consumable good, arbitrarily demarcated from other kinds of goods, but which may be regarded for practical purposes as homogeneous within itself.

A *firm* is a concern very similar to the firms of the real world, but which produces only one commodity, and is controlled by a single independent interest.

The controlling interest of a firm is an *entrepreneur*. For long-period problems the entrepreneur is conceived to require a certain reward, sufficient to induce him to continue in business, which is independent of the amount of his output.

An *industry* is any group of firms producing a single commodity. The correspondence of such an industry to the industries of the real world is not perhaps very close. But in some cases, where a commodity in the real world is bounded on all sides by a marked gap between itself and its closest substitutes, the real-world firms producing this real-world commodity will conform to the definition of an industry sufficiently closely to make the discussion of industries in this technical sense of some interest.

A *demand curve* represents a list of prices at which various amounts of a certain commodity will be bought in a market during a given period of time. Such conceptions as the amount of raw cotton bought in the world per year, or the number of motor cars bought in England per month, or the number of silk stockings bought in Berwick Market per day, may be represented by a demand curve.

Similarly a *supply curve* represents the amounts of output of a commodity, during a given period of time, which will be associated with different prices.

---

[1] These definitions are constructed appropriately to the analysis which is to follow. For other purposes different definitions might be required.

C

The demand curve is an objective conception, looked at from the point of view of the sellers of the commodity. The supply curve is an objective conception, looked at from the point of view of the buyers.

A *utility curve* is subjective from the point of view of the buyer. But the concept of utility does not have to be introduced until later in the argument. In the first half of the book we are concerned only with the decisions of sellers. The subjective conditions of demand reveal themselves in the objective demand curve, and the concept of utility has no place in the scheme. In the second half, when we come to consider the decisions of buyers, utility will be defined.

The *elasticity* of a curve is a geometrical conception. It measures the proportional change of the abscissa divided by the proportional change of the ordinate, at any point on the curve, when the changes are small. Thus the *elasticity of demand* at any price or at any output is the proportional change of amount purchased in response to a small change in price, divided by the proportional change of price. Similarly, *elasticity of supply* is the elasticity of a supply curve. It is convenient to adopt the convention of regarding the elasticity of a falling curve as positive, and of a rising curve as negative. A curve of elasticity numerically less than unity is described as *inelastic*, and a curve of elasticity greater than unity as *elastic*. When the elasticity is equal to zero the curve is said to be *perfectly inelastic*, and when the elasticity is equal to infinity the curve is said to be *perfectly elastic*.[1]

Perfect competition prevails when the demand for the output of each producer is perfectly elastic. This entails, first, that the number of sellers is large, so that the output of any one seller is a negligibly small proportion of the total output of the commodity, and second, that buyers are all alike in respect of their choice between rival sellers, so that the market is perfect.

The problem of defining *factors of production* has raised a considerable amount of controversy on a number of points, but the difficulties lie in finding convenient definitions of the total supply of factors. Since this book is only concerned with single commodities considered separately these problems need not delay us.

---

[1] A perfectly inelastic curve will be parallel to the y axis, and a perfectly elastic curve will be parallel to the x axis.

The factors of production are conceived to consist of the services of *productive units*, a man-day of labour, a manager-month, an entrepreneur-year, an acre-year, and so forth. These are the *natural units* of the factors, and may be arbitrarily chosen to correspond as closely as possible to the conditions of the real world. Each unit is only employed in the production of one commodity at a time. The degree of abstraction involved in the conception of such units of factors is considerable, since in the real world a single firm often produces many commodities, so that a single productive unit, for instance a man engaged upon some preparatory process, may be contributing to the production of several commodities at once. Moreover in the real world an individual entrepreneur may have a foot in a large number of industries at the same time, and may begin to produce in a new industry without leaving those in which he is already employed. But in the world depicted in this book an entrepreneur is an indivisible unit, whose function is to take decisions upon the price and output policy of a firm, which can only take part in the production of one commodity at a time. The natural unit of capital, for long-period problems, is a certain sum of money controlled for a certain time. In the short period—the lifetime of the physical embodiment of capital, machines or buildings —it is convenient to treat fixed capital in the same terms as land, and to regard the natural unit as a machine-year or machine-day. It is the services of the productive units, not the units themselves, which are factors of production, but for simplicity the time dimension of a productive unit is omitted in the following pages. The natural units of land will be referred to simply as acres, the natural units of labour as men, and so forth.

It has been customary to speak of four factors of production: Land, Labour, Capital, and Enterprise. This traditional demarcation of factors is convenient. Each of the four traditional titles refers to a category of productive units with certain obvious characteristics in common. In the argument of Books VII., VIII., and IX. such phrases as "the factor land" must be taken to mean a certain number of productive units all having the general characteristics of land, of which the most important is a unique position in space. "The factor labour" will mean a number of units having the characteristics of labour, of which the most important is that it is provided by an individual human being.

And so forth. A more precise conception of "a factor" will be introduced as the argument demands. Any single productive process will require some units out of each of the four categories. That is to say, any single process of manufacture, transport, or marketing must require space, labour, implements, and directing control.

The above definitions represent a considerable degree of abstraction, but more realistic definitions, though cumbrous to handle, would not require any fundamental alteration in the technique of analysis.

3

The following explanations may be found useful for reference as the argument proceeds:

Demand Curves.—The demand curve for a particular commodity in a given market represents a list of the amounts of that commodity which would be bought at various prices (per day or per year, or for any other interval of time), all other conditions remaining unchanged. Marshall instructs us to draw up a demand schedule on the assumption that the prices of all other things are fixed. This not only cuts off all hope of drawing realistic demand curves, but is somewhat illogical in itself. A change in the actual price of a commodity will alter the demand curve for any commodity to which it is a rival or to which it is supplementary. This change in demand will alter their prices unless they are produced under constant supply price for the relevant amounts. Marshall's method therefore would apply only in two cases. Firstly, in the case of a commodity which had no rivals and was not used jointly with any other, and since in the last resort all uses of money are rivals to each other in so far as they are not co-operative, and co-operative in so far as they are not rival, such a commodity would be impossible to find. Secondly, it would apply to one commodity provided that all others were produced under constant supply price, a situation which we would not expect to find. The proper course is that suggested by Professor Pigou:[1] to assume, not the prices, but the conditions of supply of all other commodities to be fixed. This still leaves of course many difficulties, but the usefulness of such a method is far wider.

[1] *Economic Essays and Addresses*, p. 64.

The phrase *individual demand curve* means, not the demand curve of an individual buyer, but the demand curve for the product of an individual firm. Complications are introduced into the problem of the individual demand curve by the existence of advertising, but these have been ignored. It may be assumed that expenditure on advertisement necessary to increase the sales of a firm can be treated as equivalent, from the point of view of the entrepreneur, to a reduction in price having the same effect upon sales.[1]

In an industry which is conducted in conditions of imperfect competition a certain difficulty arises from the fact that the individual demand curve for the product of each of the firms composing it will depend to some extent upon the price policy of the others. Thus if one raises its price the demand curves for the others will be raised. This may cause them to raise their prices also, and the rise in their price will react upon the demand for the commodity of the first firm. In drawing up the demand curve for any one firm, however, it is possible to take this effect into account. The demand curve for the individual firm may be conceived to show the full effect upon the sales of that firm which results from any change in the price which it charges, whether it causes a change in the prices charged by the others or not. It is not to our purpose to consider this question in detail. Once the demand curve for the firm has been drawn, the technique of analysis can be brought into play, whatever the assumptions on which the demand curve was drawn up.

It is frequently convenient to refer to a demand curve as the *average revenue curve* of a seller.

Supply Curves.—The supply curve of a commodity shows, for each amount of the commodity, the price per unit which it is necessary to pay in order that that amount of it shall be produced. The notion of a supply curve presents innumerable difficulties, some of which are discussed in the following chapters. A short-period supply curve may have a definite meaning, but the notion of a long-period supply curve represents a high degree of abstraction from real conditions. The main difficulty arises from the fact that, in actual cases, costs of production,

---

[1] But see Kahn, *Economic Journal*, December 1932, p. 660, and Shove, " The Imperfection of the Market ", *Economic Journal*, March 1933, p. 114, for a complication which is introduced into the analysis by the existence of marketing costs.

and therefore the supply price of the commodity, do not depend merely upon the amount that is being produced at any moment, but will be influenced by the past history of the industry.[1] The conception of a curve which shows a unique relationship between the amount of output and its supply price is therefore highly unreal. In our abstract analysis, however, we make use of this unreal conception. The cost curves which we employ are not historical curves showing at what costs actual outputs are produced; they show the effect upon costs of an alteration in output, all other conditions remaining unchanged. Changes in the technique of production entailed by a change in the scale of output are admitted, but changes in technique which arise from invention or the application of new methods which might equally well have been applied to a different scale of production are not an element in the cost curve, but alter the position of the whole curve.[2]

The output of an industry is increased by the addition of indivisible units of the factors, for instance by the entry of a new firm. Thus a supply curve, whether it is rising, falling, or constant, will contain small waves, but when the output of the industry requires a large number of units of the factors these waves may be neglected.

Time.—Many of the most formidable difficulties of economic analysis are connected with time. These will be glanced at as occasion arises in the course of the argument, but for the most part we shall be obliged to leave them on one side. Upon the side of supply we shall suppose that production is carried on by firms which are in conditions of static equilibrium. On the side of demand, we assume that when we are dealing with individual demand curves it is permissible to represent them in two dimensions. We ignore, that is to say, the fact that the price charged at any one moment may alter the position of the demand curve in the future. It may be objected that this is an unnecessary restriction and that it would be possible to draw a long-period demand curve connecting each price with the amount that will be sold when that price has had time to exercise its full effect upon demand. But this would not serve our turn. If an individual seller knows that a high price at the

---

[1] Cf. Marshall, *Principles.* p. 808.
[2] See Pigou, *Economics of Welfare,* p. 218.

present time will lead to a lower demand curve in the future he
has a choice between a higher profit now, with less profit in the
future, and a lower profit now with more profit in the future.
What we require is not a long-period two-dimensional demand
curve but a curve showing, at each point, the discounted future
rate of selling which may be expected at each price. This conception is distressingly vague, since it involves both the guess-
work of the producer as to the future effect upon sales of his
present price policy and the rate at which he discounts future
prospects, but it is obviously some such conception which an
intelligent entrepreneur must have in mind when he is deciding
what price policy to adopt. In the course of the following argument these complications will be ignored, and we shall assume
that it is legitimate to make use of a two-dimensional demand
curve, without inquiring how it is drawn up. These difficulties do
not arise in connection with the demand curve for the output of
a competitive industry; they apply only to the individual demand curve.

Shapes of Curves.—In the following pages the convention is
adopted of describing a curve as concave when it is concave
from above, that is to say, when its convex side is towards the
x axis, and as convex when it is convex from above and its
concave side is towards the x axis.[1]

The greater part of this book is written in very technical
language. This makes it possible to put forward the results in a
precise and condensed manner, but it is important at every
stage to retranslate the technical language into terms of common sense. When a demand curve is described as concave or
convex, this means, in the former case, that a given absolute
fall in price induces a larger and larger absolute increase in the
amount sold as the price falls, and in the latter, that the
response of sales becomes less and less as price falls.

It seems on the whole probable that the demand curve of an
individual buyer for most ordinary commodities will be convex,
since it is likely that his demand will usually reach saturation at a positive price, so that the lowest part of the demand
curve is vertical. Thus the demand curve of a whole market

---

[1] In the language of the differential calculus, a curve will be described as
concave if $\frac{d^2y}{dx^2}$ is positive and as convex if $\frac{d^2y}{dx^2}$ is negative. Cf. Figs. 47 and 48.

for any commodity is only likely to be concave when the market is composed of individuals of differing wealth, so that a fall in price not only induces those who, at a higher price, consume some of the commodity to buy more, but also induces new buyers to come into the field. The same effect would be produced if the taste for the commodity was unequally distributed amongst the buyers. The concavity of the demand curve will be increased if each successive group of buyers with a smaller income, or with less desire for the commodity, is larger than the group before it, so that a larger number of new buyers are attracted to the commodity by each successive fall in price. The demand curve is likely to be convex if the market is composed of buyers all alike in wealth and in their taste for the commodity, and it is likely to be convex over the range where the price is so low that even the poorest and least ardent buyers purchase some of the commodity.

In an imperfect market, where the imperfection is due to transport costs, and where the buyers are evenly distributed over the area concerned, the demand curve for each individual producer is likely to be concave, since each successive drop in price charged by any one of them will cause a wider ring of customers to buy from the firm which makes it. On the other hand, when there is a dense population of buyers in the neighbourhood of each separate firm, and a sparse population in the regions between them, the demand curve for the individual firm will tend to be convex, since as the price is first reduced below the level at which the firm sells nothing, buyers from its own neighbourhood will be attracted to it in large numbers, but each succeeding reduction in price will meet with a smaller and smaller response as the output of the firm penetrates further and further afield, until it begins to invade the densely populated regions around the rival firms. Similar considerations will apply when the imperfection of the market is due to preferences on the part of groups of buyers for particular firms. In every case the shape of the demand curve can be interpreted in the light of the conditions which affect it.

Similarly the shapes of the cost curves will depend upon the conditions of production. For instance the supply curve of a perfectly competitive industry will be concave when economies of large-scale production occur at a diminishing rate as output

increases, or when the increase of costs due to the existence of
a scarce factor occur at an increasing rate. This is the state of
affairs which we should normally expect to find, but a convex
supply curve, on which costs fall at an increasing rate or rise
at a falling rate, is not impossible.

A curve is a straight line when a given absolute change in
amount is associated with the same absolute fall in price or in
cost for all amounts of output. There is no reason to expect that
such curves are to be found in any actual case, but they provide
us with an analytical device of which we shall make great use in
the succeeding argument.

The Entrepreneur.—In the following pages the entrepreneur
is personified and referred to as an individual. But in a joint-
stock company no single individual is responsible for the final
control of the firm. Responsibility rests nominally upon the
shareholders, whereas actual control is commonly left entirely
to the directors, and the initiation of the concern may have
been due to a company promotor. Moreover, the "reward of
the entrepreneur" may not be received by the individuals who
actually carry out the functions of entrepreneurship. The
policy of the concern will be dictated by its most influential
directors, while the resulting profits or losses will fall to the
shareholders. These complications are here disregarded, and
the entrepreneur is treated as an indivisible unit of control
and of interest.

CHAPTER 2

THE GEOMETRY

1

THE first tool required for the monopoly analysis of value is a pair of curves, marginal and average. The conceptions of average and marginal value can be applied to costs of production, utility, revenue, the productivity of factors of productions, and so forth.[1] In the present chapter we shall for purposes of illustration call the quantities under discussion cost and output, but the discussion can be applied equally to any other two quantities of which one is determined by the value of the other. Marginal cost represents the rate at which total cost increases as output increases; thus the marginal cost of n units of output is the total cost of n minus the total cost of $(n-1)$. Average cost is the total cost of n units of output divided by n. It is therefore possible, if the average costs of any two successive amounts of output are known, to calculate the marginal cost. Thus:[2]

---

[1] Some parts of the technical apparatus set out in this chapter are derived from the work of Professor Pigou (see Appendices, *Economics of Welfare*). The algebraical formulation of the relations of marginal and average curves (p. 36) is derived from Mr. Harrod ("The Law of Decreasing Costs", *Economic Journal*, December 1931). Other writers, to whom I am not myself indebted, have published parts of the apparatus at various times, *e.g.* Dr. H. v. Stackelberg ("Grundlagen einer reiner Kostentheorie", *Zeitschrift für Nationalökonomie*, May 1932); Prof. Amoroso, ("La curva statica di offerta", *Giornale degli Economisti*, 1930); Dr. E. Schneider (*Reine Theorie monopolistischer Wirtschaftsformen* and "Das Verteilungs- und Kostenproblem in einer vertrusteten Industrie", *Schmollers Jahrbuch*, vol. 19); Prof. T. O. Yntema ("The Influence of Dumping on Monopoly Price", *Journal of Political Economy*, December 1928).

[2] In this numerical illustration considerable changes in amount ($\frac{1}{10}$, $\frac{1}{11}$, $\frac{1}{12}$, etc.) are shown, for the sake of clarity, but such large changes introduce an

* *The reader who is acquainted with the elements of marginal analysis is recommended to use this chapter for reference as it is required. Other readers are recommended to study the first two sections, and to return to the more complicated relationships displayed in the remaining sections at a later stage.*

Units of Output.	Average Cost.	Total Cost.	Marginal Cost.
10	20	200	—
11	21	231	31
12	22	264	33
13	23	299	35

or

Units of Output.	Average Cost.	Total Cost.	Marginal Cost.
10	20	200	—
11	19	209	9
12	18	216	7
13	17	221	5

The first example shows rising costs, the second falling costs. If costs are constant, marginal and average cost are equal. Thus:

Units of Output.	Average Cost.	Total Cost.	Marginal Cost.
10	20	200	—
11	20	220	20
12	20	240	20

If marginal cost is greater than average cost, average cost must be rising. For if it costs more to add, say, a 12th unit to output than the average cost of 11, the average cost of 12 will be higher than the average cost of 11. Similarly if marginal cost is less than average cost, average cost must be falling, for if it costs less to produce a 12th unit than the average of 11, then the average cost of 12 will be less than the average cost of 11. To maintain the average at the same level, the marginal cost of the 12th unit must be as great as the average cost of the 11 units. Thus, so long as marginal cost is greater than average cost, average cost increases with output, and so long as marginal cost is less than average cost, average cost is falling. If marginal cost is equal to average cost, average cost is constant. But it is

inaccuracy into the calculation. More precisely, marginal cost is only equal to the increase in total cost, due to an increment of output, divided by the increment of output, if the increment is infinitesimal. Marginal cost
$$= \frac{d \text{ (total cost)}}{d \text{ (output)}}.$$

possible for average cost to be falling while marginal cost is rising, and *vice versa*. If the rate of fall of average cost diminishes as output increases, it is possible that, after a certain point, marginal cost will begin to rise. Thus:

Units of Output.	Average Cost.	Total Cost.	Marginal Cost.
8	22	176	—
9	21	189	13
10	20	200	11
11	19	209	9
12	$18\frac{1}{2}$	222	13
13	$18\frac{1}{4}$	$237\frac{1}{4}$	$15\frac{1}{4}$
14	$18\frac{1}{8}$	$253\frac{3}{4}$	$16\frac{1}{2}$

2

These relationships can be represented diagrammatically by means of marginal and average curves. According to the usual convention, output is measured on the x axis and cost per unit (average or marginal) on the y axis. As we have seen, so long as the marginal curve lies below the average curve, the average curve must be falling; and so long as the marginal curve lies above the average curve, the average curve must be rising. If the average curve is at first falling and then rising, the marginal curve will cut the average curve at its lowest point, for the

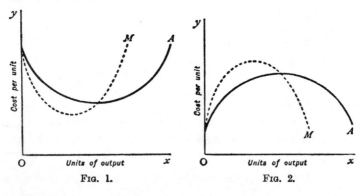

FIG. 1.   FIG. 2.

average curve can only fall while the marginal curve lies below it, and only rise while the marginal curve lies above it. Similarly, if an average curve is at first rising and then falling, the marginal curve will cut it at its highest point.

The two curves must leave the y axis at the same point, since the average and marginal cost of an indefinitely small output are the same.

It is possible, as we have seen, to calculate marginal cost if the average costs of two successive outputs are known, or in other words, if the slope of the average cost curve is known. But in order to derive average cost from marginal cost it is necessary to know the course of the marginal curve up to the output in question. We can find the total cost of n units if we can calculate the cost of 1 unit, *plus* the additional cost of the 2nd, *plus* the additional cost of the 3rd, and so forth up to the additional cost of the nth unit. The total cost of any output is thus shown by the area lying below the curve of marginal costs for all outputs up to the output in question. Then, by dividing by n, we can find the average cost.

3

We must now explore the geometrical relationships between these two curves. The fundamental relationship between average

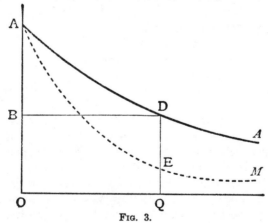

FIG. 3.

and marginal curves is that for any given output (OQ in Fig. 3) the area lying below the marginal curve (AEQO) is equal to the rectangle (BDQO) subtended by the average curve.

From this it is possible to deduce the following relationships. If the curves are straight lines, a perpendicular from any point on the average curve to the y axis will be bisected by the marginal curve.

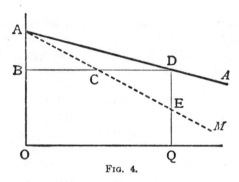

Fig. 4.

Draw DB and DQ perpendicular to the y and x axes respectively from a point D on the average curve.
Let the marginal curve cut DB in C and DQ in E.
Let the marginal and average curves cut the y axis in A.
It is required to prove that BC = CD.
The area BDQO = the area AEQO, since each is equal to the total cost of the output OQ.
∴. △ABC = △CDE in area.
But ∠B = ∠D = a right angle.
And the opposite angles at C are equal.
∴. △ABC = △CDE in all respects.
∴. BC = CD.

Thus BC is equal to half BD. By the same proof it follows that AB is equal to DE. This is equivalent to saying that, for straight lines, the rate of fall (or rise) of the marginal curve is twice the rate of fall (or rise) of the average curve.

There is no reason to expect that the curves with which we shall have to deal should be straight lines, but the simple case of straight line curves enables us to discover the fundamental relationships upon which all the geometry of marginal and average curves is built up. We can already make some useful deductions from them. First of all, without leaving the realm of straight-line curves, we can see from the above proof that if two or more straight-line average curves cut at a point, the corresponding marginal curves cut half-way from the y axis and on the same horizontal level.

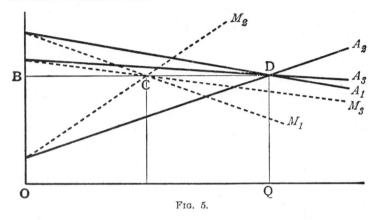

FIG. 5.

In Fig. 5, the marginal curves all cut in C, and BC is equal to CD.

When we are dealing with the analysis of monopoly we often need to consider the behaviour of two or more pairs of average and marginal curves. This relationship between pairs of straight-line curves will then be of service.

4

Further, the fundamental relationships set out above provide us with a very simple diagrammatic method of deriving marginal from average curves. When the curves are straight lines the method is obvious. We know that the perpendicular drawn from any point on the average curve to the y axis is bisected by the marginal curve, so that when the average curve is known the corresponding marginal curve can immediately be drawn. When the average curve is not a straight line the case is more complicated. The method for deriving the marginal curve from it depends upon the fact that the marginal value corresponding to any point on the average curve is the same as the marginal value corresponding to the tangent at that point. This must be the case, since the rate of change of cost is the same at this point

on the tangent and on the curve, and when we are calculating
the increase in total cost due to a small increase of output at this
point it is a matter of indifference whether we calculate the
increase from the curve or from the tangent.

Marginal value can therefore be derived from average value
as follows:

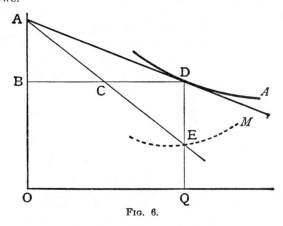

FIG. 6.

Let AD be the tangent to an average curve at D.

Draw DB and DQ perpendicular to the y and x axes
respectively.

The marginal cost for the output OQ is the same for the
curve to which AD is the tangent at D, and for the tangent
itself.

Let AE bisect BD in C and cut DQ in E.

Then, treating the tangent AD as an average curve, AE is
marginal to it. Hence the marginal curve passes through E.
This device of drawing a marginal curve to a tangent will
be of service in the succeeding argument. AE may be described as the *correspondent* to the tangent at D.

AB equals DE and QE is the marginal cost of the output OQ.

We are now provided with a method of finding the marginal
curve corresponding to an average curve of any shape. In
order to construct a diagram it is not necessary to draw the
correspondent (AE) to the tangent, for we know that the distance AB (in the above diagram) is equal to the distance DE.
Thus by drawing a tangent at any point on the average curve,

we can immediately find the corresponding point on the marginal curve. To find the point on the marginal curve corresponding to a point on the average curve, draw a tangent to the average curve at that point and a perpendicular from the point to the y axis. The marginal curve will lie below the average curve by the distance cut off on the y axis (AB) by the tangent and the perpendicular.

By this means, we can follow an average curve whatever its shape, and draw the corresponding marginal curve at all points.

It follows from the fact that the marginal value corresponding to any point on an average curve is the same for the curve and for its tangent at that point that if a number of average curves are tangential to each other at a certain point the corresponding marginal values must be the same for all the curves. That is to say, at the output at which the average curves are tangential, the marginal curves must cut.

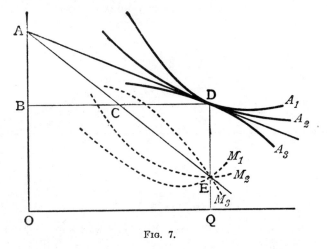

Fig. 7.

In Fig. 7, the three average curves A_1, A_2, and A_3 have a common tangent (AD) at D.

The marginal value QE (which is equal to QD *minus* AB) is the same for all the curves and for the tangent, and the marginal curves cut each other in E.

Further, it can be seen that if two average curves, instead of touching, cut each other at any point, D, then the marginal

D

curve corresponding to the less elastic curve must cut the line DQ below the point at which it is cut by the marginal curve corresponding to the more elastic average curve, and the marginal curves must cut each other to the left of the line DQ.

5

The relationship between a particular average curve and the corresponding marginal curve will depend upon the elasticity[1] of the average curve. When the average curve is rising the marginal values must be positive whatever the elasticity of the curve, and when the average curve is falling, but its elasticity is greater than unity, so that an increase in output leads to an increase in total cost, the marginal values must be positive; but if the elasticity of the average curve is equal to unity, so that total costs are unchanged by an increase in output, marginal cost is equal to zero, and if the average curve has an elasticity

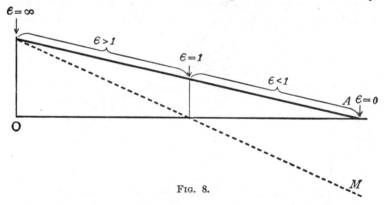

Fig. 8.

of less than unity the corresponding marginal curve will show negative values.[2]

---

[1] See p. 18 for the definition of elasticity.

[2] We have so far taken our examples from cost curves, and if the average curve which we are considering shows the costs of output to any business unit it is impossible that it should have an elasticity of less than unity, for it is impossible for the total cost of a greater output to be less than the total cost of a smaller output. But we are here studying the relationships of marginal and average curves as such, only taking cost curves as an example for the sake of convenience. The fact that when an average curve is inelastic the marginal values are negative is of importance when we come to consider average and marginal revenue (see p. 53, below).

The case for straight lines is illustrated in Fig. 8.

For any average curve the elasticity is infinite where it cuts the y axis, and at that point the marginal curve coincides with it. The elasticity is zero where it cuts the x axis. The elasticity is unity for a straight line at the half-way point. Above this point the average curve is elastic, and the marginal values are positive; below it the average curve is inelastic, and the marginal values are negative.

It is possible to see, quite generally, how the exact vertical distance between the marginal and average curves will depend on the elasticity of the average curve. The greater the elasticity of the average curve at a given point, the closer will the marginal curve lie to it.

Thus, in Fig. 6 above, the greater the elasticity at a given point D, the smaller will be the slope of the tangent AD, the smaller will be the distance AB, and the nearer will E lie to D. If the average curve is perfectly elastic, it will lie parallel to the x axis, the marginal curve will coincide with it, and costs will be constant. The extra cost of producing one more unit at each

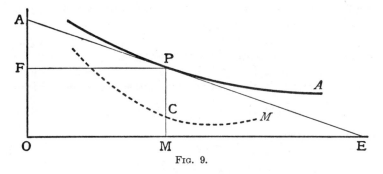

FIG. 9.

point is then equal to the average cost of the output at that and every other point.

The relationship between average value, marginal value and elasticity can be precisely formulated.

[*Footnote continued*]

An average cost curve of unit elasticity is not theoretically impossible. If the outlay necessary to produce the minimum unit of output will serve for an indefinitely large output without any additional cost, we should have an average cost curve of the form of a rectangular hyperbola, and the marginal curve would coincide with the y and x axes. Broadcasting to various numbers of listeners might, perhaps, afford an example of such an average cost curve.

(Fig. 9). Let PM be the average value for any output OM, and CM the marginal value.

Draw a tangent to the average curve at P to cut the y axis in A and the x axis in E.

Then the elasticity[1] of the average curve at P is $\dfrac{PE}{AP}$.

Now the triangles APF and PEM are similar.

$$\therefore \frac{PE}{AP} = \frac{PM}{AF}.$$

But AF = PC.

$$\therefore \text{ the elasticity at P} = \frac{PM}{PC}$$

$$= \frac{\text{average value}}{\text{average value} - \text{marginal value}}.$$

If elasticity is ϵ, average value A and marginal value M,

then $\epsilon = \dfrac{A}{A-M}$, $A = M\dfrac{\epsilon}{\epsilon-1}$,   and $M = A\dfrac{\epsilon-1}{\epsilon}$.

From this formula the ratio of the marginal to the average value can be deduced as soon as the elasticity of the average curve is known. Thus, for instance, if the average curve is a rectangular hyperbola asymptotic to the axes, so that elasticity is equal to unity for all outputs, then the marginal value is zero for all outputs, that is to say, the marginal curve coincides with the axes. If the elasticity of the average curve is equal to infinity, $\dfrac{\epsilon-1}{\epsilon}$ is equal to unity, and the average and marginal values are equal.

If $\epsilon = 2$, $M = \frac{1}{2}A$,
if $\epsilon = \frac{1}{2}$, $M = -A$, and so forth.

The elasticity of a rising curve is regarded as negative.[2] For a rising curve the marginal value is greater than the average value.

Thus if $\epsilon = -\frac{1}{2}$, $M = 3A$,
if $\epsilon = -1$, $M = 2A$,
if $\epsilon = -2$, $M = \frac{3}{2}A$, and so forth.

[1] Marshall, *Principles*, p. 102.
[2] This is illogical, but convenient. It makes no difference to the results whether the elasticity of a rising curve is regarded as positive or negative, provided that it is treated as of opposite sign to the elasticity of a falling cuvre.

6

Next we must show the relationship of marginal and average curves in certain peculiar cases. These are of importance, both because they contribute to an understanding of the general relationships, and because they will be necessary to us in our

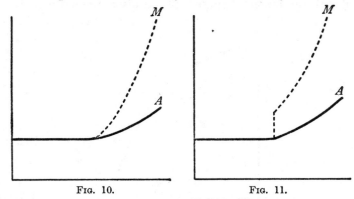

FIG. 10.   FIG. 11.

subsequent analysis. For instance, if average cost remains constant up to a certain point and then begins to rise gradually, the marginal curve will diverge from it gradually (Fig. 10). If the average curve begins to rise suddenly it will be said to contain a

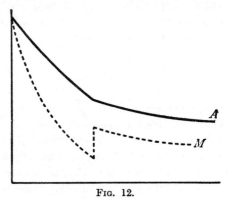

FIG. 12.

kink,[1] and the marginal curve will contain a discontinuity (Fig. 11).

---

[1] The existence of a kink in a curve entails a discontinuity in its slope.

Similarly a kink may occur in a falling average curve. If, for instance, the slope of the average curve, which has hitherto been falling steadily, suddenly diminishes, as in Fig. 12, the marginal curve will rise discontinuously and then pursue its normal course.

If the slope of the average curve suddenly increases (as in Fig. 13), the marginal curve will fall discontinuously.

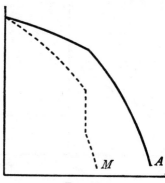

FIG. 13.

The presence of a kink in the average curve may be regarded as an extreme example of the case where the slope of the curve undergoes a rapid change over a small range of output, and where the marginal curve without any actual discontinuity rises or falls very steeply over this range.

7

There is one further possibility which we have not yet considered. Marginal cost may be constant while average cost is falling. This will occur when cost is composed of two elements, a sum which varies directly with output and a fixed sum which does not vary with output at all. This is clearly seen in the familiar example of the die and medals. Suppose that a die costs £100, and that to strike a medal from it costs £1. Then marginal and average costs would be as follows:

Medals.	Total Cost.	Average Cost.	Marginal Cost.
	£	£	£
1	101	101	—
2	102	51	1
3	103	$34\frac{1}{3}$	1
4	104	26	1
..	...	..	.
100	200	2	1

In this case marginal cost is constant and average cost falls as output increases. The average curve is a rectangular hyperbola subtending an area equal to the fixed cost (£100 in the above example) and the marginal cost curve is a horizontal line to which the average curve is asymptotic.[1]

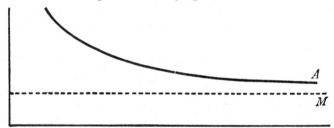

FIG. 14.

Curves of this type are useful in the analysis of short-period cost, where overhead expenses represent a fixed element and prime costs a variable element. When average prime cost is constant for the relevant amounts of output the situation illustrated in the above diagram will occur.

8

We must now return to the study of curves of a simpler type. We found, in Section 3, that when an average curve is a straight line, a perpendicular drawn from it to the y axis, at any point, is bisected by the marginal curve. The corresponding relationships, when the curves are not straight lines, can also be discovered.

If a falling average curve is concave,[2] the perpendicular is cut by the marginal curve to the left of its middle point.

---

[1] The marginal cost curve must be regarded as coinciding with the y axis at zero output, and as meeting the average cost curve at infinity.

[2] See p. 23.

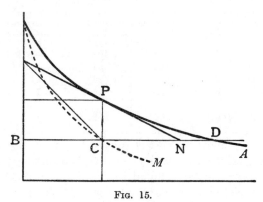

FIG. 15.

Draw the tangent to an average curve at any point P. Then the correspondent[1] cuts the marginal curve vertically below P in C.

Draw BC parallel to the x axis, to cut the y axis in B, the marginal curve in C, the tangent in N, and the average curve in D. Then BC = CN.[2]

Since the curve is concave, D must lie outside BN.

∴ CD>CN.

But CN = BC.

∴ BC<½BD.

If a concave average curve is rising, the tangent will lie to the right of the curve, so that BC is greater than ½BD. If an average curve is falling, but convex, BC is greater than ½BD, and if the curve is rising, but convex, BC is less than ½BD. The ratio of BC to BD depends upon the slope and the curvature of the average curve.[3]

---

[1] See p. 32.   [2] See p. 30.

[3] An approximate value of the ratio can be obtained as follows for the case where the curvature is small:

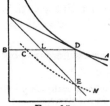

FIG. 15A.

Let the correspondent to the average curve at D cut BD in L so that BL = LD.

If $y = f(x)$ is the equation of the average curve, the slope of the correspondent is $2f'(x)$ (p. 30). The equation of the marginal curve is

$y = f(x) + xf'(x)$, and the slope of the marginal curve is $2f'(x) + xf''(x)$.

If $f''(x)$ is small the marginal curve can be treated as a straight line between C and E, and it follows that

9

In much of what follows we shall have to deal with the intersections of pairs of marginal and average curves. The above propositions help to disclose the relationship between such intersections. When we were studying straight-line curves **we**

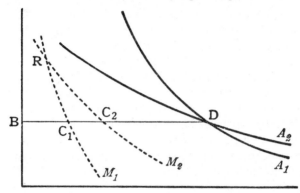

Fig. 16.

found[1] that if two average curves cut at a point, the marginal curves must necessarily cut each other at a point midway between the y axis and the point of intersection of the average curves and on the same horizontal level. When the curves are not straight lines this will no longer be generally true, as the above relationships will show. In each particular case the

[*Footnote continued*]

$$\frac{LD}{CD} = \frac{2f'(x) + xf''(x)}{2f'(x)}$$

$$= 1 + \frac{xf''(x)}{2f'(x)}.$$

But $\dfrac{BC}{CD} = \dfrac{2LD - CD}{CD}$

$$= 2\frac{LD}{CD} - 1.$$

$$\therefore \quad \frac{BC}{CD} = 1 + \frac{xf''(x)}{f'(x)}.$$

$\dfrac{xf''(x)}{f'(x)}$ may be regarded as a measure of the *adjusted concavity* of the average curve.

I am indebted to Mr. R. F. Kahn for this proof.

[1] See p. 30.

results will depend upon the *adjusted concavities* of the curves, which determine the ratios of BC to BD.

(FIG. 16). Let two falling average curves, A_1 and A_2, cut at D.
    Draw BD parallel to the x axis.
    Let the corresponding marginal curves, M_1 and M_2, cut BD in C_1 and C_2, and cut each other in R.

Then if the average curves are concave, BC_1 and BC_2 are both less than $\frac{1}{2}$BD, and if they are convex, BC_1 and BC_2 are both greater than $\frac{1}{2}$BD.

It is therefore clear that when the average curves are concave, the point R, at which M_1 and M_2 cut each other, may either lie above BD at a horizontal distance from the y axis of less than $\frac{1}{2}$BD, or below BD at a distance which may be less than, equal to, or greater than $\frac{1}{2}$BD. And when the average curves are convex, the point R may either lie below BD at a distance from the y axis of more than $\frac{1}{2}$BD, or above BD at a distance which may be less than, equal to, or greater than $\frac{1}{2}$BD. In the same way it can be shown [1] that if a convex average curve is falling and a concave average curve rising, the point of intersection of the marginal curves must be more than midway from the y axis, but the level may be above or below the level of the point of intersection of the average curves, and so forth. Thus the relationships between pairs of curves of all possible shapes can be derived from the propositions set out in Section 8.

10

It is further necessary to consider the movements of curves. We shall be mainly concerned with changes in the position of average curves. These may be of various types. An average curve may be raised so that its slope, at a given output, is the same as before. The tangents, at that output, are then parallel. Or it may retain the same slope at any given price. The tangents, at that price, are then parallel. Or the curve may move in such a way that its elasticity, either at a given output or at a given price, is the same as before, in which case its slope will be different.[2] If the elasticities are the same at one output, it can

---

[1] The reader unacquainted with the technique is recommended to illustrate this and the following relationships by drawing diagrams for them.
[2] For a reader unacquainted with the relationship between slope and elas-

be shown that the tangents, at that output, will meet on the x axis. Similarly, if the elasticities are the same at one price, the tangents, at that price, will meet on the y axis.[1] Average curves which stand in this relationship to each other will be found of service in the succeeding argument, and it is convenient to have a name for them. Two average curves which have the same elasticity at a given price are described as *iso-elastic* at that price.

Average curves, of course, may also move in any other way, so that neither the slopes nor the elasticities are the same at any price or at any output, but the above relations, so to speak, map out the field of possible changes.

11

The use of the geometrical relationships which have been set out in this chapter will become clear in succeeding chapters. They will be applied to various problems and reference will be made to them at many points in the following argument. At the same time, as our analysis proceeds, some further relationships will be required, and will be deduced, as occasion arises, from the propositions contained in this chapter.

ticity the following exercise may be useful : Consider two parallel straight-line falling curves. The slope of these two curves is the same. A line through the origin will cut the two curves at points of equal elasticity. A line perpendicular to the x axis will cut the higher curve at a point of greater elasticity than the lower curve. Conversely a line perpendicular to the y axis will cut the lower curve at a point of greater elasticity than the higher curve.

[1] The converse of this proposition is proved on p. 68, below.

BOOK II

MONOPOLY EQUILIBRIUM

of variable ... are already in existence long-period and quasi-long-
period ... and costs are the same. The difference between the
long period and the quasi-long period only arises from the fact that
in the long period the number of firms producing a given commodity may alter, while in the quasi long period it cannot alter.
In given conditions of demand price and output will be
determined by marginal cost and the function of average cost

CHAPTER 3

MONOPOLY EQUILIBRIUM

1

THE first problem to be solved is the determination of the output of the individual seller, given his costs of production, and given the conditions of demand for his commodity.

The problem may be considered either from the point of view of the *short period*, or the *quasi-long period*. In the short period the productive equipment of the firm is fixed, and part of the cost of production is fixed irrespective of output. The costs which need not be incurred if no output is produced (for instance, the cost of labour, raw material, and power) are known as *prime costs*. In the quasi-long period the productive equipment is conceived to be adapted to changes of output, and all costs except the minimum reward of the entrepreneur may vary with output. In the true *long period* the firm itself may be created or may disappear.

The cost curve which will be relevant to this inquiry is the curve of marginal cost to the individual firm.

The curve of marginal cost may be adapted to deal with short period or quasi-long period problems, and from the point of view of a firm already in existence long-period and quasi-long-period marginal costs are the same. The difference between the long period and the quasi-long period only arises from the fact that in the long period the number of firms producing a given commodity may alter, while in the quasi-long period it cannot alter.[1]

In given conditions of demand, price and output will be determined by marginal cost, and the function of average cost will be to show whether, with a given price and output, the entre-

[1] See p. 92, below.

* *A reader not interested in technique is recommended to omit Sections 5 and 6 and the latter part of Section 7.*

preneur is earning a profit or not, and therefore whether he will
continue to produce. As long as he continues in business at all,
the level of average cost will not affect the amount of his output.

The importance of average costs in determining the profitability of production often leads, by a confusion of thought, to
the view that they are also important, in a given situation, in
determining price. For instance, business men often complain
that some foreign rival has an advantage in competition because
his overhead costs are lower. It is true that a firm whose overhead costs are low will be able to survive when low prices are
ruling, while one with high overhead costs would be ruined, but
as long as both continue to produce, the price is unaffected by
the overhead costs.

A more sophisticated observer would be accustomed to look
not at average total cost but at prime cost, as influencing price
at any moment. Yet clearly it is not average but marginal prime
cost that governs short-period price. Thus the rule that price is
governed by marginal cost applies equally in the short period,
when productive capacity is fixed, and in the quasi-long period,
when it may be altered. In the short period marginal total cost
is simply marginal prime cost, for it is only prime cost which
alters when output alters. The distinction between prime and
overhead costs is thus not of much significance in itself;[1] it is the
distinction between average and marginal cost that is important, whatever the period may be which is under discussion.

2

Marginal cost may either fall or rise, as output increases, or
it may be constant. In general we should expect that marginal
cost for an individual concern would at first fall, and then rise
or remain constant as output increases. This is likely to be true
whether the technique of production is adapted to the change
in output or not. In the quasi-long period, when the technique
of production may be altered, there are likely to be economies of
large-scale production. When there are no further economies of
large scale to be gained from an increase in output, then, in the
absence of scarce factors, marginal costs will be constant, so

---

[1] Average prime cost is important in determining whether (with given
equipment) a business will produce something or nothing in any given conditions of demand.

long as it is possible for the entrepreneur to increase his output without incurring diseconomies of large-scale management. Or marginal cost may be constant for a certain range of output if there is an exact balance between the economies and diseconomies entailed by increasing output. After a certain point diseconomies of large scale may outweigh the economies, and marginal costs may rise.[1]

In many cases when marginal cost is constant, or even rising, average cost will be falling. There will always be a fixed element in total cost, the reward of the entrepreneur, and in many types of production, such as railways, the distribution of gas, or wireless broadcasting, the minimum unit of plant necessary for the smallest output has a very large capacity. In such cases average costs must necessarily be falling, over a considerable range, with increases of output, and this has led some writers to suppose that in such cases price must necessarily fall with increases of demand.[2] But this is a false deduction, for the fact that average cost is falling does not entail that marginal cost is falling, and it is marginal cost which determines output and price in any given situation.

A similar type of case is frequently met with in the short period when the capacity of the plant in existence in an industry is in excess of the output which is being produced, for the marginal prime cost is often constant up to capacity output. Consider, for instance, the case of a cotton mill which is working under capacity owing to a decline in demand. Either the whole mill may be worked for a few days a week, so that increases of output, up to the point at which a full week is being worked without overtime, bring about no rise in marginal cost. Or the mill may be worked every day, but part of the looms or spindles may be left idle; thus, if the machines are all equally good, there will again be no rise in marginal cost with increases of output up to the point where every machine is in use and further increases can only be made by working overtime or by reducing the number of machines tended by each worker. In either case marginal cost will be constant over a considerable range of output.[3]

[1] This treatment of the cost curves of a firm is based upon Mr. E. A. G. Robinson's *Structure of Competitive Industry.*

[2] *E.g.* Marshall, *Principles*, p. 485.

[3] In the second case, though not in the first, average prime cost will fall with increases of output, but this does not affect the argument.

Falling marginal costs in the short period are probably not so common as the frequent claim that an increase of output will lead to a lower price would lead us to expect. It is possible, however, that in some cases the technical efficiency of production is much impaired by working an organisation at less than the output for which it was designed, so that there are falling marginal costs up to the designed output. This may be the case, for instance, in the iron and steel industries, where there are large technical economies to be gained by working plant to its designed capacity. In general, however, it may be supposed that in the short period marginal costs begin to rise at a fairly low level of output, as a result of the limitation of plant and organisation, and in any case there must always be some level of output at which they begin to rise.

For our present purpose it makes no difference for what reason marginal costs are constant, or are rising or falling, though the nature of the average cost curve corresponding to any given marginal cost curve, and therefore the amount of profit, would be different in each case. And our analysis can be applied equally to quasi-long or to short-period cases provided that for each problem those curves are drawn which are relevant to the period under discussion.

3

The demand curve for the output of the individual firm will normally be falling. Its elasticity will depend upon many factors, of which the chief are the number of other firms selling the same commodity and the degree to which substitution is possible, from the point of view of buyers, between the output of other firms and the output of the firm in question. If there are few or no other firms producing closely similar commodities, the distribution of wealth among buyers, the conditions of supply of rival commodities, the conditions of supply of jointly-demanded commodities,[1] and all the innumerable factors which affect the demand for any one commodity will influence the demand curve for the individual producer. But when the number of firms producing any one sufficiently homogeneous commodity is large it is the competition of

[1] Marshall, *Principles*, p. 383.

these rival firms which will have the preponderating influence upon the demand curve for any one of them. The elasticity of demand for any one of them will be greater than the elasticity of demand for the commodity as a whole; for although each producer may have certain customers who prefer, for one reason or another, to buy from him, a rise in his price will drive some of them to buy from his competitors before it will drive them to give up buying the commodity altogether.

When, the number of firms being large, so that a change in the output of any one of them has a negligible effect upon the total output of the commodity, the commodity is perfectly homogeneous in the sense that the buyers are all alike in respect of their preferences (or indifference) between one firm and its rivals, then competition is perfect, and the elasticity of demand for the individual firm is infinite. That is to say, any one producer will be able to sell as much as he pleases at the current market price. If he lowers his price, by however little, he will be able to capture the whole market, while if he raises his price, by however little, he will be unable to sell at all.

Perfect competition is never likely to prevail in the production of any actual commodity, but it provides a limiting case of imperfect competition which is of considerable service in analysis. Conditions approximating closely to perfect competition are likely to occur, for instance, in an organised produce market, such as the corn exchange in a large market town.

4

It is assumed to be the aim of the producer to fix that price at which the excess of gross receipts or *revenue* over costs will be at a maximum. He will achieve this if he regulates output in such a way that the addition to his total revenue from selling an additional unit is exactly equal to the addition to his costs caused by producing that unit. If he sold one unit less, he would lose more of revenue than he saved of cost, and if he produced one unit more, he would incur more of cost than he gained of revenue.

The addition to total revenue produced by selling an additional unit of output is *marginal revenue*.[1] The seller is assumed

---

[1] This conception is in no way connected with Professor Pigou's "marginal demand price" (*Economics of Welfare*, p. 137, note, and p. 806).

always to equate marginal revenue to marginal cost. He may be conceived to do this either by estimating the demand price and the cost of various outputs, or by a process of trial and error.[1] For the sake of simplicity the individual producer may be referred to as a *monopolist*.

The marginal revenue curve of the monopolist is marginal to the demand curve for his product, and can be derived from it by the method shown in Fig. 6.

The demand curve represents his average revenue. If he can sell 1000 units at 10s. each, 10s. is his average revenue for 1000 units, and his total revenue from selling 1000 units is 10,000s. His marginal revenue will be the difference between his total revenue when he sells 1000 units and 1001 units. As output is increased selling price is reduced, so that average revenue declines as output increases. Marginal revenue will therefore be less than average revenue. Thus:

Units.	Price or Average Revenue.	Total Revenue.	Marginal Revenue.
10	20	200	—
11	19	209	9
12	18	216	7

The determination of output can be illustrated thus:

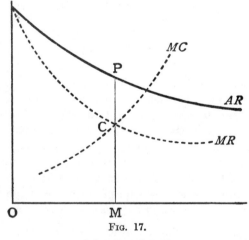

Fig. 17.

---

[1] See p. 56, below.

AR is the average revenue or demand curve.

MR is the marginal revenue curve.

MC is the marginal cost curve.

OM is the most remunerative output, and MP its price.

If the demand curve is inelastic, marginal revenue will be negative.[1] Thus:

Units.	Price.	Total Revenue.	Marginal Revenue.
20	10	200	—
21	9	189	− 11
22	8	176	− 13

In such circumstances, it would pay the monopolist to contract output, for even if an addition to output costs him nothing, his revenue is reduced by each addition to his sales. If the demand curve were inelastic throughout its length, it would

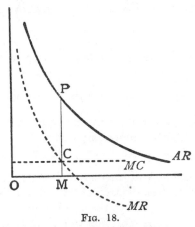

Fig. 18.

pay him best to produce an infinitesimal amount and sell it for an infinite price. A demand curve which continues to be inelastic, however high the price, is obviously an absurdity. There must be some point at which sales begin to fall off rapidly as price is raised, and if a monopolist finds himself faced with an inelastic stretch of the demand curve, he will raise price until the demand begins to become elastic (as in Fig. 18).

[1] See p. 34.

If the demand curve is perfectly elastic marginal revenue and

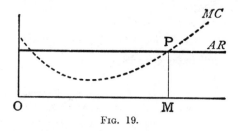

price are equal,[1] and the output will be such that marginal cost is equal to price (as in Fig. 19).[2]

5

The price of the monopoly output will stand in a certain relation to its marginal cost.

If ϵ is the elasticity of demand, then we know[3] that the price is equal to marginal revenue multiplied by $\dfrac{\epsilon}{\epsilon-1}$. But for the monopoly output marginal revenue is equal to marginal cost. Thus monopoly price is equal to marginal cost multiplied by $\dfrac{\epsilon}{\epsilon-1}$. This must be true whatever the shape of the cost curve, since marginal revenue will always be equal to marginal cost to the monopolist, at the monopoly output.

The same relationship can be expressed in another form:

> Let PM be the price of the monopoly output, OM, MC being the marginal cost and marginal revenue for the output OM. Let AP be the tangent to the demand curve at P. Then the correspondent AC is marginal to the tangent AP.[4]

---

[1] See p. 27.

[2] It is clear that the marginal method of analysis will produce exactly the same results as the method, used by Marshall, of finding the price at which the area representing "monopoly net revenue" is at a maximum, since net revenue is at a maximum when marginal revenue and marginal cost are equal. Both methods can be applied to problems of competition and of monopoly. Marshall introduced into his system of analysis an artificial cleavage between monopoly and competition, by treating competitive problems only by the "marginal" method, and monopoly problems only by the "areas" method; cf. p. 6.

[3] See p. 36.   [4] See p. 32.

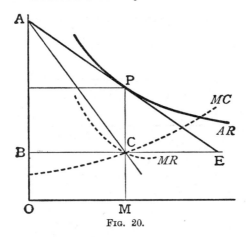

FIG. 20.

Draw BC perpendicular to the y axis, to cut it in B.
Let the tangent AP cut BC in E.
Then BC $=\frac{1}{2}$BE.[1]
AEB and PEC are similar triangles.
$\therefore$ CP $=\frac{1}{2}$AB.
$\therefore$ MP $=$MC $+\frac{1}{2}$AB.
Alternatively—
    since MC $=$OB and AB $=$OA $-$OB,
        MP $=\frac{1}{2}$(OA $+$MC).

Thus monopoly price is equal to the marginal cost of the monopoly output *plus* half the distance cut off on the y axis by the
marginal cost of that output and a tangent to the demand curve
at that output. Or, alternatively, monopoly price is equal to
half the sum of the intercept of the tangent on the y axis and the
marginal cost. This relationship also will prove of service in the
succeeding argument.

6

It remains to consider the amount of monopoly profit, or net
receipts. This will be equal to the difference between the area
lying under the marginal revenue curve (aggregate revenue)
and the area lying under the marginal cost curve (aggregate
costs). Monopoly profit can also be discovered by considering
the average cost curve, which will be introduced at a later stage

See p. 32.

in the argument. Monopoly profit is the difference between average cost and average revenue, multiplied by output. Thus:

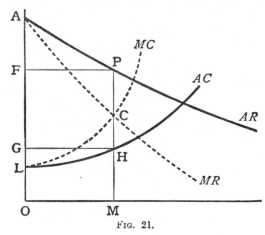

FIG. 21.

Monopoly profit is equal to the area ACL, and to the area FPHG, when MH is the average cost of the output OM.

7

It is natural to object that this method of analysis is highly artificial. Of what use, the reader may ask, to discuss fine points of analysis which depend upon the shapes of demand curves when no everyday monopolist has any such ideas in his mind, and when even the most up-to-date businesses have only the vaguest notion of what kind of demand curves they have to deal with?[1]

It is true enough that no monopolist will hit upon the exact point at which his net revenue will be greatest unless he has an accurate and enlightened system of cost accounting and a good knowledge of the market conditions in which he has to sell. But if the conditions of demand and supply remain constant over a fairly long period, the monopolist will be able to hit upon the exact monopoly output merely by balancing marginal receipts against marginal cost. We need not imagine that he is able to

[1] Certain firms actually calculate the sales which they could make at various prices, and claim that their estimates turn out to have a high degree of accuracy, but such cases are probably exceptional.

plot the demand and cost curves throughout their length, but
merely that he can see whether selling a little more of his product than he does at present will increase or decrease his net
gains. As long as marginal revenue exceeds marginal cost, there
will be a tendency for him to increase output, and as long as
marginal revenue falls short of marginal cost, there will be a
tendency for him to contract output, and he will be in equilibrium at the monopoly point.

It may happen, however, that there are several points of
equilibrium, and if he hits upon one of them there will be no

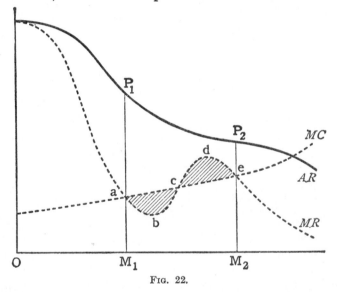

Fig. 22.

tendency for him to move, even though a greater net revenue
could be gained at some other point.

Cases of multiple equilibrium may arise when the demand
curve changes its slope, being highly elastic for a stretch, then
perhaps becoming relatively inelastic, then elastic again. This
may happen, for instance, in a market composed of several groups
of consumers each with a different level of incomes. There will be
several critical points at which a decline in price suddenly brings
the commodity within the reach of a whole fresh group of consumers so that the demand curve becomes rapidly more elastic.
The marginal revenue curve corresponding to such a demand

curve may fall and rise and fall again,[1] and there will be several points of monopoly equilibrium.

Moreover, even if the marginal revenue curve falls consistently, the shape of the marginal cost curve may be such that there are several points of equilibrium.

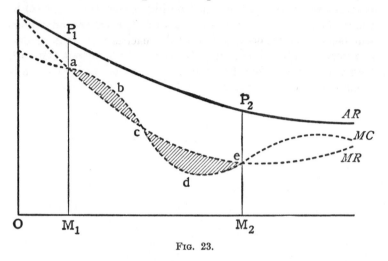

FIG. 23.

OM_1 and OM_2 are possible monopoly outputs, and M_1P_1 and M_2P_2 are the corresponding prices.

The net monopoly revenue at each point would be different, but it is unlikely that any monopolist would have sufficient knowledge of the situation to enable him to choose the greatest one from among them. If the monopolist had reached one equilibrium point there would be no influence luring him towards another at which his gains might be greater.

If the course of the marginal cost curve and marginal revenue curve is known between the points of monopoly equilibrium it is possible to judge which of them will yield the largest monopoly revenue. The net revenue of the monopolist, at any output, is the total revenue *minus* the total costs. Now the total revenue for any output is shown by the area lying below the marginal revenue curve, and the total costs are shown by the area lying below the marginal cost curve. Thus the difference between the

[1] See p. 38.

net revenues appropriate to OM_2 and OM_1 is shown by the area (c d e in Figs. 22 and 23) where the marginal revenue curve lies above the marginal cost curve, *minus* the area (a b c) where the marginal cost curve lies above the marginal revenue curve. Any small increase of output beyond OM_1 will reduce the monopolist's revenue, but when he has passed the point (c) at which the marginal curves cut each other for the second time it will begin to increase again until he reaches OM_2, the second equilibrium point. The monopoly profit for the output OM_2 will be greater or less than for OM_1, according as the area c d e is greater or less than the area a b c.

CHAPTER 4

CHANGES IN DEMAND

1

THE next stage in our inquiry is the study of the effect of changes in demand upon the price charged by the individual seller.

Monopoly price, as we have seen,[1] is a function of the marginal cost of production and the elasticity of demand. The effect of a change in demand upon price will therefore depend upon the change in marginal cost and the change in elasticity of demand.[2]

Let us first consider a case in which marginal costs are constant, so that whatever change in output may be brought about by a rise in demand there will be no change in marginal cost. Then if the demand curve is raised in such a way that its elasticity at the original price is unaltered, the monopoly price will not be changed; the larger output will be sold at the same price as before. This can readily be seen from the formula

$$\text{Price} = \text{Marginal Revenue} \times \frac{\epsilon}{\epsilon - 1}$$ (where ϵ is the elasticity of

demand). In the new position of equilibrium the marginal revenue must be the same as in the old position, for the marginal cost is the same; and since the elasticity of demand at the old price is also unchanged, the price will not alter. It naturally follows that, with constant marginal costs, if the demand curve

---

[1] See p. 54.

[2] The whole of this analysis is conducted upon the assumption that the demand curve and the cost curve of the firm are independent of each other, see p. 21, note.

* *Some of the geometrical argument in this chapter is complicated, but the results are simple and congenial to common sense. The reader who is not interested in technique may prefer to omit the geometry and be content with the summaries of the results on p. 61, and p. 68. Section 3 and the latter part of Section 4 will only be of interest to readers with an appetite for purely technical questions.*

becomes less elastic at the old price as it is raised, the price will rise, and if it becomes more elastic, the price will fall.

Two curves which have the same elasticity as each other at a certain price are said to be *iso-elastic*[1] at that price. It can be seen that two demand curves will be iso-elastic over a certain range if the amounts bought, at any value of the price within that range, are in a constant ratio to each other. For elasticity is measured by the proportionate change in amount due to a certain proportionate change in price. If at each price the amounts bought are in a constant ratio, the elasticities at each price must be the same. The proportionate change from 100 to 105 is the same as the proportionate change from 200 to 210. If the market for a certain commodity were increased by the addition of new customers exactly like the old, the demand curve would be raised in this way. That a rise in demand should leave the elasticity at the old price unaltered is not, therefore, a very improbable case.

If the rise in demand which we are considering is of this nature, and marginal costs are not constant, it is clear that the monopoly price will be altered. If marginal costs are falling the rise in demand will cause the price to fall, and if they are rising it will cause the price to rise.

We have thus already advanced some way in our inquiry. The results so far obtained may be summarised thus:

> If the demand curve is raised in such a way that the second demand curve is iso-elastic with the first, the price will be increased, reduced, or remain the same according as marginal costs are rising, falling, or constant.
>
> If marginal costs are constant, and the new demand is less elastic than the old (at the old price), the price will rise; if it is more elastic, the price will fall.

Moreover, it is clear that if marginal costs are falling, the price will remain constant provided that the second demand is less elastic than the first to an extent sufficient to offset the fall in marginal cost. If it has more than this elasticity, the price will fall; if less, the price will rise. If costs are rising, the price will rise unless the second demand curve is more elastic than the first to an extent sufficient to offset the rise in marginal costs.

[1] See p. 43.

2

It is thus obvious that in many cases the change in price will be the result of two forces tending in opposite directions, for instance, when marginal costs are falling but the demand becomes less elastic. It will then be impossible to say immediately whether the price will rise or fall. A further consideration of the problem is therefore necessary.

The relationship between the two prices can be discovered as follows:

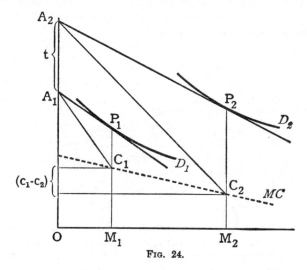

Fig. 24.

Let D_1 and D_2 be any two demand curves, D_2 being the higher demand curve (this convention will be maintained throughout the present discussion).

Let MC be any marginal cost curve.

Let P_1M_1 be the monopoly price appropriate to D_1, and P_2M_2 to D_2, and let M_1C_1 and M_2C_2 be the marginal costs of the outputs OM_1 and OM_2.

Let the tangent to D_1 at P_1 cut the y axis in A_1 and the tangent to D_2 at P_2 cut the y axis in A_2.

Then we know[1] that $P_1M_1 = \frac{1}{2}(OA_1 + M_1C_1)$,

and $P_2M_2 = \frac{1}{2}(OA_2 + M_2C_2)$.

[1] See p. 55.

$$\therefore P_2M_2 - P_1M_1 = \tfrac{1}{2}(OA_2 - OA_1 + M_2C_2 - M_1C_1)$$
$$= \tfrac{1}{2}(A_1A_2 + M_2C_2 - M_1C_1).$$

For M_1C_1 and M_2C_2 write c_1 and c_2.

For A_1A_2 write t.

Then the rise in the monopoly price due to the rise in demand from D_1 to D_2 will be equal to $\tfrac{1}{2}\{t - (c_1 - c_2)\}$, that is, to half the difference between the intercepts of the tangents on the y axis *minus* half the difference between the marginal costs of the two outputs.

We have now established the fact that a rise in demand will raise or lower price according as t is greater or less than $(c_1 - c_2)$.

A general method for testing in every case whether a rise in demand will raise or lower price can be devised.

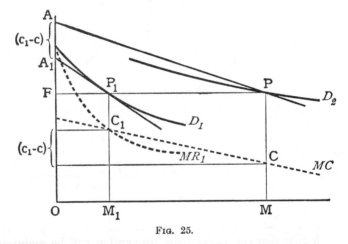

FIG. 25.

Through P_1, representing the monopoly price appropriate to D_1, draw a line parallel to the x axis to cut D_2 in P and to cut the y axis in F. Measure the difference between the marginal cost of the output appropriate to D_1 (M_1C_1 or c_1) and the marginal cost of the output of which MP is the price (MC or c). If costs are constant, this difference will be zero; if rising, it will be negative; if falling (as in Fig. 25), it will be positive.

Draw the tangent to the curve D_1 at P_1, and let it cut the y axis in A_1. Take a point A on the y axis such that A_1A

equals the difference between the two marginal costs $(c_1 - c)$. If costs are constant, A_1 and A coincide; if costs are rising, A lies below A_1, and if falling, A lies above A_1.

We are now able to establish three propositions.

If AP is the tangent at P to the new demand curve (D_2), then MP is the monopoly price appropriate to D_2, and the price is not changed by the rise in demand.
If AP cuts D_2 at P from below, then the price will be raised, and if AP cuts D_2 at P from above (as in Fig. 25), the price will be lowered.

These propositions can be proved as follows:

$P_1C_1 = A_1F.$[1]
But $PC = P_1C_1 + (c_1 - c)$.
$\therefore PC = A_1F + (c_1 - c)$
    $= AF$.
$\therefore$ the marginal curve corresponding to AP passes through C.
$\therefore$ the marginal curve corresponding to any curve to which AP is the tangent at P passes through C.

It immediately follows that if AP is a tangent at P to D_2, then OM is the output appropriate to D_2 and MP the price, and the price is unchanged by the rise in demand. If AP cuts D_2 from below, then the elasticity of D_2 at P is less than the elasticity of AP, consequently the marginal revenue curve corresponding to D_2 cuts PM below C. Hence the output appropriate to D_2 is less than OM, and the price must rise. If AP cuts D_2 from above, then the elasticity of D_2 at P is greater than the elasticity of AP, and the price must fall.

3

The direction of the change in price thus depends upon the elasticity of the new demand curve at the old price, given the change in marginal cost. The exact amount of the new price can only be determined by considering the shape of the new demand curve.

[1] See p. 30.

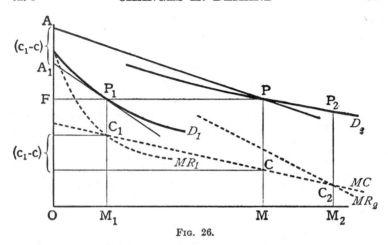

FIG. 26.

AP cuts D_2 from above, therefore P_2 will lie below P. The exact position of P_2 will depend upon the shape of D_2.

It would be possible to show that when the price is raised by the increase in demand, the rise in price will in general be greater if the new demand curve is concave than if it is a straight line with the same slope at the old price; and the rise in price will in general be less if the demand curve is convex. The exceptions to this rule involve very peculiar conditions in the change of demand and very rapidly falling marginal cost.[1] In the cases where the increase in demand leads to a lower price, the price will be reduced by more for a concave curve, and by less for a convex curve, except in the unlikely case when the fall in price has occurred in spite of rapidly rising marginal costs. Thus, in general, the effect of concavity in the new demand curve is to enhance either the rise or the fall in price.

4

We have so far examined the effect of a rise in demand upon price, rather than upon output. The absolute change in demand at the old price is measured in Fig. 26 by the distance P_1P, and when the price is unchanged, this will be the increase in output.

---

[1] The reader is recommended to illustrate these relationships by drawing diagrams for them.

F

In all those cases where price falls it is obvious that output must increase by more than P_1P, and in all those cases where the price is raised, output must increase by less than P_1P. In those cases where the price will fall it can easily be seen that the increase in output will be greater the greater is the concavity of the new demand curve (given its slope at the old price). In those cases where the price will rise the effect is somewhat more complicated. Consider a demand curve having any given slope at the point P. Then the greater the concavity of the demand curve the further to the left will the corresponding marginal revenue curve cut the line P_1P (produced to the y axis). Thus if the marginal cost curve cuts the marginal revenue curve below the line P_1P, it is certain that the increase in output will be less for a concave demand curve, and greater for a convex demand curve, than for a straight line having the same slope and, in general, the increase in output will be less the greater the concavity of the curve. But if the marginal cost curve is falling so rapidly (relatively to the demand curves) that it cuts the marginal revenue curve above P_1P, it is possible that the output for a concave curve may be greater than for a straight line, and the output for a convex curve less. It is, however, improbable that a case should occur in which the price would rise in spite of rapidly falling marginal cost. We may therefore say, in general, that the effect of concavity is to enhance the difference between the actual output and the increase in demand at the old price.

In some cases the increase in demand will actually reduce output. This can easily be seen. If the higher demand curve is steeper than the lower, the marginal revenue curves may cut each other.[1] Then if the marginal cost curve cuts the marginal revenue curves below their point of intersection, the output appropriate to the higher demand curve will be less than that appropriate to the lower demand curve.

[1] If the demand curves are convex, or are straight lines, the marginal revenue curves will only cross in this way if the slope (at any price) of the second demand curve is greater than the first, but if the higher demand curve is concave the marginal revenue curves may cross each other even if the slope of the new curve (at the old price) is less than that of the old.

5

It remains to discover in various types of case whether price will rise, fall, or remain constant when demand is increased. It is clear that for any change in marginal cost (due to the change in output) there will be a certain change in the elasticity of demand which will be just sufficient to ensure that the price remains unchanged. If we can isolate, in each case, this critical elasticity of the new demand curve, for which the price would remain constant, it will at once be possible to say in what conditions the price would rise or fall. If the new elasticity at the old price is less than this critical value the price will rise, and if it is more the price will fall. We shall therefore employ the device with which we equipped ourselves in Section 2 to discover, for various types of marginal cost curve, the nature of the change in demand which will maintain the price unaltered.

It is possible in the first place to establish by this method the proposition, enunciated above,[1] that when marginal costs are constant the new demand curve must be iso-elastic with the old if the price is to remain unchanged. If marginal costs are constant, $(c_1 - c)$ is equal to zero, and A and A_1 coincide (see Fig. 25). We therefore require to prove that if AP_1 is a tangent to D_1 at P_1 and AP is a tangent to D_2 at P (P_1P being parallel to the x axis), then the elasticity of D_2 at P is the same as the elasticity of D_1 at P_1.

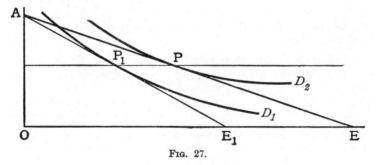

FIG. 27.

Let AP_1 cut the x axis in E_1, and let AP cut it in E.

[1] See p. 61.

Then $\dfrac{E_1P_1}{P_1A}$ is the elasticity of D_1 at P_1, and $\dfrac{EP}{PA}$ is the elasticity of D_2 at P.

But $\dfrac{E_1P_1}{P_1A} = \dfrac{EP}{PA}$.

Therefore the elasticities of D_1 and D_2 (at P_1 and P) are equal.

Thus with constant marginal costs the elasticity of demand (at the old price) has to remain constant if the price is to be unchanged. If the elasticity increases the price falls, and if it is reduced the price rises.

When marginal costs are rising the elasticity of demand must be increased if the price is to remain unchanged. The extent to which it must increase will depend on the rate at which costs are rising and the amount of the increase in demand. Beyond a certain point it will be impossible for the increase in elasticity to be sufficient to maintain the same price; for if the new demand curve cuts the marginal cost curve at the point where the marginal cost is equal to the old price, the price must rise unless demand becomes perfectly elastic at that price, and if the new demand curve cuts the marginal cost curve above the old price, the price must necessarily rise, no matter how elastic the demand becomes.

When marginal costs are falling, the elasticity of demand must be reduced if the price is to remain unchanged, and the amount by which the elasticity must be reduced will depend upon the rate of fall of the marginal cost curve and the amount of the increase in demand.

It can be proved that if the rate of fall of the marginal cost curve is less than the slope of the old demand curve, then, to maintain the same price, while the elasticity of demand must decrease, the slope of the new demand curve (measured by the tangent at the old price) must be less than of the old.[1] The rate of fall of the marginal cost curve is measured by the slope of the chord joining the points corresponding to the old output and to the output which would be bought at the old price under the new conditions of demand. It will be sufficient to show that

---

[1] For the relations between slope and elasticity see p. 42, note.

if the slope of the demand curve at the old price is unchanged the price must rise.

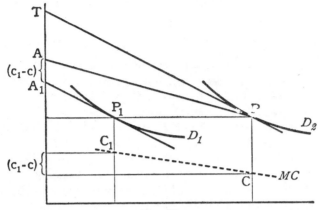

FIG. 28.

Let the tangent to D_2 at P cut the y axis in T, and let TP be parallel to A_1P_1, the tangent to D_1 at P_1.

Then, in the case where the slope of C_1C is less than the slope of the parallel tangents A_1P_1 and TP, $(c_1 - c)$ will be less than TA_1, and therefore A must lie below T. It follows that AP must cut D_2 from below, and the price must rise.

In the same way, it can be seen that if the rate of fall of marginal costs is greater than the slope of the old demand curve, then, to maintain the price unchanged, the elasticity of the new demand must be reduced so much that the slope of the new demand curve (at the old price) is greater than the slope of the old demand curve.

Finally, if the rate of fall of marginal cost is equal to the slope of the old demand curve (so that the chord of the marginal cost curve is parallel to the tangent to the old demand curve), then the price will be unchanged if the slope of the demand curve is unchanged.[1]

[1] The result that when the slope of the demand curve is unchanged the price will rise or fall according as the slope of the marginal cost curve is less or greater than the slope of the demand curves was employed (for the case of straight-line curves) by Dr. Zeuthen in connection with a somewhat different inquiry; but he expressed it by saying that the price will rise or fall according as the rate of fall of average costs is less or more than half the rate of fall of the demand curves. *Problems of Monopoly*, p. 19.

In each case, if the elasticity of demand is not reduced sufficiently to maintain the old price, the price will fall, and if it is more than sufficiently reduced the price will rise.

6

We have so far considered changes in demand in a purely formal manner. The results which we have obtained will only be of interest if we are able to say what type of change in demand is likely to be found in actual cases.[1]

An increase in the demand for the output of an individual firm may come about in various ways. Firstly, there may be an increase in the number of buyers. If new buyers are added to the market and if the separate demand curve of each new buyer is perfectly inelastic, then, if the old buyers continue to act exactly as before, a constant volume of purchases will be added to the demand at each price, and the slope of the demand curve, at any price, will be unaltered.[2] The new buyers may be supposed, for instance, each to take only one unit of the commodity, however low its price falls. But this is clearly an unlikely case. If the separate demand curves of the new buyers have any elasticity, the slope of the demand curve will be reduced. And if the separate demand curves of the new buyers are exactly like those of the old buyers, then (as we have seen) the slope of the demand curve will be so much reduced that at each price its elasticity is the same as before. In any case it is impossible that the mere addition of new buyers should increase the slope of the demand curve.

Secondly, an increase in demand may come about through an increase in the wealth of the existing group of buyers. An increase in wealth is likely to make the demand of the individual buyer of any particular commodity less elastic. Thus an increase in demand due to an increase of wealth is likely to reduce the elasticity of the demand curve, and may reduce the elasticity so

[1] The character of the demand curves for various commodities and the effect of changes in demand upon their shape present a fascinating and largely unexplored field for investigation. The few remarks here set out are very slight and very tentative.

[2] Dr. Zeuthen makes use of demand curves which fall without any change of slope when he is considering the case where a monopolist loses part of his market to rival sellers whose output is independent of the monopolist's price (*op. cit.* pp. 15-23).

much that the slope of the curve is increased. An increase in the taste of the existing buyers for the commodity would have much the same effect as an increase in their wealth.

Thirdly, an increase in the demand for the output of any one firm may be brought about by the disappearance of rival sellers. Here there are two opposite effects. The disappearance of alternative sources of supply will tend to make the demand of the existing customers of the firm less elastic, but the buyers who formerly preferred the output of the firms which have now disappeared may be indifferent between the firms which remain, and this will tend to make demand for the remaining firms more elastic. It will largely depend upon the number of surviving competitors whether the first or second effect will prevail. If only one firm is left in the field, it is almost certain that the elasticity of demand for its output will be reduced; if many survive, the elasticity of demand for any one of them is likely to be increased. In any case it seems, on the whole, unlikely that the disappearance of rival firms would reduce the elasticity of demand sufficiently to increase the slope of the demand curve.

Fourthly, an increase in demand may occur because some rival commodity has become more expensive. This will reduce the elasticity of demand, and may, in some cases, increase the slope of the demand curve.

A combination of these and other factors may produce any effect upon demand, and it would be rash to say that any sort of change in a demand curve is impossible; but it appears on the whole most probable that an increase in demand will be accompanied by a reduction in the elasticity of the demand curve, but a reduction insufficient to prevent the slope of the curve from being reduced.

If we may take, as the common case, an increase in demand which reduces both the elasticity and the slope of the demand curve (at the old price), we are able to say which of the possible effects of a rise in demand upon price are likely to be found in practice.

First, when marginal costs are rising or constant, since we are supposing that the elasticity of demand will be reduced, price must be raised by an increase in demand. In short-period cases marginal costs are on the whole unlikely to be falling;

thus we may say that in the short period an increase in demand is likely to lead to an increase of price.

Second, when marginal cost is falling, and the slope of the marginal cost curve is greater than the slope of the demand curve in its first position, then (since we are supposing that the slope of the demand curve is reduced) the price must fall. At first sight it may appear unrealistic to contemplate a rate of fall of marginal cost greater than the slope of the demand curve; but if a particular firm is selling in close rivalry with others, the elasticity of demand for its product may be very great, and there is no reason to suppose that an impossibly rapid rate of fall of marginal costs is required to fulfil the condition that the slope of the marginal cost curve is greater than the slope of the demand curve.

Finally, if marginal costs are falling, but the slope of the marginal cost curve is less than the slope of the demand curve, it is impossible to say whether the price will rise or fall. If the elasticity were unchanged, the price would fall, and if the slope of the demand curve were unchanged, the price would rise; but since we are assuming that both the elasticity and the slope of the curve are reduced, the price may either rise or fall.

For long-period cases, therefore, when the marginal costs of the individual firm are likely to be falling, it is impossible to say in general terms whether an increase in demand is more likely to raise or to lower price, and each particular type of case must be examined on its merits by the method here set out.

7

Our inquiry into the effect of changes in demand may be turned to account in examining two problems which are of some interest at the present time.

In the first place, it helps to explain a phenomenon which has sometimes puzzled economists. Firms are occasionally found to raise prices when trade is bad and the demand for their goods has fallen.[1] This is at first sight surprising, and the explanation which the business men give of their conduct only serves to make it still more puzzling. Their explanation usually is that as

---

[1] For instance, many American motor-manufacturers raised their prices at the beginning of the slump in 1929.

output has fallen off each unit has to bear a higher share of the overhead cost than before. But overhead cost is fixed, however large or however small the output, and it would be the height of folly for the business men to regulate prices in the way which they describe themselves as doing. It must pay them to fix the price at which profits are greatest (or losses least) whether that price happens to be greater or less than the average total cost of the output which they are producing, and the attempt to charge average total cost would merely involve them in a loss which they might avoid or give them a profit less than they might make.[1] But our examination of the effect of changes in demand upon price has provided us with a rational explanation of their conduct.

In all those cases where we have found that an increase in demand would lower price, a decrease in demand would raise price. There are two factors which will lead to a rise in price when demand falls. If marginal costs are falling, the reduction in output (due to the fall in demand) will raise marginal cost, and there will be a tendency for the price to be raised. And if the demand becomes less elastic as it falls there will be a tendency for the price to be raised. We found that on the whole it is likely that an increase in the demand for a particular commodity will reduce elasticity, but the reverse effect may also be found. A fall in demand due to a cyclical movement of trade is likely to be accompanied by a reduction in elasticity in the case of durable goods, the replacement of which can be postponed to better times, for only the most urgent demands for the goods will be effective during the slump even if price is considerably reduced. A rise in price may therefore be the appropriate response to a fall in demand, and not a mere act of folly on the part of the producer.

A second service which our examination of changes in demand can do for us is to throw light upon the arguments advanced in favour of closing down surplus productive capacity under certain rationalisation schemes, such as that undertaken by the British shipbuilding industry. Let us suppose, in order to

---

[1] It might happen that the most profitable price was also the price at which total average costs were covered. This will be the case in conditions of full long-period equilibrium (see p. 95, below), but it is only brought about as the result of what, from the point of view of the individual business, are the accidents of external circumstance.

simplify the problem, that no changes in productive technique are to be introduced, but that the industry is to be relieved of part of its surplus capacity by the destruction of redundant plant. The argument is advanced in favour of the rationalisation scheme that demand will be concentrated upon that part of the plant which is not broken up, and that since the surviving firms will be working nearer to full capacity, they can afford to charge a lower price.

Let us look at the matter from the point of view of one of the surviving firms. Customers formerly attached to some of the condemned firms will now place orders with it, and the demand curve for its product will be raised. The argument of the rationalisers that it will therefore lower its price seems at first sight highly unreasonable, and when it is backed up by the familiar claim that overhead costs will now be spread over a larger output, we begin to suspect that it must be false.

But the analysis of the preceding pages enables us to make out a better claim for the rationalisers than they make for themselves. We found that, in general, a rise in demand will raise price in the short period, but this is not necessarily always the case. In the first place, if it can be shown that marginal prime costs are falling (with increases of output) in the firms in question[1] there is a certain presumption that the price of the product will fall when demand is concentrated on a smaller number of firms. To determine whether, in a particular case, marginal costs are falling would require an intimate knowledge of the technique of the industry in question.[2] There is no way of saying *a priori* whether it is a probable state of affairs or not.

Secondly, even if marginal costs are constant, the claim that prices will fall can be made good if it can be shown that the demand for the output of particular firms becomes more elastic when some of the firms are closed down. If competition is perfect this is impossible. When competition is not perfect the change in elasticity will depend upon the nature of the market imperfection. In so far as it is due merely to differences of transport cost the effect of closing down firms will be different according to which firms are closed. If the remaining firms are situated

---

[1] It is only possible for marginal cost to the individual firm to be falling if competition is not perfect (see p. 95, below).

[2] See p. 50.

close together, so that the industry becomes geographically more concentrated, the imperfection of the market will be reduced by the elimination of firms. But if firms are weeded out here and there, so that the industry becomes geographically more scattered, the opposite effect will be produced; the market will become less perfect and there will be a presumption that prices will be raised by the concentration of demand. In so far as the imperfection of the market is due to goodwill, there is a certain presumption (as we have seen) that the elimination of firms will cause the market to become more perfect. The faithful customers of the condemned firms, once dislodged from their adherence to them, may be presumed to choose with greater nicety between the remaining firms, so that each of the remaining firms will have added to their market a fringe of customers whose demand for their particular output is more elastic than the demand of their old customers. If this is the case, prices will be reduced by the concentration of demand, unless marginal costs are rising sufficiently rapidly.

It is only by considering all the factors in the situation in this manner that it is possible to discover whether a scheme for rationalisation is likely to raise or lower the price of the particular commodity concerned.

CHAPTER 5

1

THE analysis of the effect of a change in cost upon the price of a single producer is at once simpler and more complicated than the analysis of the effect of changes in demand. It is simpler because an increase in marginal cost will always reduce output, and so, with a given demand curve, raise price, while, as we have seen, an increase in demand may either raise or lower price. It is more complicated because the change in cost may take many more forms than the change in demand. A change in cost which is the result of a change in technique will be likely to alter the whole shape and course of the cost curve, and a change which is due to an alteration in the price of one of the factors of production may lead to a change in technique. In order to simplify the problem we will suppose (following tradition) that an increase of cost comes about in the simplest possible way, for instance by the imposition of a tax of a constant amount per unit of output. The average and marginal cost curves will then both be raised uniformly by the amount of the tax, and there will be no change in the shape of the curves.

2

Let us first consider the case in which the demand curve is a straight line.

Let the marginal revenue curve be cut by the old marginal cost curve, MC_1, in C_1 and by the new marginal cost curve (raised by the amount of the tax), MC_2, in C_2.

* *This chapter is not of great importance except for readers interested in the technique of analysis.*

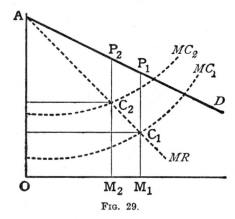

Fig. 29.

Now we know that the old price, M_1P_1, is equal to $\frac{1}{2}M_1C_1$ (the old marginal cost) *plus* $\frac{1}{2}OA$, the intercept on the y axis of the straight-line demand curve.[1] And the new price, M_2P_2, is equal to $\frac{1}{2}M_2C_2$ (the new marginal cost) *plus* $\frac{1}{2}OA$. Therefore the rise in price due to the imposition of the tax is equal to half the increase in marginal cost.

When marginal costs are constant for all amounts of output the rise in marginal cost is equal to the tax, and the price is therefore raised by half the tax.

When marginal costs are rising, it is raised by less than half the tax, the price being unaltered in the extreme case where the cost curve is completely inelastic.

When marginal costs are falling the price is raised by more than half the amount of the tax, the extent to which it is raised being greater (with any given demand curve) the more rapid is the rate of fall of marginal cost with increases of output. The price will rise by exactly the full amount of the tax when the rate of fall of the marginal cost curve is sufficiently great for its slope (as measured by the chord joining the points corresponding on the old marginal cost curve to the old and new outputs) to be the same as the slope of the demand curve. This can be proved as follows:

Let M_2C be the old marginal cost of the new output.
Then C_2C is equal to the amount of the tax.

---

[1] See p. 55.

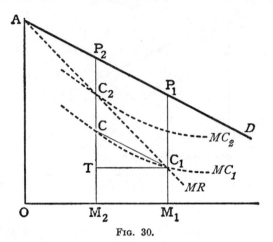

FIG. 30.

Draw C_1T parallel to the x axis to cut M_2C in T.

Let CC_1 be parallel to the demand curve.

Now the slope of the marginal revenue curve is twice the slope of the demand curve.[1]

Therefore (since the slope of MC_1 is assumed to be equal to the slope of the demand curve) the slope of CC_1 is half the slope of the marginal revenue curve. Hence C_2T is equal to twice C_2C. That is, M_2C_2 (the new marginal cost) is greater than M_1C_1 (the old marginal cost) by twice C_2C, which is the amount of the tax. But we have just seen that the price is raised by half the rise in marginal cost. Therefore the price is raised by the amount of the tax.

If the slope of the marginal cost curve is greater than the slope of the demand curve, the price is raised by more than the full amount of the tax.

It is impossible for the slope of the marginal cost curve to be greater than the slope of the marginal revenue curve, since if it were, there would be no equilibrium. If the slope of the marginal cost curve is very close to this limiting value, a small tax would produce a very large rise in price.[2]

[1] See p. 30.

[2] This is the case mentioned by Marshall (*Principles*, p. 482), who expresses it by saying that a small rise in average cost will produce a large decline in output when the total monopoly net revenue is very nearly independent of the amount of output.

3

We must now examine the effect of the concavity of the demand curve.

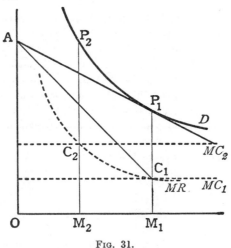

Fig. 31.

Let AP_1 be the tangent to the demand curve at P_1, the old price.

Now, the more concave[1] is the demand curve the further to the left of the correspondent AC_1 will the marginal revenue curve lie.

Thus, for any given rise in the marginal cost curve, the reduction in output will be greater the more concave is the demand curve.[2] Moreover, for any given output the price will, in general, be higher the more concave is the demand curve.[3] Thus for two reasons the effect of the tax will be greater the

---

[1] That is to say, the greater is the "adjusted concavity" of the demand curve; see p. 40, note.

[2] This is on the assumption that the new marginal cost curve cuts the marginal revenue curve below the level of P_1, and therefore, *a fortiori*, below the intersection of MR and the correspondent AC_1. If the tax is sufficiently greater than P_1C_1 (the difference between marginal revenue and price for the old output), or if marginal costs are falling sufficiently rapidly, the effect of concavity may be to mitigate the reduction in output due to the tax.

[3] So that even in those cases where the reduction in output is less for a concave curve than for a straight line it is unlikely that the rise in price will be less.

more concave is the demand curve, and less the more convex is the demand curve.

4

We found that when the demand curve is a straight line and marginal costs are constant for all amounts of output the rise in price is equal to half the tax. It now appears that if the demand curve is concave and marginal costs are constant, the rise in price will be greater than half the tax. It is further possible to isolate the case in which the rise in price is equal to the full amount of the tax when marginal costs are constant. This will be found when the concavity of the demand curve is so great that the slope of the marginal revenue curve is equal to the slope of the demand curve, the slopes being measured by the chords joining the points corresponding to the old and the new outputs. This can easily be seen.

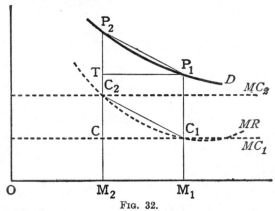

Fig. 32.

Let P_2P_1, the chord of the demand curve, be parallel to C_2C_1, the chord of the marginal revenue curve.
Let perpendiculars from P_1 and C_1 to P_2M_2 cut it in T and C.
Then P_2P_1T and C_2C_1C are congruent triangles.
$\therefore$ P_2T (the rise in price) is equal to C_2C, the rise in marginal cost, which is equal to the amount of the tax.

5

We found that the effect of the tax in raising price will be less the more convex is the demand curve. In the extreme case the price may be unaltered. If the change in slope of the demand curve is so rapid that it contains a kink, there will be a discontinuity in the marginal revenue curve;[1] and if the old and new marginal cost curves both cut the marginal revenue curve vertically below the kink in the demand curve, there will be no change in price. Thus:

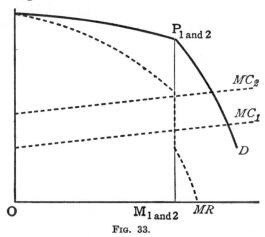

FIG. 33.

A demand curve of this form might be found where a monopolist is subject to potential competition. A monopolist may have some advantage over his rivals, whose costs are higher than his, but he may be aware that if he raises his price beyond a certain critical level his rivals will find it profitable to produce and will begin to invade his market. Above this critical price, therefore, his demand curve suddenly becomes very elastic, and even when his costs are augmented by the tax he will not find it worth while to raise his price above this critical level, provided that his rivals are not also subject to the tax.

6

We have found that the effect of a tax per unit of output is in general to raise the price by something less than the full amount of the tax. Only when the marginal cost curve is falling

[1] See p. 38

G

faster than the demand curve, or when the demand curve is sufficiently concave, will the rise in price be equal to or greater than the amount of the tax. If marginal costs are rising with increases of output, or if the demand curve is convex, the effect of the tax upon price will tend to be small; and in the extreme cases where the supply is perfectly inelastic or where the convexity of the demand curve is infinite, so that there is a kink in the curve, there will be no rise in price at all.

But these results can only be applied within a narrow sphere. If we are considering a firm selling in rivalry with others, and if the tax is imposed on all the rival firms, then all will raise their prices, and the demand curve of each will be raised. The results here worked out upon the assumption that the demand curve is unaffected by the imposition of the tax will therefore not be applicable.

The tax which we have been discussing may be taken to stand for a rise in marginal costs brought about by a rise in wages. Our results can then be applied if the rise in wages affects only one firm. But if there is a general rise in wages the demand curve of any one firm is likely to be raised by the rise in the price charged by its rivals. The results obtained in this chapter can thus only be applied to a single firm considered separately, and the study of the effects of a rise in cost upon price, assuming the demand curve to be constant, are of less general interest than the study of the effect of a rise in demand, assuming the cost curve to be constant.

BOOK III
COMPETITIVE EQUILIBRIUM

CHAPTER 6

1

WE have now completed our analysis of price and output for a
single firm. We must next discuss the supply curve of a commodity produced by a number of firms. The supply curve for a
commodity represents a list of amounts of the commodity which
will be associated with various prices. A supply curve tells us that
if such and such an output is to be produced, this will be the
price. And if the conditions of demand are such that this amount
of the commodity is demanded at this price, then this is the output that will be produced. We can imagine that we move along
the supply curve by means of successive increases of demand.
As the amount demanded increases, the supply price may rise,
remain constant, or fall, but each separate amount has a certain
price which it is necessary to pay in order to call forth that
amount of output. If the price secured by the sale of this amount
of output were less, a smaller output would be produced. And
if a higher price were secured by the sale of this output, a larger
output would be produced. In every case a larger total sum must
be offered to call forth a larger total output. A larger output will
cost a larger total sum to produce, and a larger total offer must
be made in order to procure it. This must be true even though
average cost may fall as output increases.

The quasi-long-period supply curve (the supply curve of a
fixed number of firms) presents no difficulty so long as competition is perfect. Under perfect competition price is equal to
marginal cost, and the output produced at any given price is
the sum of the outputs of the separate firms for which marginal
cost is equal to the given price.[1] The notion of a supply curve

---

[1] The costs of an individual firm may alter with a change in the scale of
the industry. The manner in which this may occur is discussed in Chapter 9.

has always been associated with the notion of perfect competition, but if we are to study conditions in which competition is not perfect the orthodox conception of a supply curve must be reconsidered.

First, there is the obvious fact that if the market is imperfect the same commodity may be sold at different prices by different producers.[1] This presents an initial difficulty in drawing up the supply curve which could be disposed of if we assumed that the cost curves of all firms are exactly alike, that the individual demand curves are all alike, and that individual demand curves all move in the same way when the total demand increases. Then in spite of the imperfection, a single price will rule throughout the market for each position of the total demand curve.

But a more fundamental difficulty would remain. When competition is not perfect, the demand curve for the output of each individual producer is not perfectly elastic, and each producer will sell that output at which his marginal cost is equal to his marginal receipts. Marginal revenue will not be equal to price; it is marginal revenue, not price, which determines the output of the individual producer, and any number of different prices are compatible with the same marginal revenue.[2]

The relationship between marginal revenue and price will depend upon the shapes of the individual demand curves, and the effect of a given increase in the total demand for the commodity upon output will depend upon the manner in which it affects the individual demand curves. We may assume that any increase in the total demand for the commodity would be distributed evenly between all the individual firms, so that the individual demand curves all move in the same way. But there are many possible ways in which they might move, and before we can say what effect an increase in the total demand will have upon output it is further necessary to postulate the particular way, out of all the possible ways, in which the individual demand curves will move. We might postulate, for instance, that each

for the case in which the number of firms alters. The results there obtained may be applied, with the necessary modifications, to the case in which the number of firms is fixed.

[1] Further there are considerable difficulties, as we shall see in a moment, in talking of the "same commodity" when the market is imperfect.

[2] Competition may be imperfect either because the market is imperfect or because the number of firms is small. The case of a small number of firms selling in a perfect market raises some difficulties, which are not here discussed.

curve is raised vertically, so that a constant sum is added to the
price which would be paid for each amount on a given individual
demand curve. Or that each curve is moved to the right, so that
a constant quantity is added to the amount that would be
bought at each price on a given individual demand curve. Or
that the elasticity of the curves remains the same when they are
raised, so that the amount that would be bought at each price
on a given individual demand curve is increased by a constant
proportion. And so forth. Any number of such assumptions
might be made, and upon any one of them it would be possible
to draw up a supply curve, which would show the response of
supply to a given increase in the total offer for the commodity.
A certain price would be associated with each output, but the
result would be different on each of the different possible
assumptions. Thus, although it is possible to draw up a supply
curve on any one of these assumptions, there will be a different
supply curve on each different assumption. We cannot say what
increase in the total offer is necessary to induce a given increase
in supply unless we know in which of all the possible ways
the increase in the total offer affects the individual demand
curves.

And even when the curves are assumed to move in a certain
way, so that it is formally possible to draw up a supply curve,
it is still necessary to recognise that the increase in supply is
governed by the rise in the marginal revenue curves of the
individual producers. It is only if we have, so to speak, tethered
the demand curves to the marginal revenue curves by an
arbitrary assumption, that the increase in output appears to be
associated with the rise in the total demand curve. In reality,
the increase in output is not immediately associated with the
rise of the total demand curve, but with the rise of individual
marginal revenue curves.

The alternative assumptions which make it possible to preserve the appearance of a supply curve on which a given output
is associated with a given price are all equally unplausible. There
is no reason to choose one rather than another, and in fact a
given increase in the total demand for a commodity is unlikely
to be associated with any one of them.

Moreover, our initial assumption that a given increase in
demand is distributed evenly between the individual firms is

also unplausible. When the total demand increases some firms
may find that their individual demand curves are raised more,
and some less; some that they are raised but made more elastic,
some that they are raised and made less elastic; or the increase
of demand may be concentrated wholly upon a few producers.
Even if it happened by chance that the same price was charged
throughout the whole market, it would be impossible to predict
what output would be associated with that price unless we knew
exactly how the demand was distributed between the individual
markets. Moreover, when the cost curves of the individual firms
are not all alike, a further source of variation is introduced. A
given increase in demand will produce different increases in
output, according to whether it is concentrated mainly upon
firms whose marginal costs are relatively low or on firms whose
marginal costs are higher.

In short, the effect of a given increase in total demand upon
total output will vary according to its effect upon the demand
for the individual producers. An increase in total demand will
show itself in a rise of the individual demand curves, but it may
change their shape in any number of ways, and it may affect
some demand curves more than others. The effect upon output
will be different in each different case. A given rise in total
demand will produce a smaller or greater effect upon output
according to its effect upon the individual marginal revenue
curves. It is even possible, if it so happened that each individual
demand curve became less elastic as it was raised, that a decrease
in output would be the result of a rise in total demand.[1]

The simple notion of a single price associated with a single
output from the industry can only be retained if there is a
unique relation which links marginal revenue to price. The
fundamental relationship is between marginal revenue and
output, not between price and output.

2

The traditional assumption of perfect competition is an
exceedingly convenient one for simplifying the analysis of price,
but there is no reason to expect it to be fulfilled in the real
world. It depends, in the first place, upon the existence of such

[1] Cf. p. 66.

a large number of producers that a change in the output of any one of them has a negligible effect upon the output of the commodity as a whole, and it depends, in the second place, upon the existence of a perfect market. The first condition may often be approximately fulfilled, but the existence of a perfect market is likely to be extremely rare in the real world.

If the demand curve for an individual producer is perfectly elastic, he is able by the least reduction in price to attract an indefinite amount of custom, and by the least rise in price he will forfeit the whole of his sales. Thus the notion of a perfect market is based upon the assumption that the customers who make up the market all react in the same way to differences in the prices charged by different sellers. But in actual markets the customer takes into account a great deal besides the prices at which rival producers offer him their goods. Quite apart from the inertia or ignorance which prevents him from moving instantly from one seller to another, as soon as a difference appears between the prices which they charge, he has a number of good reasons for preferring one seller to another. And these reasons will affect different individuals differently.

In the first place, the customer must take costs of transport into account. This will show itself in a retail market in a reluctance of the customer to go far afield when he is shopping, and in the wholesale market in actual differences in the freights which he must pay to obtain delivery from one producer rather than another. And the relative distances of the location of different firms will be different for different customers.[1] Secondly, the different customers will be differently influenced by the guarantee of quality provided by a well-known name. Thirdly, they will be influenced in varying degrees by the difference between the facilities provided by different producers—quickness of service, good manners of salesmen, length of credit, and the attention paid to their individual wants. In some cases (most disconcertingly from the point of view of analysis) the

---

[1] Marshall (*Principles*, p. 325) defines a market as a region in which the same price rules for the same commodity allowing for differences in the cost of transport, but this definition will not serve our turn, since market imperfection due to differences in transport cost, as between one buyer and another, have just the same effect as inertia or "goodwill" in making the individual demand curve less than perfectly elastic. Cf. Sraffa, *Economic Journal*, March 1926, p. 543.

customer will be influenced by the actual price, since he will sometimes take a high price to be a sign that the article in question is a good one, and reject a cheaper substitute because its very cheapness makes him suspect that it is inferior. Lastly, the customer will be influenced by advertisement, which plays upon his mind with studied skill, and makes him prefer the goods of one producer to those of another because they are brought to his notice in a more pleasing or more forceful manner.

Thus there are many reasons why a customer buys from one producer rather than another besides the simple one of a difference in the prices which they charge, and since the rival producers make it their business to exploit all these influences upon the customer's choice, the very existence of competition, in the plain sense of the word, ensures that the market will not be perfect. Rival producers compete against each other in quality, in facilities, and in advertisement, as well as in price, and the very intensity of competition, by forcing them to attract customers in every possible way, itself breaks up the market and ensures that not all the customers, who are attached in varying degrees to a particular firm by the advantages which it offers them, will immediately forsake it for a rival who offers similar goods at an infinitesimally smaller price.[1]

---

[1] The existence of competition which takes the form of providing facilities to the customer, of improving the quality of goods, of advertisement, or any other form than a simple lowering of price, is awkward from the point of view of theoretical analysis for two reasons. In the first place, it very much enhances the difficulty of deciding what precisely we mean by a commodity. Even if all the more obvious difficulties are disposed of, and we are able to decide exactly what we mean by a motor car or a tin of cocoa, the fact remains that, from the point of view of a particular customer, a tin of cocoa sold by Jones is not necessarily the same thing as a tin of cocoa sold by Brown, and if they are not the same it is impossible to sum the demand curve for Brown's cocoa and Jones' cocoa so as to obtain the demand curve for cocoa as such. A second and even more perplexing difficulty arises because all forms of competition except a mere lowering of price involve a change in the costs of production. The demand curve for the product of the individual firm depends partly on the outlay made by the firm in order to attract customers. This difficulty would be less intractable if the outlay could be treated as sales cost entirely separate from the costs of manufacture, but actually it often takes the form of changes in the quality of goods and is intimately bound up with the ordinary expenses of production. The fact that in the real world the demand curve and the cost curve of individual firms are not independent presents a very formidable problem to economic analysis, and no attempt is made to solve it here. (Cf. p. 21.)

3

There are a further set of difficulties in drawing up the supply curve, arising from the passage of time. At any one moment all the firms in an industry may not be in equilibrium (from a long-period or quasi-long-period point of view), some may be growing, and others declining, and yet the industry as a whole may be in equilibrium. It might be possible therefore to draw an industry's supply curve without assuming each firm to be of equilibrium size. The attempt to do so introduces many formidable difficulties which we have not considered, and they have received more attention from economists than the difficulties connected with the imperfection of markets. Various devices have been suggested to overcome them, of which the most familiar is Marshall's Representative Firm.[1] Since these devices are not designed to deal with the fundamental difficulty involved in the notion of a supply curve under imperfect competition, they must be taken to represent an attempt to deal with an imaginary world in which the market is perfect, but in which firms take time to reach their equilibrium size. This does not appear to be a very satisfactory method of approach. It would be impossible to tell how rapidly firms would grow or contract in a perfect market. The influences which prevent firms from growing are closely interrelated with the influences which make markets imperfect, and it may even be that in a perfect market there are no impediments at all to the growth of firms. A more fruitful line of attack appears to be to solve first the most abstract problem, in which there is neither time nor market imperfection; then to deal with cases in which the market is imperfect but in which firms are imagined always to be in individual equilibrium; and, finally, to introduce the element of time, and to study cases in which firms are tending to grow (or contract) towards the position of individual equilibrium. Last of all, factors connected with ignorance, inertia and the "human element" generally would have to be fitted into the scheme.

[1] Professor Pigou has postulated an imaginary equilibrium firm which may be different from any actual firm in the industry (*Economics of Welfare*, p. 788), but this does not appear to provide a solution of the problem, for if the actual firms are not in equilibrium, their costs will bear no relation to the costs of this imaginary firm. Mr. G. F. Shove has suggested a system of three dimensional cost curves; see "A Symposium on Increasing Returns and the Representative Firm," *Economic Journal*, March 1930, p. 111.

CHAPTER 7

COMPETITIVE EQUILIBRIUM

1

WE have so far considered only a given number of firms. It remains to consider the reaction of monopoly profit on the number of firms producing a given commodity. A change in the number of firms will alter the demand curve for any one firm, and may alter its costs. It is customary to regard the level of profits in an industry as governing the entry of new firms. *Normal profits* is that level of profit at which there is no tendency for new firms to enter the trade, or for old firms to disappear out of it. Abnormally high profits earned by existing firms are regarded as inducing new firms to begin to produce the commodity, and abnormally low profits, by leading to a cessation of new investment, are regarded as leading to a gradual decline in the number of firms in the industry.[1]

Such an account of the matter is somewhat artificial, in so far as the expansion of an industry is concerned. An increase in the demand for the commodity attracts new entrepreneurs to the industry directly, by opening up some new possibility of profitable investment, rather than indirectly, by making their mouths water at the sight of the high profits of the existing firms. The abnormal profits are a symptom rather than a cause

---

[1] There is likely to be a considerable difference between the level of profits just sufficient to maintain the existing productive equipment of an industry and the level of profits sufficient to lead to expansion. If an increase in demand raises profits within these limits there will be no increase in the number of firms engaged in the industry. For industries, such as railways or iron and steel, where the initial investment is necessarily large, it may be that no level of profits likely to occur in practice will be sufficiently great to attract new firms. In such cases the quasi-long-period analysis must be applied. The problem of the conditions influencing the entry of new firms, in response to a rise in demand, or the disappearance of old firms, in response to a fall in demand, presents an interesting and largely unexplored field of inquiry.

of the situation in which new firms will find it profitable to enter the trade. But the artificial device of regarding the abnormal profits as a causal factor is of great assistance in simplifying the formal argument, and provided that its artificiality is recognised, it seems permissible to make use of it.

Only the expansion of an industry in response to abnormally high profits will be considered here, and it will be assumed that by a similar process industries decline when profits are less than normal. The level of normal profits must be defined in respect to the particular industry. The difficulties of entering the trade will be reflected in the level of profits, just as the difficulty of becoming a doctor or a civil servant is reflected in the incomes earned by doctors and civil servants. The level of normal profits in trades which are easy to enter, for instance, retail selling on a small scale, are likely to be low relatively to the normal profits of industries requiring a very large initial investment or peculiar efficiency or peculiar facilities of various kinds, just as the earnings of successful crossing-sweepers are low relatively to the earnings of successful doctors.[1]

In trades into which there is no possibility of entry, such as the provision of public-houses in a district where a fixed number of licenses is granted, there is no upper limit to profit, though there must be a lower limit at the level of profits which is just sufficient to maintain the existing number of firms in business.[2] The analysis of such a case may be conducted in the manner discussed in the last chapter.

An industry is said to be in *full equilibrium* when there is no tendency for the number of firms to alter. The profits earned by the firms in it are then normal.[3]

In order to discover whether profits are normal or not it is necessary to introduce into our analytical apparatus the average cost curve of the firm. Average cost must include the average per unit of output of the normal profit of the entrepreneur. The average cost curve must therefore be falling (even if there

---

[1] Further complications, which are ignored in this analysis, arise because a change in the total demand for the commodity is likely to alter the conditions which determine the degree of difficulty of entry into the trade.

[2] Firms producing patent goods, or using patent processes, also belong to this class.

[3] See Chapter 9 for the complications introduced by differences in the efficiency of different firms.

are no economies of large-scale production) for small outputs. The fixed sum representing normal profits will be averaged out over a larger number of units of output as the firm expands in size. In addition there are likely to be technical economies due to the increased scale of operations.

The demand curve for each firm is assumed to be independent of its costs. This is an unrealistic assumption, since advertising and other marketing costs will affect the demand curve of the firm in actual cases.[1]

Profits will be normal when price is equal to average cost. The total receipts of the firm are then exactly equal to total costs including normal profits. But the firm is in individual equilibrium when marginal revenue is equal to marginal cost. Full equilibrium thus requires a double condition, that marginal revenue is equal to marginal cost, and that average revenue (or price) is equal to average cost.

The double condition of full equilibrium can only be fulfilled when the individual demand curve of the firm is a tangent to its average cost curve. For if the demand curve everywhere lies below the average cost curve no output can be produced at normal profits. And if the demand curve anywhere lies above the average cost curve there will be a range of outputs at which an abnormal profit can be made; among these outputs the firm will choose the most remunerative, and profits will be more than normal. Only when the demand curve is a tangent to the average cost curve will profits be normal. Thus whenever the demand curve of the individual firm lies above its average cost curve, new firms will be attracted into the industry by the abnormal profits, and their competition will lower the individual demand curve again until it is once more tangential to the average cost curve.

For the output at which the demand curve and the average cost curve are tangential the marginal revenue curve must cut the marginal cost curve.[2]

In each diagram AC and MC are the average and marginal cost curve of the firms. AR is the demand curve, or average revenue curve. MR is the marginal revenue curve.

---

[1] It is further necessary to assume that the cost curve of the firm is independent of the conditions of demand. This assumption also is unrealistic; see p. 21, note.   [2] See p. 33.

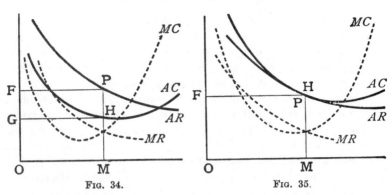

FIG. 34.   FIG. 35.

OM is the output produced when the firm is in individual
equilibrium, MH is the average cost of the output OM, and
MP is the price. In Fig. 34 the firm is making abnormal
profits. Then, although the firm is in equilibrium, the industry is not. The abnormal profit is shown by the area
FPHG. In Fig. 35 profits are normal. H and P coincide
(average cost is equal to price), and the area FPHG disappears. The double condition of equilibrium is thus fulfilled when the individual demand curve is a tangent to
the average cost curve.

2

Now, when competition is perfect, marginal revenue is equal
to price. Marginal cost must therefore be equal to price. But
for full equilibrium price must be equal to average cost. Full
equilibrium can therefore only be attained, under perfect competition, when marginal cost is equal to average cost. Marginal
and average cost are equal at the minimum point on the average
cost curve.[1] It follows that under perfect competition there
must be a minimum point on the average cost curve, that is to
say, there must be a certain output beyond which the average
costs of the firm begin to rise.

It may appear fantastic to deduce a fact about the nature of
the costs of a firm from a purely geometrical argument. But upon
reflection the paradox disappears. Mr. Robinson[2] has shown
that there may be cases in which average costs for a firm do rise

---

[1] See Fig. 1, p. 28.   [2] *Structure of Competitive Industry*, chap. iii.

after a certain output has been reached. Now if average costs are continually falling, as the firm expands, and never reach a minimum point, marginal cost will always lie below average cost. Marginal costs may be rising (over a certain range of outputs) or may be falling. If marginal costs are rising it will be possible for the firm to reach equilibrium, where price is equal to marginal cost. But price will be less than average cost, profits will be less than normal, and the industry will not be in equilibrium. And if marginal costs are falling the firm will continue to expand. The expansion of one firm (or the growth of the firm by amalgamation with others) will reduce the number of firms until competition ceases to be perfect. Thus, under perfect competition, marginal and average cost must be equal in equilibrium and average cost must be at a minimum, simply because, if this condition is not fulfilled, competition is not perfect.

Equilibrium under perfect competition is illustrated in Figs. 36 and 37:

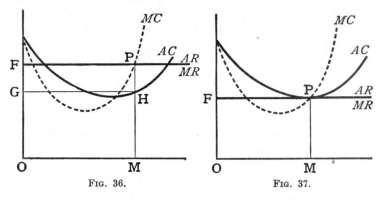

FIG. 36.   FIG. 37.

MP is the price of the output OM, and MH is its average cost. In Fig. 37 the industry is in full equilibrium; in Fig. 36 it is not, and an abnormal profit (FPHG) is being earned by the firm.

3

In a perfectly competitive industry each firm, in full equilibrium, will produce that output at which its average costs are a minimum. Each firm then will be of *optimum size*. It is sometimes supposed that the optimum size of the firm is that which is most profitable to the entrepreneur, so that the entrepreneur has a motive for wishing his firm to be of optimum size.[1] But this view is mistaken. It is no disadvantage to the entrepreneur to produce more than the optimum output. Indeed it is when profits are abnormally high (because new firms are failing to enter the industry to a sufficient extent to keep profits at the normal level) that the firms are of more than optimum size. The entrepreneur will have no desire to return to the situation in which his profits are reduced to normal, and the fact that, at the optimum size, his average costs would be at a minimum will not influence his conduct. Of course it is to the interests of every entrepreneur to produce whatever output he may be producing in the most efficient way, and we are assuming throughout this analysis that an entrepreneur will always produce any given output in such a way that the cost to him of that given output is at a minimum. But it is not to his interest to choose from all possible outputs that output whose average cost is least. It is to his interest to choose the output for which (in the existing conditions of demand) marginal gain to him is equal to marginal cost.

If competition is imperfect the demand curve for the output of the individual firm will be falling (Fig. 35) and the double condition of equilibrium can only be fulfilled for some output at which average cost is falling. The firms will therefore be of less than optimum size when profits are normal. When the conditions which produce equilibrium obtain, it is not profitable for the firm to expand, and the entrepreneur has no reason for wishing to produce the optimum output, since any increase beyond the equilibrium output would involve a marginal cost greater than marginal revenue. It is only if conditions of perfect competition prevail that firms will be of the optimum size, and there is no reason to expect that they will be of optimum size in the real world, since in the real world competition is not perfect.

4

We may now attempt to draw up the supply curve of an

---

[1] *E.g.* Schneider, "Das Verteilungs- und Kostenproblem in einer vertrusteten Industrie", *Schmollers Jahrbuch*, vol. 19, p. 55; Hicks, *Theory of Wages*, p. 37.

H

industry in conditions of full equilibrium, where price is equal to average cost for the firms.

In order to isolate the effect upon the output of a single firm, and upon its cost, of changes in the number of firms, it is necessary to make certain simplifying assumptions.

To eliminate the problems connected with time we may assume first that the efficiency and the costs of individual firms do not alter with the passage of time, but only with changes in the scale of output; and secondly, that each firm is always in individual equilibrium, in the sense that it is always able to produce that output at which its marginal gains are equal to its marginal costs.

To isolate the effect of changes in the individual demand curves upon supply price it is necessary to assume that there is no change in the cost curves of the firms when the industry expands.

Finally, in order to dispose of the difficulties discussed in the last chapter and to simplify the problem, we may assume that all firms are alike in respect of their costs and of the conditions of demand for their individual outputs.[1]

Now, starting from a position in which the industry is in equilibrium, suppose that the total demand for the commodity is increased. The individual demand curves will then be raised, and since all firms are assumed to be always alike in respect of conditions of demand, all the demand curves will be raised in the same way. The output of each firm will then increase. The price of the commodity may rise, fall, or remain constant, but in any case the firms will receive a surplus profit in excess of the normal profit which is included in average cost (cf. Fig. 34). New firms will now be attracted into the industry, and, in the conditions postulated, these new firms will have the same costs as the old. The total output of the commodity will be further increased, and the competition of the new firms will lower the individual demand curves of old firms. A new position of long-period equilibrium will be established when the individual demand curves are once more tangential to the average cost curves.

---

[1] This does not of course entail that the firms are alike from the point of view of individual buyers. If they were, the market would be perfect. But individuals with different scales of preferences, as between any one firm and the others, are assumed to be grouped symmetrically so that the demand curves of the separate firms are all alike.

In the new position, will the price of the commodity be greater or less than before? Clearly the answer depends upon the manner in which the demand curves move as they fall back towards an equilibrium position. If the individual demand curve does not alter its slope it will fall back to exactly the same position as before. The output of each firm will be the same in the new position as in the old, and the increase in the number of firms will be in proportion to the increase in the total output.[1] Since the output of the firm is unchanged, its average cost and the price of the commodity will be unchanged. If the individual demand curve is less elastic in the new situation it will reach equilibrium with its point of contact with the average cost curve to the left of its old position. The output of each firm in the new situation will be smaller than in the old situation. The increase in the number of firms will therefore be more than in proportion to the increase in output. Since the output of the individual firm has decreased, its average cost will be raised, and the price of the commodity will be raised.

Conversely, if the individual demand curve is more elastic in the new situation the price of the commodity will be lowered.

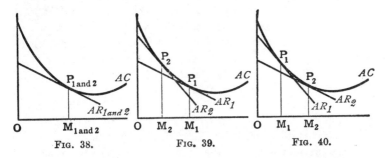

FIG. 38.   FIG. 39.   FIG. 40.

In each diagram AC is the average cost curve of the firm. AR_1 and AR_2 are the old and new demand curves. OM_1 is the output of the firm in the old situation and M_1P_1 its price. OM_2 is the output in the new situation and M_2P_2 its price. In Fig. 38 M_2P_2 is equal to M_1P_1. In Fig. 39 M_2P_2 is greater than, and in Fig. 40 less than, M_1P_1.

---

[1] This will occur in the special case of perfect competition, but it may also occur when competition is not perfect.

From this analysis we can obtain the answer that, in the conditions postulated, an increase in the total demand for the commodity may either raise or lower its price, or leave it unchanged.[1]

5

But less purely formal considerations must also be taken into account. We must inquire what type of change in demand will lower price and what types would raise it or leave it unaltered. A full discussion of this topic would lead us far afield and we will here do no more than examine one example of each type.

First consider the case in which price is unchanged. This might occur if the increase of demand came about by the addition to the market of a new group of customers. As new firms are set up these additional buyers, whose demand was temporarily satisfied by the old firms, may be supposed to forsake them for the new firms; the demand curves of the old firms would then fall back to their former position, and the new demand would be satisfied by the new firms. For example, suppose that the imperfection of the market is due to differential transport costs, and that the increase in demand comes entirely from a fringe of newly established suburbs on the outskirts of a town. The inhabitants of the suburbs would at first buy from the various firms in the centre of the town, but as soon as firms were set up in their own districts they would transfer their custom to the new firms. The elasticity of the individual demand curve would then be the same as before.

Next consider the case in which price is raised by the increase in demand. This would occur, whatever the nature of the initial rise in demand, if the new firms, when they enter the industry, attract away all the most fickle customers of the old firms, and leave only those who are more strongly attached to them. The individual demand curves would then become less elastic. There may have been, for instance, a fringe of customers attached to the market of each firm who were never

---

[1] Professor Pigou has published a confirmation and generalisation of these results, in analytical form, in the *Economic Journal*, March 1933 (pp. 108-12). Mr. Shove (*ib.* pp. 115-17) has made some criticisms on my analysis which appear to suggest that he would disagree with the proposition that, when competition is imperfect, the firm must be producing under conditions of falling average cost in full equilibrium; but the apparent conflict arises from a difference between Mr. Shove's interpretation of cost and my own.

provided for in the manner which they would really have preferred (for instance, the location of the old firms may have been inconvenient or, if we relax the assumption that the commodity is perfectly homogeneous, the types of article produced by the old firms may all have been equally unsatisfactory to buyers with peculiar tastes). They were therefore indifferent between the old firms. But the increase in total demand has called into existence firms which exactly meet their various requirements. The indifferent fringe of the old markets now disappears, and the new firms are each provided with a group of buyers whose preference for their wares is strong. The elasticity of the individual demand curves is then less than before.

Lastly, consider the case in which the price falls. This would occur if the increase in demand were spread evenly over the whole market, for instance by a uniform increase in the density of population, and if the new firms were set up, so to speak, in between the old firms (either geographically or in respect of special qualities which appeal in various degrees to different customers). The difference, from the point of view of buyers, between any one firm and the next would thus be reduced, the customers of each firm would become more indifferent, and the elasticity of demand would be increased.

There are some grounds for supposing that the last type of change in demand is the most frequent. It may therefore be considered probable that an increase in total demand will lower price rather than raise it. It is worth while to remark, however, that successive increases of demand of this type would ultimately remove market imperfection altogether and establish the optimum size as the equilibrium size of the firms; but in considering the imperfection of the market as independent of the action of the firms we have drawn a highly simplified picture of the conditions which prevail in the real world. In the real world when a firm finds that the market is becoming uncomfortably perfect it can resort to advertisement and other devices which attach particular customers more firmly to itself. If a number of firms all act in this way the market is broken up again and the equilibrium size of the firms is reduced.

CHAPTER 8

1

BEFORE we can proceed with the second part of the analysis of the supply curve, and consider the reactions of a change in the output of an industry on the costs of the firms composing it, we must pause to consider a particular kind of cost of which the nature is not obvious.

The essence of the conception of *rent* is the conception of a surplus earned by a particular part of a factor of production over and above the minimum earnings necessary to induce it to do its work. This conception of rent, both verbally and historically, is closely connected with the conception of "free gifts of nature". The chief of these free gifts of nature (of which the essential characteristic is that they do not owe their origin to human effort) is space, and for this reason they have usually been referred to simply as "land"—land being understood to comprise all the other "free gifts" besides mere space. Consequently the term rent, which in ordinary speech means a payment made for the hire of land, was borrowed by the economists as the title of the sort of surplus earnings which the free gifts of nature receive. The whole of the earnings of *land* in the economist's sense is *rent* in the economist's sense, for it follows from the definition of the free gifts of nature that they are there in any case, and do not require to be paid in order to exist.

But the conception of rent has often been too closely interwoven with the conception of land. Particular units of factors of production which belong to the other three broad categories, labour, entrepreneurship, and capital, may also earn rent. A man who finds himself born into the world must earn what he can get. The minimum payment which is necessary to induce him to continue to work with any given intensity is the real income which will maintain his physiological efficiency at an adequate level. The necessary minimum for an entrepreneur is the level of earnings which is sufficient to prevent him from relapsing into the ranks of employed labour. And many men obviously receive a real income greater than this necessary minimum. The question of what level of earnings is necessary to induce a man to be born is another matter, into which we need not here inquire.[1] Further, it is obvious that capital also often receives a surplus over the necessary minimum. Many individuals would still be prepared to save and to lend a given amount of money if the payment they received for it was less than it actually is, and some might save and lend even at a negative rate of interest. Thus, in each of the broad categories of factors, particular pieces of factors may be found which earn rent.

The same point may be made clear if we look at the matter from another angle. It is obvious that no part of a factor will earn rent if the factor in question is in perfectly elastic supply for all amounts. An imaginary example of a factor in perfectly elastic supply may be constructed as follows: Suppose that individuals are prepared to save and to lend money to any extent provided that they receive five per cent. on it. And suppose that a lower rate will fail to induce them to lend at all. Then the rate of interest can never depart from five per cent. If the rate rises above five per cent. such a flood of savings will be put on to the market for loans that the rate must fall again. And if the rate falls below five per cent. no new loans will be forthcoming and the stock of capital will gradually be depleted until it once more earns five per cent. Money capital would then be in perfectly elastic supply, and each particular part of the factor capital would be receiving no more than its necessary minimum earnings. Now the extraordinarily unreal nature of this example makes it obvious that not even capital is in perfectly elastic supply in the real world. And it is still more obvious that factors belonging to the other broad categories are not likely to be in perfectly elastic supply. It is therefore clear that factors of any type are often likely to receive rent.

[1] This whole treatment is over-simplified. See Robertson, "Economic Incentive", in *Economic Fragments*, for a full discussion.

But all this is quite beside the purpose of our present inquiry. This book does not deal with the question of output as a whole. It is confined to the study of the output of a particular commodity considered in isolation. Now from the point of view of an industry producing a particular commodity the necessary minimum payment for a factor is not the payment which will cause that factor to exist, but the payment which will cause it to take service in that particular industry rather than in another.[1]

The cost of any unit of a factor, from the point of view of one industry, is therefore determined by the reward which that unit can earn in some other industry. A worker, an entrepreneur, or an acre of land, will be transferred to one use from others when the reward that it can earn in the one use is higher than in the others (allowing for various impediments to movement which we shall consider later on). Thus when we are studying the supply of a factor to any one industry we are not concerned with the total supply of the factor, but with the level of earnings which is necessary in order to induce units of the factor to transfer themselves from other uses to the industry in question. The price which is necessary to retain a given unit of a factor in a certain industry may be called its *transfer earnings* or *transfer price*, since a reduction of the payment made for it below this price would cause it to be transferred elsewhere; and any particular unit of a factor may be said to be *at the margin of transference*, or to be a *marginal unit*, if the earnings which it receives in the industry where it is employed are only just sufficient to prevent it from transferring itself to some other use.[2] A unit which would remain in the industry for a smaller payment than it actually receives may be called an *intra-marginal unit*.

Now it is quite possible, even when the total supply of a factor is perfectly inelastic, for its supply to any one industry to be perfectly elastic.

A second imaginary example will make this clear. Consider a world in which all land is alike in every respect, but limited in amount relatively to the economic demand for it. Then there

---

[1] See Henderson, *Supply and Demand*, p. 94, and Shove, "Varying Costs and Marginal Net Products", *Economic Journal*, June 1928, p. 259.

[2] See Henderson, *loc. cit.*

will be a certain flat rate of rent per acre paid for all land in all uses, and the supply of land will be absolutely inelastic. No increase in the price paid for it, however great, will call forth an increased supply. Now suppose that the demand for one commodity increases. The makers of this commodity, by paying a rent very slightly greater than that 'offered by the other employers of land, can obtain as much as they please.

The general level of rent, in this illustration, represents the transfer earnings of land from the point of view of each use considered separately. The factor, land, is in perfectly elastic supply to each use considered separately, and from the point of view of each industry it earns no rent.

2

But although the total supply of factors has nothing to do with the case it is clear that there may be pieces of factors which earn more in the industry in which they are employed than would be just sufficient to induce them to take service in it. When this occurs it is consonant with the general notion of rent to describe the difference between the actual earnings of the unit of the factor and its transfer earnings as rent from the point of view of the industry.[1] A third artificial example will illustrate the point.

Imagine a certain strip of the coast which is suitable for seaside hotels, and for which the only possible alternative use is grazing sheep. Suppose that an acre under hotels can earn £20, and under sheep £2. Then the transfer price of an acre of land is £2, and its rent £18. Next suppose that the demand for hotel accommodation is less strong, and that the price which will be offered by would-be hotel proprietors for the use of an acre of land is only £10. No owner of the land (unless influenced by æsthetic considerations) will prefer to let his land to sheep farmers. The amount of land under hotels will be the same as before, and as before, the transfer price of an acre of land will be £2, but the rent is now only £8. Next suppose that some revolution in sheep-farming raises the earnings of grazing land to £12. Now the land-owners will prefer to let to the farmers,

---

[1] This conception was developed by Mr. Shove from the work of Mr. Henderson; see Shove, *loc. cit.*

and the transfer price from the point of view of sheep-farming will be £10, and the rent £2.

Thus each piece of land will have a hierarchy of possible uses, and each would be, in a frictionless world, devoted to its most profitable use. As demands and methods of production change, the hierarchy alters and the use to which the site is put will alter. It is a mistake to suppose that one use of a factor is more profitable than another *per se*. The Strand is more profitably devoted to building hotels than to grazing sheep, but the Wiltshire Downs are more profitably devoted to grazing sheep than to building hotels. Moreover it is clear that the units of a factor which it will first cease to be profitable to employ in a certain use, when there is a decline in demand for the commodity produced with their aid, are not necessarily inferior to the rest. The marginal units in a particular industry may be those which have the best chance of finding profitable employment elsewhere, and are just as likely to be the best as the worst units in the industry. It may well be that if the Strand were under grass it would produce fatter sheep than the Downs.

The unit which will first go out of employment, when demand declines, is that for which the efficiency-price is highest, but the efficiency price may be high either because the unit is very good, but very expensive, or because the unit is inferior from the point of view of this industry, but can command a good price elsewhere. This distinction is well illustrated by entrepreneurship. In some industries, which demand no special gifts, those entrepreneurs will be marginal who have the greatest general ability, for it is they who can find the most profitable alternative employment. In other industries in which great capacity has a chance to earn high rewards, the best entrepreneurs will be the last to transfer themselves to industries in which their talents give them a smaller advantage over the common fry, and the marginal entrepreneurs will be the least competent, for it is they who will be first driven by a decline in earnings to transfer themselves elsewhere.

Land which is "marginal" in the classical sense has no alternative use to the one to which it is actually put, and for it the transfer price is zero; but for units of factors belonging to the categories labour and enterprise there will be a minimum level of earnings below which the individuals providing the factors cannot survive, that is to say, in no use will transference earnings be zero.[1]

This is Mr. Shove's jig-saw puzzle.[2] Each individual unit of each factor will be fitted into the place where its earnings will be greatest; when its earnings in that use fall it will retreat to its next most profitable use, and if there is an appreciable difference between its actual earnings and its earnings in the next most profitable use to which it could be put it will be receiving rent. If each productive unit is like its neighbour, both in respect to their efficiencies in the industry employing them and in respect to their efficiencies in alternative uses, there will be no rent.

3

But a jig-saw puzzle is an end in itself. It is not a useful instrument. So long as we continue to look at the matter as a jig-saw puzzle we shall find it extraordinarily hard to solve the problems which await us. To reduce those problems to manageable dimensions it is convenient to make use of the notion of a supply curve of a factor to a particular industry. But it is necessary to recognise that no difference can be made to the real situation by the terms in which we choose to describe it. And if the artificial instrument, the supply curve of a factor, turns out to be so treacherous that we cannot use it to solve our problems we shall always be able to fall back upon the jig-saw puzzle and pass our time in fitting it together.

[1] It is important to realise that this distinction between transfer earnings and rent in the industry has nothing to do with the distinction between those expenses of production which correspond to the *real costs* of human effort and sacrifice and those which merely represent exchanges within society. From the point of view of society, land, by definition, is provided free, and the whole rent is a surplus and none of it is a real cost. From the point of view of a particular industry, transfer payments are as much a part of supply price as any other element of cost, and from the point of view of an individual competitive producer the whole of rent is a cost of production. These distinctions give the clue to the somewhat confused appearance of Marshall's treatment of the subject. He is mainly concerned with questions of real cost, and from this point of view the distinction between rent in industry and transfer earnings becomes irrelevant. Mr. Henderson's attempt to preserve an appearance of orthodoxy by calling transfer payments a real cost only led to further confusion.

[2] *Economic Journal*, March 1930, p. 99: "To me, at any rate, the economic problem presented by the real world seems to be . . . a question of sorting out and fitting each into its appropriate niche a vast number of heterogeneous individuals and activities . . . a jig-saw puzzle rather than a problem in hydrodynamics".

The attempt to draw up a supply curve of a factor involves two steps. First, we must collect together different actual productive units into whatever groups are convenient, calling each group a single factor. The productive units fall naturally into four categories—land, labour, capital, and enterprise.[1] It would be unwise to put two units belonging to different categories into the same group. An acre of land, fifty-nine men, and two hundred pounds' worth of capital would not make a very convenient factor. Each factor must consist of units from only one of the four categories and any particular unit must be placed whenever possible in the same factor as the other units which are most like it.[2] Any two units which are perfect substitutes for each other must be included in the same factor. In many cases the factors will define themselves without trouble. We may find, for instance, a large body of unskilled workers, between whose capabilities there are only small differences, while there is a clearly marked difference, on the one hand, between the quality of the best of them and of the least capable worker outside the group, and on the other hand, between the quality of the worst of them and of the most capable worker outside the group. Such gaps in nature make the demarcation of factors quite simple. But there will be many doubtful cases, and we must not be too meticulous in putting dissimilar men or dissimilar acres into separate factors. If we take too strict a view of the degree of similarity between units which will justify us in grouping them together we shall have so many separate small factors that any productive process would require an enormous number of them, and most of our problems would become intractable.

Our groups must be large enough to reduce the number of factors employed in any one process to reasonable proportions. But we are bound to follow the rule that one factor consists of productive units out of only one category. And since every process must have some units out of each of the four categories,

---

[1] See p. 19. These four categories are traditionally called factors, but the division of all productive units into only four factors belongs properly to the analysis of output as a whole, and for the problems of a single industry a finer division is necessary.

[2] In some cases an individual, for instance a small employer who provides some labour as well as entrepreneurship in his business, may belong to several categories of factors. The services of such individuals must be divided up and allocated to separate factors.

land, labour, capital, and enterprise, the number of factors must in any case be inconveniently great.[1] We must therefore always enlarge the groups of units as generously as possible. When there is no very marked gap in the chain of productive units which can be substituted for each other, providing an obvious line of demarcation which it would be foolish to ignore, it will be wise to make each factor large and to include in it such a number of units that each factor is employed in a number of different industries.

The second step in drawing up a supply curve of a factor is to choose a unit in which to measure it. The problem of finding the unit is discussed at some length in the Appendix. The general outline of the provisional solution there suggested is as follows: two portions of a certain factor—a number of men, if the factor belongs to the category, labour, of acres if it belongs to the category, land, and so forth—will be counted as consisting of an equal number of *efficiency units* if they can be substituted for one another without altering physical productivity. The efficiency unit must be determined with reference to the industry for which we are drawing the supply curve of the factor. The same actual productive unit may occur in the supply curves of different industries as different numbers of efficiency units. If, by good fortune, we are able to compile a factor which consists of units closely similar to each other in efficiency from the point of view of the industry for which we are drawing the supply curve, the natural unit (a man or an acre) for the factor will coincide with the efficiency unit.

If the firms composing the industry form a perfectly competitive market for the factors,[2] the price of each efficiency unit of a factor must be the same. If one unit of the factor is cheaper than others, relatively to its efficiency, it would be advantageous to employ it, rather than a more expensive unit, and its price would be bid up by rival employers to the same level as the rest. Thus at any given scale of the industry the efficiency earnings of each unit will be equal to the efficiency

---

[1] The analysis of Book VII. is made on the assumption that there are only two, or only three, factors engaged in producing a commodity, and even with such a small number of factors the analysis is sufficiently complicated.

[2] The assumption that this is so is retained throughout the first part of this book. The removal of it carries us into the field of monopsony which is discussed in the second part.

earnings of a unit which is marginal at that scale of the industry. The earnings of entrepreneurs are received, in the form of profit, and not paid out by an employing agency, but as we shall see in the next chapter the same principles can be applied to entrepreneurs as to units of any other factor. The difference between the earnings actually received by a certain unit of a factor and its transfer price is its rent from the point of view of the industry.

Now if the supply curve of a factor, drawn up on these principles, is perfectly elastic to an industry we shall know that none of the units contained in it are earning rent from the point of view of that industry. And if the supply curve is rising we shall know that there is a possibility that rent may be present. But the essential nature of rent in the industry is only to be understood by considering Mr. Shove's jig-saw puzzle, and we must always return to the jig-saw puzzle in order to explain it.

4

Our next task is to discover in what circumstances the supply curve of a factor to an industry may be rising. A factor which is in imperfectly elastic supply to an industry may be called a *scarce factor* from the point of view of that industry.

First consider a case in which the whole of one factor consists of units which are all closely similar to each other both in respect to the industry in which they are employed and in respect to their possible alternative uses. Then if there is a marked natural gap between this factor and others it may happen that there will be a certain small group of industries all of which are competing for the use of this homogeneous factor. Now if any one of these industries expands, the amount available for the others is reduced. If the expanding industry only employs a negligible proportion of the factor, the reduction in the amount available for the rest will not have an appreciable effect upon the price of the factor, and its supply to the expanding industry will be perfectly elastic. But if this industry absorbs a considerable proportion of the factor, then its value to the others is raised as this industry expands, and the transfer earnings of units of it are increased. Its supply price to the industry is therefore rising as the industry expands, but since all the productive units composing the factor are similar from the point of view of the relevant industries the transfer earnings of all units will be the same, and will be equal to their prices, and none of them will earn rent. Thus a rising supply curve of the factor to an industry is not a sufficient condition, although it is a necessary condition, for the existence of rent from the point of view of that industry.

Of course we can regard as a separate industry any group of producers that we find it convenient to class together. If we are interested in an industry which employs only part of a factor of the type that we have just been discussing, the factor, as we have seen, earns no rent from the point of view of that industry, while from the point of view of a larger industry it may earn rent. If, in a certain town, all the sites suitable for retail shops could be classed together as one factor, clearly demarcated on all sides by a gap in the chain of productive units which can be substituted for each other—so that no site not included in the factor was at all suitable for a shop—but within which all sites were not appreciably different from each other, then if we chose to regard only the grocers' shops as a single industry, the factor earns no rent in the grocers' shop industry, but if we regard all retail shops as a single industry, the factor earns rent in that industry, since sites which were not used for shops would be less profitably employed in some other industry.

If there is no marked natural gap differentiating this factor from all others it is likely that an expansion of any one industry employing it will be met by a transference of productive units from a large number of other industries, even if the expanding industry is of considerable size, and the transfer price of any given productive unit will then be independent of the scale of the expanding industry, and the supply of the factor to the industry will be perfectly elastic.

5

Next consider a factor which is homogeneous from the point of view of the industry for which we are drawing its supply curve, so that in that industry all natural units are of the same efficiency, but which is heterogeneous from the point of view of other uses. In this and the succeeding cases we shall assume that the transfer cost of any given natural unit of the factor is independent of the scale of the industry for which the supply curve is being drawn; that is to say, we shall assume that as the industry expands it draws productive units from such a wide range of other industries that its expansion has a negligible effect upon the transfer earnings of the productive units that it employs.

In this case, as the industry expands it attracts to itself natural units of a factor which, from the point of view of this industry, are like those already employed. But the units which successively find themselves at the margin of trans-ference will have successively greater transfer prices, for they can be put to successively more profitable uses in other in-dustries. The supply curve of the factor will therefore be rising, and there will be rent in the industry. For instance, as the num-ber of grocers' shops in the town increases, the sites which they occupy, though no better for grocers than those already em-ployed, may be progressively more eligible in other uses, so that their transfer costs are progressively higher. Sites whose transfer costs are less than those of marginal sites will then earn rent. In the case which we are now considering the natural unit and the efficiency unit coincide, and it is this case which is most congenial to the notion of a supply price of a factor to an industry and which puts least strain upon our artificial device for drawing up the supply curve of the factor.

Next consider the case of a factor which is heterogeneous from the point of view of the industry for which the supply curve is being drawn. If the other industries from which the factors are transferred into this industry as it expands are similar to it in their methods of production, the relative efficiencies of different natural units will be the same in these other industries as in the industry which is expanding. The transfer earnings of the particular natural units of the factors will then stand in the same ratio to each other as their efficiencies, and the supply curve, in efficiency units, will be perfectly elastic. For instance, the sites which the grocers call into service may be progressively less efficient as the industry expands further and further, but if the relative efficiencies of different sites are the same in the industries from which they are drawn as in the grocers' shop industry, their transfer costs will also be progress-ively less as the industry expands. It will employ worse sites, but it can acquire them at correspondingly lower prices. The supply of the factor to the industry is perfectly elastic, and the units composing the factor earn no rent. The heterogeneity of the factor, from the point of view of the industry, is not a sufficient condition that the supply curve of the factor should be rising and that there should be rent in that industry.

If, however, the factor is homogeneous from the point of view of other industries although heterogeneous from the point of view of this industry, the price of all the natural units will be the same, but the supply curve measured in efficiency units will be rising, and the factor will earn rent. For instance, the grocers may pay the same price for sites as the number of their shops increases, but the profitability of the sites to grocers may be progressively less.

Finally, consider the case in which the factor is heterogeneous, both from the point of view of the industry for which we are drawing the supply curve and from the point of view of other industries, but in which there is a difference between the relative efficiencies of natural units in the industry and their relative efficiencies in the industries from which they are drawn. Then there will be a rising supply curve of the factor and rent in the industry.

6

Our search for scarce factors has been rewarded by cases of three types—all of which, of course, may be exemplified by the same factor at once. First, the transfer costs of units of the factor may rise as more of it is employed. Second, as the industry expands it may be obliged to employ units of the factor successively less and less well adapted to its particular needs, and yet there may be no compensating difference in the transfer earnings of the units of the factor. Third, it may be able to call into employment units of the factor which are at least as efficient as those already employed from its own point of view, but which are put to more profitable uses elsewhere. As the demand for the factor increases, the industry will then be obliged to lure away units which are successively better and better off where they are; it must pay a progressively higher price as it comes to compete with successively more profitable rival uses for the factor, and there is no compensating difference in the efficiency of the units which it employs.

I

A further point remains to be considered; even if the relative efficiencies of different units of the factors are the same in the industries from which they are drawn as in the expanding industry, their cost, relatively to their efficiency, may rise, for another reason, as more are employed. Certain people may have a taste for the trade in question, and may be prepared to work in it even though they might make a larger income elsewhere. Thus their transfer cost to this industry will be lower than it would otherwise have been, and when the supply of such persons is exhausted transfer costs will rise, because to obtain a further increase in the supply of labour and entrepreneurship it will be necessary to tempt into the trade those to whom it offers no special attractions, or even those who (apart from the greater income they are able to earn in it) positively dislike the occupation. Such preferences may arise either from a view of the "net advantages" of the trade, its healthiness, security, social prestige, and so forth, which will be differently evaluated by each individual, or from a hereditary connection with the trade, or from personal fancy. Moreover, ignorance, or the difficulty of moving from one occupation to another, or mere reluctance to do so, may prevent units of the factors from reacting to differences in the earnings which they can obtain in different industries.[1]

7

The influences which lead to the occurrence of rent in an industry will apply with varying force to factors of production belonging to the four main categories of factors. The supply of entrepreneurship is certainly heterogeneous, but it is on the whole likely that the qualities which make enterprise efficient in one industry will be equally valuable in a

---

[1] The foregoing treatment of scarce factors is mainly derived from Mr. Shove's contribution to the "Symposium on Increasing Returns and the Representative Firm" (*Economic Journal*, March 1930) and from his teaching in Cambridge, and I am much indebted to him for allowing me to make use of ideas which he has not himself published in a fully developed form. His more realistic account of the matter has been drastically simplified by the omission of the complications which arise on the one hand from time and on the other from the imperfection of the market in factors of production within the industry. Moreover, Mr. Shove rejects the notion of a supply curve of a factor to an industry (*loc. cit.* p. 100), which is retained in the present discussion; see Section 8 below.

large number of others. In the same way the relative efficiencies of different workers will often be the same in a large
number of occupations. The definition of an industry would
have to be very wide before it would cover a region bounded
on all sides by a gap in the chain of alternative employment for the men concerned. But it is certainly possible that
there should be industries which require peculiar gifts, either
from enterprise or from labour, that are quite differently
evaluated in all other industries. For the factor land it is even
more likely that there are numerous uses which require some
special qualities in the soil, in the geographical situation, or in
a combination of the two, so that the relative values of different
pieces of land may be different in one quite small industry from
their relative values in all other industries. Only for the factor
capital must all uses be alike in the qualities which they require.
For money capital is perfectly homogeneous, and can be turned
into whatever form is required in each industry.[1]

In the importance which must be attached to differences due
to preference the order of the factors must be reversed. In the
case of land, where the effect of heterogeneity is strongest, the
effect of preference is weakest. Some land-owners may prefer to
receive a lower price from the National Trust than a higher
price from a building company, but in general we should expect
that a piece of land will (apart from frictions) always take
service in the industry in which its earnings are greatest. The
human factors, labour and entrepreneurship, will obviously be
more strongly subject to differences of preference than land.
And they will also be impeded from moving readily from one
industry to another by distrust of the unknown. Capital, which
is homogeneous from the point of view of efficiency, may
also be subject to differences due to preference or ignorance.
Each industry may have certain sources (notably its own profits)
from which capital may be readily drawn, and when these
supplies are exhausted it may have to attract capital, by the
prospect of a higher reward, from investors who have no particular preference for the industry in question or knowledge of its
possibilities.

It thus appears that factors belonging to any of the four categories may be scarce. Such questions cannot be answered by

[1] See p. 19.

a priori methods, but our analysis has made it clear that there is no presumption that rent from the point of view of a single industry is any more confined to the factor land than is rent from the point of view of society as a whole.

8

It has been the intention of this book to avoid wanton controversy. But the recent controversy over "the laws of returns"[1] is too important to be ignored, and it will be helpful to the reader to understand the points of difference between the system set out in this chapter and the systems of Mr. Shove on the one hand and Mr. Sraffa on the other.

This system is founded upon Mr. Shove's system, and the two only differ in so far as this system is drastically simplified by the omission of any reference to time, and in so far as Mr. Shove rejects the notion of a supply curve of a factor. The difference between them is neither a difference of analysis nor a dispute as to facts. It is merely a difference of optimism. It is obvious that the actual nature of individual productive units (men and acres), the actual earnings which will cause them to move from one industry to another, and the actual rents that they receive can be in no way affected by the manner in which we choose to define a factor of production. And Mr. Shove's jig-saw puzzle is a convincing account of the real world. But Mr. Shove's map is on too large a scale to serve our present purpose. By reducing the scale of the map we may hope to catch a glimpse of the outline of our continent, though we shall fail to see every bay and every promontory on its coasts, while Mr. Shove must be for ever poring over his ordnance survey, sheet by sheet. The device of drawing supply curves of factors is merely a reduction in the scale of the map, which sacrifices its accuracy to its usefulness. It does not involve any fundamental difference of opinion with Mr. Shove.

The difference from Mr. Sraffa is of another kind. In Mr. Sraffa's world it is the usual rule that any particular unit of a factor is like its neighbours, both in respect to its efficiency in

---

[1] See *Economic Journal*, March 1930, p. 79, where a list of the relevant articles is given. Of these the most important for our present purpose are Mr. Sraffa's article of 1926 and Mr. Shove's contribution to the "Symposium".

the industry in which it is employed and to its efficiency in
neighbouring industries. Perfectly elastic supply of factors to
each industry is therefore the rule. But in this sea of homogeneous factors of production there float here and there lumps
of heterogeneity, such as coal-bearing land or soil particularly
suitable for root crops. Each of these lumps of factors is homogeneous within itself but unlike all other productive units. Mr.
Sraffa thus only recognises two out of all the possible types of
conditions of supply of factors which are included in Mr. Shove's
jig-saw puzzle.

It was in connection with such lumps of factors that Mr. Sraffa
posed his famous dilemma. Some of them are absorbed into a
single industry and cause no trouble. But some of them, as we
have seen, will be employed in several industries. Suppose that
there is a certain limited area of land suitable for roots. Turnips,
swedes, and mangold-wurzels all require it, and its efficiency for
other crops is very small. Now if, say, the turnip industry is
employing a very small proportion of this limited supply of land,
it can expand without causing a perceptible rise of its price.
But if it is employing a large proportion, then when it expands the price of the land rises. The output of the other root
industries is reduced, and the prices of swedes and mangold-
wurzels go up. Now it is very likely (though by no means necessary) that commodities which are alike in requiring some highly
specialised factor will be alike in the uses to which they can be
put. This is certainly true of turnips and swedes. If the price of
swedes and mangold-wurzels go up, the demand curve for their
substitute, turnips, will be raised. The demand curve for turnips
therefore infringes the first canon of behaviour for a demand
curve. It is not independent of the supply curve of its own
commodity. This was Mr. Sraffa's dilemma. If we are interested
in an industry which is sufficiently small to use only a small
proportion of the specialised lump of the factor, the factor will
not be scarce. And if the industry is sufficiently large for the
factor to be scarce our tools will break in our hands.

The damage to the demand curve caused by the second horn
of Mr. Sraffa's dilemma is not perhaps as great as appears at
first sight. It does not apply to every case; and even when it
does apply it does no irremediable damage. Provided that
we know in what way the conditions of supply in other in-

dustries are likely to alter as a result of a change in the output
of the industry we are considering, and provided further that
we know the shift in the demand curve brought about by the
change in the prices of other commodities, we can redraw the
demand curve for each scale of the industry. Thus the wound in
the demand curve caused by this blow from the horn of Mr.
Sraffa's dilemma can be bound up if we have sufficient knowledge of the conditions of the problem.[1]

But however that may be, it is quite clear that the difference
between Mr. Shove and Mr. Sraffa arises out of the picture of the
world at which they are looking.[2] It seems undeniable that
Mr. Shove's more complicated picture is a better likeness of the
real world than Mr. Sraffa's simplified picture. But, this is a
question which it is idle to debate by *a priori* methods. The
answer to it must come from a statistical examination of actual
factors of production. Mr. Sraffa, no doubt, is perfectly content
to await the verdict of the statisticians. For he was not concerned
to defend a particular view about the real world. His purpose
was quite a different one. He was concerned to show that
economists who make use of the competitive analysis of value
have a strong unconscious bias in favour of rising and falling
supply price, simply because, if supply price is always constant,
their analysis has nothing interesting to say. The monopoly
analysis of value, inaugurated by Mr. Sraffa himself, has no axe

---

[1] That is to say, when an additional unknown is introduced into a problem
the problem can be solved by introducing an additional equation and (for
geometrical presentation) an additional dimension.

[2] The world envisaged by Professor Pigou appears to be different from
either. His factors of production are always perfectly homogeneous within
themselves, but are often scarce to particular industries. They may be fitted
into Mr. Sraffa's world if his picture is modified to allow for more frequent
lumps of factors, and if his dilemma is neglected. Some of Professor Pigou's
illustrations suggest the notion (at least to an unwary reader) of a very large
homogeneous factor, say all land, and of an industry, say wheat-growing,
absorbing so large a proportion of it that the price of land rises as wheat-
growing expands (cf. *Economics of Welfare*, p. 805). But such a notion is
erroneous. The expansion of any one industry (unless we are concerned with
an increase of output as a whole, which is not the province of the analysis of
value) must come about by a change of relative demands. If more wheat, and
less of other commodities, is demanded, the output of other commodities
contracts. Land is released from their industries which becomes available for
wheat, and since this land is like all the rest there is no guarantee that the
price of wheat will rise. But there is no reason to attribute to Professor Pigou
the mistake of his unwary reader. And his conclusions are not dependent on
the particular image of the world at which he happened to be looking when
he arrived at them.

to grind in the matter. If the statisticians assure Mr. Sraffa that he is right, and that almost every industry works under conditions of constant costs, the task of the monopoly analysis will be much simplified. But it will lose none of its validity, and will gain considerably in charm.

CHAPTER 9

THE SUPPLY CURVE UNDER PERFECT COMPETITION

1

WE must now introduce into our analysis the effects upon the costs of a firm of an increase in the scale of the industry. In order to draw up a supply curve it is always necessary to make some assumption about the movement of the individual demand curves of the firms, and on every possible assumption there is a different supply curve.[1] The simplest assumption that can be made about the individual demand curves is that they are horizontal and that they always move upward and downward without changing their slope. In short, the simplest assumption to make is that competition is perfect. To isolate the effects of a change in the scale of the industry upon costs it is therefore convenient to discuss the case of a perfectly competitive industry. Under perfect competition, as we saw in Chapter 7, the firms must be of optimum size when profits are normal.

We will first consider the case in which there are no economies of large-scale industry, and in which all factors, including entrepreneurship, are in perfectly elastic supply to the industry. The effect of an increase in demand for a commodity produced under perfect competition is then easily seen. The firms will all be alike. When the demand increases, the price will be temporarily raised, and each firm will increase output to the point at which its marginal cost is equal to the new price. Price will now be greater than average cost, a surplus profit will be made, new firms will come into the industry, and the price will consequently fall. It follows from the assumption that all factors are in perfectly elastic supply that the new firms will be like the old, and the new average cost for a larger output will be the same as

---

[1] See p. 88.

the old average cost for a smaller output. In equilibrium conditions with normal profits, price will be equal to average cost for the industry, and to both average and marginal costs for each separate firm. For each individual seller marginal revenue will be equal to marginal cost, and both will be equal to price. Since average cost does not alter as the output of the industry expands, supply price will be constant.[1]

2

But, as we saw in the last chapter, it is possible that factors of production may be scarce from the point of view of a particular industry. An expansion in the size of the industry will then lead to a rise in the price of the scarce factors.

In these conditions what determines supply price? For simplicity of exposition we will suppose that there is only one scarce factor, but the argument applies equally when there are several. Rent from the point of view of the industry is, as we have seen, the difference between the transfer earnings of intra-marginal efficiency units of the factors and the earnings of units which are on the margin of transference. Given the supply curves of the factors, the amount of rent is determined by the position of the margin. Rent is therefore not a causal element in the situation, and to find the supply price of the commodity we must study what is the cost of production in a situation where no element of rent is present. That is to say, we must study *cost at the margin* in order to discover both the supply price of the commodity and the amount of rent in the industry.

Consider a firm which employs only marginal units of the factors, that is, units which would cease to be employed in the industry if their earnings were slightly reduced. For instance, if the scarce factor is land, we must consider a firm working on a site which is on the margin of transference from the point of view of the industry. In the costs of such a firm there will be no element of rent, and its cost per unit of output will be the *cost at the margin* of the industry. Now the cost of such a firm must be equal to the price of the commodity. For if price were greater than this cost it would be profitable to employ more expensive

---

[1] This is an example of the special case, discussed in Chapter 7, in which the increase in the number of firms is proportional to the increase in output.

units of the factors, and the units employed by this firm would
not be marginal units. And if price were lower than this cost
the transfer earnings of the factors would not be covered by
price, and these units of the factors would lie outside the
margin.

We must also consider the *intensive marginal cost*. *Intensive
marginal cost*, when any given output is being produced by the
industry, is the cost of making a unit increase [1] in the output
produced with the aid of any given portion of the scarce factor
by increasing the amount of the other factors. For instance, if
the scarce factor is land, we must consider the cost of increasing the output produced on any given site. In this cost also
there is no element of rent. And this cost also must be equal to
the price of the commodity. For if the price were greater than
this cost it would be profitable to increase the output produced
with the aid of the given portion of the scarce factor, until the
intensive marginal cost rose to equal the price; and if price
were less than this cost it would be profitable to lower the
intensity of cultivation of the scarce factor by employing less of
the other factors with the given portion of the scarce factor,
until the intensive marginal cost fell to equal the price.

Thus both cost at the margin and intensive marginal cost
must be equal to price, and consequently both must be equal to
the supply price of the commodity. As the demand for the
commodity increases, more of all the factors are called into
employment in the industry. When more of any scarce factor is
called into use the price of a marginal unit is raised, and the price
(including rent) of all units of the factor must remain equal to the
price of a marginal unit. It is therefore profitable to increase the
employment of those factors whose price does not rise (whose
supply to the industry is perfectly elastic) relatively to the
factor whose price rises. That is to say, the scarce factor is used
more intensively as output increases, to an extent determined
by the technical possibilities of substituting factors for each
other, and the intensive marginal cost is raised. Cost at the
margin and intensive marginal cost are thus both raised and
both remain equal to the price of the commodity. Supply price

---

[1] The increment of cost due to a "unit increase" of output must be envisaged
as the increment of cost due to a small increment of output, divided by the increment of output. The phrase will be used in the following pages in this sense.

is determined at these two margins, and these two costs are always equal.

The elasticity of supply of the commodity is therefore governed by two causes. It will depend upon the elasticity of supply of the scarce factor (the rate at which the cost of a marginal unit of it rises as more is employed) and upon the elasticity of substitution,[1] which measures the technical possibility of substituting factors for each other, that is, the possibility of economising in the use of the scarce factor as its cost rises.[2]

3

What is the relationship of cost at the margin and intensive marginal cost to the costs of the individual firm? First consider a case in which the supply of entrepreneurs to the industry is perfectly elastic, and some other factor, say land, is scarce. Then each firm will be of the size at which its average cost is a minimum, for the rent of the scarce factor, land, must of course be included in the cost of the firm, and the marginal and average cost of the firm will both be equal to the price. As the industry expands and the cost of land alters, the optimum size of the firms (at which average cost is a minimum) may be changed, but, in equilibrium, the firms must always be of optimum size. As the cost of land rises, more of the other factors, as we saw, will be employed with each unit of land. Each firm therefore will employ less land as the cost of land rises.

Next consider the case where entrepreneurship is the scarce factor and all other factors are in perfectly elastic supply. Then cost at the margin is the cost of a firm controlled by an entrepreneur on the margin of transference, and it will be equal to

[1] Defined on p. 256 below.

[2] Let E be the elasticity of supply of the commodity, E_t the elasticity of supply of the scarce factor, η the elasticity of substitution, and k the ratio of the cost of the scarce factor to total cost.

When all other factors are in perfectly elastic supply,

$$E = -\frac{(1-k)\eta - E_t}{k}$$

$$\text{or } (-E) = \frac{(1-k)\eta + (-E_t)}{k}.$$

$(-E)$ is the numerical value of the elasticity of supply of the commodity and $(-E_t)$ is the numerical value of the elasticity of supply of the scarce factor. I am indebted to Mr. Kahn for this result.

both the marginal and the average cost of such a firm. The minimum unit of the scarce factor is now a single entrepreneur. Therefore to find intensive marginal cost we must consider the cost of increasing the output produced by any given entrepreneur and intensive marginal cost will be the marginal cost of an intra-marginal firm. Thus when entrepreneurship is the scarce factor the proposition that price is equal to cost at the margin is equivalent to the proposition that price is equal to marginal and average cost of a marginal firm. And the proposition that intensive marginal cost is equal to price is merely another form of the familiar proposition that the marginal cost of each firm is equal to the price.

For all firms marginal cost must be equal to price, but only for marginal firms will average cost be equal to the price. For any intra-marginal firm the difference between its total receipts and its total cost, including the transfer earnings of the entrepreneur, is the rent of the entrepreneur. Thus the rent of the entrepreneur, in each firm, will be the difference between marginal and average cost to the firm, multiplied by output. If we exclude this rent from the costs of the firm, and only include the transfer earnings of each entrepreneur in the costs of his firm, we are obliged to say that only marginal firms are of optimum size, since it is only for them that average cost, so defined, will be at a minimum. All intra-marginal firms, on this definition, are of more than optimum size. But to employ this definition would be misleading, for two reasons. First, it introduces an arbitrary distinction between the rent of entrepreneurs and of other factors. This distinction is clearly a natural one to make when we are looking at the matter from the point of view of a firm, but when we are studying the supply curve we are looking at the matter from the point of view of the whole industry, and for the industry entrepreneurship is a factor of production on exactly the same footing as the rest.

Secondly, the statement that intra-marginal firms are of more than optimum size carries the suggestion that it is in some way undesirable for them to be so large, and that they ought to be smaller. But of course this suggestion is quite false. The fact that when entrepreneurship is a scarce factor intra-marginal firms are larger than what, on this definition, would be called their optimum size merely shows that the differential advantages of entrepreneurs whose efficiency cost is relatively low are being fully exploited, so that the marginal cost of their output is not less than the marginal cost of the outputs of more expensive entrepreneurs. And this is obviously in no sense undesirable. The fact that, as the output of the industry expands, the output of an intra-marginal firm increases merely shows that its relative efficiency increases as the margin is extended and entrepreneurs whose efficiency is less (relatively to their transfer costs) are called into the industry. The increase in the size of an intra-marginal firm is a reflection of the fact that the scarce factor, entrepreneurship, is being used more intensively as its cost rises. And there is clearly no sense in which it is undesirable that this should occur.

It therefore appears better to include in the costs of intra-marginal firms the rent of the entrepreneur, as well as the rents of the other factors. The average cost of every firm, including rent, will then be at a minimum in equilibrium, and every firm, in this sense, will be of optimum size.

This can be illustrated as follows:

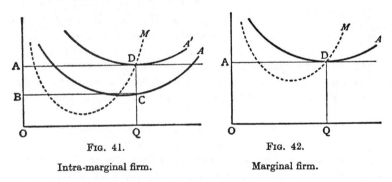

FIG. 41.   FIG. 42.

Intra-marginal firm.   Marginal firm.

Fig. 41 shows an intra-marginal firm, and Fig. 42 a marginal firm.

In each case A is the average cost of the output of the firm excluding the entrepreneur's rent, and M is the marginal cost of the firm.

DQ is the price of the commodity.

A' is the average cost of the firm including the entrepreneur's rent, and $ADCB$ is the total rent of the entrepreneur.

Since the inclusion of rent adds to total costs a lump sum which is independent of the firm's output (given the price of the commodity), the marginal cost curve cuts A', as well as A, at its minimum point.

The price of the commodity is equal both to marginal cost, and to average cost including rent.

Finally, we must consider the case in which there are several scarce factors. Rent over and above transference earnings will be earned by intra-marginal units of all the various scarce factors. The cost at the margin of the commodity will be equal to the cost of a firm using only marginal units of all factors. It is not, of course, necessary to suppose that any actual part of the product is produced at the margin from the point of view of all of the factors. An intra-marginal entrepreneur may work on marginal land. But this would make no difference to the result. If we wish to distinguish the part of the total rent going to each factor, we must discover, firstly, what surplus would arise if each piece of land were managed by a marginal entrepreneur; the whole of this surplus would then be rent of land (if there is no third scarce factor). Secondly, we must discover what surplus would arise if each entrepreneur were working on marginal land; the whole of this surplus would then be rent of entrepreneurship. And so forth. These distributional problems are not to our present purpose, which is simply to construct the supply curve which is the net result of all the payments made to the various factors.

Intensive marginal cost, from the point of view of each factor, is the cost of making a unit increase in the output produced with the aid of any given portion of that factor by increasing the amounts of the other factors. It is obvious that intensive marginal cost, for each factor, must be equal to price. This is, of course, equally true when the factor is in perfectly elastic supply and when it is not.

In every case the supply price of the commodity is equal to cost at the margin and to intensive marginal cost. Rent makes up the difference between the price and the cost of producing a unit of the commodity with the aid of intra-marginal units of the factors, and supply price is equal to average cost including rent.

4

We have so far made no reference to the influence upon the supply curve of what Mr. Shove has taught us to call "economies of large-scale industry".[1] When an industry expands in size there are various ways in which its costs may be reduced. The firms composing it may be buying some element of their equipment from a subsidiary industry which is producing under conditions of falling supply price, so that as the main industry increases its use of this equipment the price of it falls. Or it may be that as the industry expands its organisation is altered, the firms specialising upon a narrower range of productive processes; or it may be that some factor of production (for instance skilled labour) becomes better adapted to the requirements of this particular industry when a large amount of it is employed.[2] When the assumption of perfect competition is followed to its logical conclusion the scope for possible economies is found to be very narrow,[3] but they may be conceived to occur, and to complete our analysis of the supply curve they must be introduced into it. This can be done without making any fundamental alteration in it. The effect of economies of large-scale industry will be to reduce the average costs of the firms, and may alter the optimum size of the firms. At any given scale of the industry the firms will be of optimum size (in equilibrium) and the price will be equal to the marginal cost and the minimum average cost of the firms, but the costs of the firms may vary with the scale of the industry. Thus the existence of scarce factors tends to raise the average cost of a firm of optimum size as the industry expands, and economies of large-scale industry tend to lower the average cost of a firm of optimum size. On balance the average cost of a firm of optimum size may either rise or fall as the industry expands. The propositions that price must be equal to cost at the margin, and to intensive marginal

---

[1] "Symposium", *Economic Journal*, March 1930, p. 104.

[2] See Appendix, p. 341. It is also possible that in certain cases some factor deteriorates as more is employed (see Appendix, p. 347). Such "diseconomies of large-scale industry", due to a fall in the efficiency of a given portion of a factor when more of the factor is employed, not to a rise in its price, are left out of account in the present treatment of the supply curve, and in the succeeding argument, merely for the sake of simplicity, and the analysis can easily be adapted to deal with them.

[3] See Appendix, p. 340.

cost from the point of view of each factor, are unaffected by the existence of economies of large scale.

5

The chain of causation may be summarised in this way: In equilibrium price is equal to marginal and average cost to the firms. When the demand for the commodity increases its price rises; therefore marginal revenue to the firms rises, and their output expands until their marginal costs are once more equal to the price. But profits are then abnormal, new firms enter the industry, and a further increase of output occurs. Price falls again and equilibrium will be established when price is once more equal to average as well as to marginal cost for the firms. But the expansion of the industry may have altered the costs of the firms. The additional employment of the factors of production, including the additional entrepreneurship represented by the new firms, will have raised the price, per efficiency unit,[1] of any factor which is not in perfectly elastic supply to the industry; and the economies of large scale may have lowered the cost or increased the efficiency of particular items in the productive equipment of the firms, or may have led to the reorganisation of the industry in firms whose costs (abstracting from the change in price of the scarce factors) are lower than before. The net effect of these two contrary influences may establish an equilibrium position in which the average cost of a firm of optimum size is either higher or lower than before, and supply price may be either rising or falling.

It is therefore false to suggest, as some writers appear to do, that there is a mysterious difference between the mechanism by which supply price is determined when it is rising and when it is falling.[2] The essential distinctions are not between rising and falling supply price, but between perfect competition and imperfect competition, and between an analysis in which time factors are admitted and an analysis in which they are ignored.

[1] In the terminology of the Appendix this is not the efficiency unit but the "corrected natural unit". See p. 332.

[2] Marshall's exposition is complicated by a not precisely formulated consciousness of the importance of market imperfection and by an overt recognition of the importance of time. See *Principles*, p. 805: "The term 'margin of production' has no significance for long periods in relation to commodities the cost of production of which diminishes with a gradual increase in the output".

The matter has now been carried one step further. Following out the implications of the proposition that every firm must, in the nature of the case, act as a monopolist, it has been shown that the problem of the determination of supply price in a perfect market is merely a special case of the general problem of the determination of price under competitive conditions. The distinction between perfect and imperfect competition is thus seen to be only a difference of degree. The problems connected with the influence of time remain to be solved, but no attempt is here made to solve them.

6

By combining the analysis, given in Chapter 7, of the effect of a change in the total demand for the commodity upon the demand curve for the individual firm, with the analysis of the effect of a change in the scale of the industry upon the cost curve of the individual firm, given in this chapter for the special case of perfect competition, it is possible to analyse supply curves of every type, at the level of abstraction maintained in this book. But a word must be said about the interactions of the two types of change.

When the market is imperfect the process of disintegration of firms (which, as we saw, may lead to economies of large-scale industry even under perfect competition) is very much retarded, and a degree of specialisation that would be profitable under perfect competition is not profitable when competition is imperfect.[1] There is here, therefore, a reservoir of potential economies of large-scale industry; an increase in the total demand for the commodity, leading to changes in the individual demand curves, may have the effect of releasing these potential economies by making a degree of specialisation profitable which was not profitable before. In short, an increase in the total demand for the commodity, when the market is imperfect, is far more likely to lower the average cost curves of the firms than when the market is perfect.

[1] See Appendix, p. 339.

K

BOOK IV

THE COMPARISON OF MONOPOLY AND COMPETITIVE OUTPUT

CHAPTER 10

A DIGRESSION ON THE FOUR COST CURVES

1

THE next task to which our technique may be applied is to make the comparison between competitive and monopoly output: that is to say, to contrast the output of an industry when it is composed of a number of independent producers, with the output of the same industry in the same conditions of demand when it is controlled by a single authority. We have already discussed the competitive supply curve, and we know that competitive output is the output at which demand price is equal to supply price. But the cost curve which governs monopoly output may obviously be something different from the supply curve which governs competitive output, and we cannot embark upon the comparison between monopoly and competitive output until we have examined this question more closely. The present chapter therefore is devoted to a digression on cost curves.[1]

2

We have seen that the supply curve of a commodity produced under perfect competition is the curve of average costs including rent. This proposition is no more than a tautology, since it follows from the definition of rent to the industry. Aggregate

---

[1] The treatment of the four cost curves here set out owes much to Mr. Shove, but he must not be held responsible for this exposition of them, which differs considerably from his own. Mr. Shove's article on "Varying Costs and Marginal Net Products" in the *Economic Journal*, June 1928, contains his first systematic treatment of the cost curves.

The four cost curves are only used in this book for the comparisons which follow in the next three chapters, and the succeeding chapters do not require them. The reader who prefers to omit this digression, and the whole of Book IV., will therefore not lose very much. But the system of four cost curves is also useful in connection with problems which are not discussed in this book.

cost including rent is simply the total receipts of the industry, in equilibrium, and average cost including rent is necessarily equal to price. But this average cost curve is not the only curve which can be derived from the aggregate cost of the industry. There are four cost curves which can usefully be distinguished.

From aggregate cost including rent we can derive marginal cost including rent, that is, the increase in the total costs of the industry when output is increased by one unit.[1] The curve of marginal cost including rent may be called a, and the curve of average cost including rent β. This curve, β, must coincide with the supply curve of the commodity, since supply price is equal to average cost including rent.

From aggregate cost excluding rent marginal and average cost excluding rent can be derived. Marginal cost excluding rent is the increase in the costs of the industry other than rent when output increases by one unit. Average cost excluding rent is the aggregate cost other than rent, divided by the output. The curve of marginal cost excluding rent may be called γ, and the curve of average cost excluding rent δ.

Then the a curve is marginal to the β curve and the γ curve is marginal to the δ curve, each pair obeying the various laws governing the behaviour of marginal and average curves discussed in Chapter 2.

The relationships between these four curves will be different according as the transfer price of any given unit of any factor is or is not independent of the amount of that factor employed in the industry. We will first consider the case where it is independent.

If we further assume that there are no economies of large-scale industry, so that not only the transfer cost, but also the efficiency, of each unit of a factor is independent of the amount of the factor employed, then marginal cost excluding rent is equal to the cost of the additional units of the factors required to make a unit increase of output. For the addition to the amount of each factor employed consists of marginal units, and the additional cost incurred includes no element of rent. But this additional cost is the same thing as cost at the margin and is equal to the supply price of the commodity. Thus the γ curve, showing marginal cost excluding rent, coincides (upon the two assumptions which we have made) with the supply curve of the com-

[1] See p. 122, note.

modity. And as we have seen, the β curve, showing average cost including rent, coincides with the supply curve. On our two assumptions, therefore, γ and β coincide. β and γ are then marginal to δ (average cost excluding rent) and a (marginal cost including rent) is marginal to β and γ.

A numerical example may help to make these relations clear.[1]

(1). Units of Output.	(2). Total Cost excluding Rent.	(3). Average Cost excluding Rent. (2)÷(1).	(4). Marginal Cost excluding Rent. Derived from (2).
		δ	$\gamma\ (=\beta)$
9	900	100	—
10	1020	102	120
11	1144	104	124
12	1272	106	128

The γ curve, which is marginal to δ, is derived by considering the increment of cost due to a unit increase of output. For instance, when output increases from 9 to 10 units total cost (excluding rent) rises from 900 to 1020. The marginal cost (excluding rent) of 10 units is therefore 120. On the assumptions that we are now making, the γ curve coincides with the supply curve of the commodity. Column 4 therefore gives the list of supply prices of the various outputs. Thus if 10 units are to be produced the price must be 120, if 11 units are to be produced the price must be 124 and so forth. We may therefore proceed with the example, assuming each amount of output to be sold at its appropriate price.

(1).	(5). Total Cost including Rent. (4)×(1).	(6). Average Cost including Rent. (5)÷(1)=(4).	(7). Marginal Cost including Rent. Derived from (5).
		$\beta\ (=\gamma)$	a
10	1200	120	—
11	1364	124	164
12	1536	128	172

a is marginal to β, and the divergence between them represents the increase in the cost of producing the former output which is caused by a unit increase of output; that is, it shows the difference between the cost of n units when n are being produced and the

[1] Once more the example is absurd but useful; see p. 26, note.

cost of n units when $(n + 1)$ are being produced.[1] Thus when
11 units are being produced the difference between a and β is 40,
because, when output increases from 10 units to 11, average cost
is raised by 4, and the total cost of 10 units is therefore increased
by 40. a is marginal cost including rent, and γ is marginal cost
excluding rent: the increment of rent due to a unit increase of
output is therefore shown by a *minus* γ. But γ here coincides
with β. a *minus* β therefore shows the increment of rent. In other
words, on the two assumptions which entail that γ and β coincide, the increase in the cost of producing a given output
when output expands by one unit is equal to the increment of
rent. Thus when 10 units are produced and sold at the appropriate price (120), total receipts are 1200 (column 5) and total costs
excluding rent are 1020 (column 2). The rent is then 180.
Similarly, when output is 11 units the rent is 220. The increase
in rent brought about by increasing output from 10 to 11 units
is therefore 40, and this is the difference between a and β when
11 units are being produced.

The difference between β and δ is the average rent per unit of
output. Thus when there is an output of 10 units the total rent
is 180 and the difference between β and δ is 18. The total rent
can thus be regarded either as total receipts *minus* total costs
other than rent, or, since β and γ coincide, as marginal *minus*
average cost (both excluding rent) multiplied by output.[2]

[1] If A is the average cost, M the marginal cost, and O the output,

$$M = \frac{d(AO)}{dO}$$

$$= A + O\frac{dA}{dO}.$$

$$\therefore \quad M - A = O\frac{dA}{dO},$$

which is the increase in the cost of the old output, O, when output is increased
by one unit.

This relation is to be found, in a somewhat obscure form, in the *Economics of
Welfare*, p. 803.

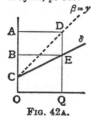

FIG. 42A.

[2] In Fig. 42A DQ is the supply price of the output OQ.
The rent can be shown either, as Marshall represents
it, by the triangular area ADC, or by the rectangle
ADEB.   DE($\beta - \delta$) = rent per unit of output.

The marginal increment of rent obviously does not enter into the supply price of the commodity. Output will always be increased if price is greater than marginal cost to the individual producer, and this will be equal to cost at the margin for the whole industry. But every increase in output will raise the rent paid by all producers. Each individually will only be influenced by the rise in the rent of intra-marginal units of the scarce factors employed by himself, that is, by his share in the increment of rent. But since (on the assumption that competition is perfect) the proportion of the total output for which any one producer is responsible must be small, the share of any one producer in the increment of rent is negligible. The increment of rent to the whole industry will have no influence on the individual producer and will therefore not enter into supply price. It is marginal cost excluding rent which is equal to supply price, and marginal cost to the industry including rent is greater than supply price.

3

We have so far proceeded upon the assumption that there are no economies of large-scale industry. We must now remove this assumption, retaining the assumption that the transfer costs of units of the factors are independent of the amounts of the factors employed in the industry.

It is argued in the Appendix on Increasing and Diminishing Returns that the economies which arise from the increase in the scale of an industry can all be treated in the same terms as apply to the simple type of external economies which arise when some item in the productive equipment, for instance a machine, becomes cheaper (without altering in nature) when more of it is employed. We will therefore only deal, in the present context, with economies of large-scale industry which are of this simple type. We will at first assume that there are no scarce factors. And we will suppose that decreasing costs arise from, say, buying machinery more cheaply when the industry expands, and so offers a larger market to machine makers, who, in turn, are producing under conditions of falling supply price.

The supply price of the commodity will be equal to the average cost of the industry, and to the average and marginal costs of each firm, and it will fall as the output of the industry expands.

On the assumption that there is no scarce factor and therefore no payment of rent, the β curve will coincide with the δ curve, both showing average cost, and the γ curve will coincide with the a curve, both showing marginal cost.

Since δ (or β) is falling, γ (or a), which is marginal to it, must lie below it.

The divergence between γ and δ measures the difference between the cost of producing n units when n are being produced and the cost of n units when $(n+1)$ are being produced. That is to say, it is the change in average cost, induced by a unit increase in output, multiplied by the former output. This difference may be described as the *induced economies* due to the unit increase in output. Thus if an increase in the output of the industry from 100 to 101 leads to economies which reduce average cost by 1, the induced economies due to the 101st unit of output are equal to 100.

Next we must consider the case where there are both economies of large-scale industry and scarce factors of production. As output increases, the cost of a marginal unit of a scarce factor increases, and consequently the cost including rent of all units of the factor increases, but, at the same time, each addition to output enlarges the scale of the industry, and reduces some other element in cost. To illustrate this case we may construct an imaginary example. Suppose, for instance, that land for growing hay is a scarce factor, but that every ton of hay added to the output of the hay-growing industry lowers the price of mowers by 0·1 of a shilling.[1] If 1000 new mowers are bought every year by the whole group of producers, then every additional ton of hay produced will reduce the aggregate expenditure on machinery by 100 shillings. That is to say, there are induced economies at the rate of 100 shillings, or £5, per ton. Suppose that the cost of producing a ton of hay on marginal land is £7. Then £7 will be the equilibrium supply price of a ton of hay, and its average cost, including rent, to all producers will be £7. But its marginal cost, excluding rent, to the industry as a whole is £7 *minus* the reduction in the cost of machinery brought about by adding a ton of hay to the total output. Thus its marginal cost, excluding rent, to the industry is £2. This artificial example illustrates the fact that when economies are

[1] An absurdly high rate of induced economies is given for the sake of clarity.

present it is no longer true that marginal cost to the industry, excluding rent, is equal to the cost of the additional factors employed when output increases. The cost of the additional factors employed, or cost at the margin, must necessarily be equal to supply price, but marginal cost to the industry, excluding rent, is now less than the supply price by the amount of the induced economies. The individual producer will only increase his output if price is greater than marginal cost to him, and marginal cost to the individual producer is equal to cost at the margin for the whole industry. But every increase in the output of one producer will have the effect of inducing economies which benefit all the other producers. The action of the individual will be influenced by his own share in these induced economies, but since we are discussing a perfectly competitive industry we must assume that the proportion of the total output controlled by any one producer is very small. His share in the induced economies will therefore be negligible, and they will not influence his conduct. It is the marginal cost to the individual which must be equal to supply price, and marginal cost to the industry, excluding rent, will be less than supply price when there are economies. β still coincides with the supply curve but γ now lies below β. a is marginal to β and γ is marginal to δ. The two pairs of curves are not connected by any marginal and average relationship, but if there are no scarce factors, a coincides with γ and β with δ. The divergence between γ and β measures the induced economies, and the divergence between γ and a measures the increment of rent, due to a unit increase of output.

4

The system of four cost curves may now be tabulated:

(1) a is marginal cost including rent;
  β is average cost including rent, and coincides with the supply curve of the commodity;
  γ is marginal cost excluding rent;
  δ is average cost excluding rent.

On the assumption that the transfer cost of any unit of a factor is independent of the amount of the factor employed, the relationships of these curves can be summarised as follows:

(2) When there are no economies of large-scale industry:
γ coincides with β;
a is marginal to γ and β;
γ and β are marginal to δ.

(3) When there are no scarce factors:
a coincides with γ;
β coincides with δ;
a and γ are marginal to β and δ.

(4) When there are no scarce factors and no economies:
γ coincides with β;
a coincides with γ;
β coincides with δ;
$\therefore$ all four curves coincide.

(5) When there are both scarce factors and economies:
All four curves are separate.
a is marginal to β;
γ is marginal to δ.

(6) $a - \gamma =$ marginal increment of rent;
$\beta - \delta =$ average rent per unit of output;
$\beta - \gamma =$ induced economies.

(7) When there are no economies but there is a scarce factor, supply price must be rising. β ($= \gamma$) must be rising, and a must lie above β. δ lies below β, and is also rising.

When there are economies but no scarce factor the supply price must be falling. β ($= \delta$) must be falling, and a ($= \gamma$) lies below β.

When there are neither economies nor scarce factors the supply price is constant and all four curves coincide and are horizontal.

(8) When there are both economies and scarce factors the supply price may be either rising, falling, or constant.

When the increment of rent $(a - \gamma)$ is greater than the induced economies $(\beta - \gamma)$, supply price will be rising, β will be rising, and a will lie above β.

Conversely, when $(a - \gamma)$ is less than $(\beta - \gamma)$, β will be falling, and a will lie below β.

If the increment of rent $(a - \gamma)$ is exactly equal to the induced economies $(\beta - \gamma)$, supply price will be constant, and a and β will coincide in a horizontal straight line.[1]

Whether supply price is rising, falling, or constant, γ will lie below β to an extent determined by the induced economies.

5

We have so far assumed that the transfer cost of any unit of a factor is independent of the amount of the factor employed. It remains to study the relationships between the four cost curves when this assumption is removed. If the factors are homogeneous, so that the transfer cost of all units is the same, there will be no rent. But the cost of the factor rises as more is employed, because its earnings in other industries increase as more of it is absorbed into the expanding industry. Since there is no rent β and δ coincide, and a and γ coincide, whether there are economies of large scale or not. β may be rising or falling, according as the rise in the cost of the scarce factors outweighs or is outweighed by economies of large scale. The divergence between $a(= \gamma)$ and $\beta(= \delta)$ will measure the difference between the cost of n units when n units are produced and the cost of n units when $(n + 1)$ are produced. When there are no economies this difference will be equal to the increased cost of the scarce factors already employed as a result of an increase in the amount employed sufficient to add a unit to output. And when there are no scarce factors it will be equal (as we found above) to the induced economies. But when there are both economies and scarce factors it will not measure either of these quantities separately.[2]

When the scarce factors are not homogeneous, so that there

[1] The difference between the type of constant supply price in which all four curves coincide, because there are no economies and no scarce factors, and the type of constant supply price in which only β and a coincide, because the rise in cost due to the scarce factors is just offset by the economies of large scale, corresponds to the difference between constant cost according to Mr. Sraffa and constant cost according to Marshall. See Sraffa, *Economic Journal*, December 1926, p. 541, note.

[2] We are here studying the type of increasing cost contemplated by Professor Pigou, and these few hints may be of service in interpreting Appendix III. of the *Economics of Welfare* to a non-mathematical reader. The conclusions of the Appendix are of course independent of the relations between the four curves, but Professor Pigou himself appears to visualise a world in which a and γ always coincide.

is rent, their cost will rise, as more is employed, both because the efficiency of a marginal unit, relatively to its price, is reduced as more of the factor is employed, and because the transfer cost of intra-marginal units is raised. β must still show cost at the margin, but it will now no longer be true that γ (marginal cost excluding rent) coincides with β when there are no economies of large scale. When there are no economies β will be rising and γ will lie between β and a; $\gamma - \beta$ will show the change of costs, other than rent, incurred in producing n units when an $(n + 1)$th unit is added to output. That is to say, it will measure the change in the transfer costs of the factors already employed when the amount employed increases sufficiently to add one unit to output. When there are also economies of large scale, γ may lie above or below β, and will coincide with it if the change in the transfer costs of the factors already employed is exactly offset by the induced economies.

CHAPTER 11

COMPARISONS OF MONOPOLY AND COMPETITIVE OUTPUT

1

WE have returned from this digression equipped with four cost curves:

a marginal cost including rent;
β average cost including rent;
γ marginal cost excluding rent;
δ average cost excluding rent.

It is now possible to make the comparison of monopoly and competitive output. We shall take as our basis of comparison a perfectly competitive industry. The conditions in which competition is perfect are not likely to be completely fulfilled in any actual case. If we are contrasting conditions of monopoly with conditions of competition in the real world—if we are interested, for example, in the effect of rationalisation on a competitive industry—we should in practice be comparing conditions of monopoly with conditions of imperfect competition. But when we take absolutely perfect competition for a starting-point we have a simple and definite notion of what we mean by competitive output, and the comparison can be made in its simplest form.

In order to make a valid theoretical comparison between competitive output and monopoly output in a particular industry it is necessary to make very severe assumptions. First, we must have a definite idea of what we mean by the commodity that we are considering. Secondly, if we wish to discuss what will happen to output and prices if a certain commodity, hitherto produced by competing firms, is monopolised, we must assume that neither the demand curve for the commodity nor the costs

143

of production of any given output are altered by the change.
These assumptions are unlikely to be fulfilled in any actual
situation, and in studying an actual case changes in demand
and in the efficiency of production must be allowed for. On the
assumption that they are unchanged, the relationship between
monopoly and competitive output can easily be discovered.

2

If there are no scarce factors and no economies of large scale,
all four cost curves coincide in a horizontal line. The monopolist
equates marginal cost to him with marginal revenue; under
competition average cost is equal to price, and marginal cost to
the monopolist is equal to average cost to him and to the competitive industry. It follows from the geometrical relations set
out in Chapter 2 [1] that monopoly output is half competitive
output when the demand curve is a straight line, less than half
when the demand curve is concave, and more than half when
the demand curve is convex.

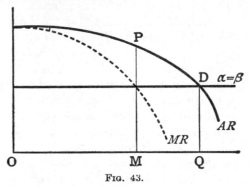

FIG. 43.

Fig. 43 represents a case in which the demand curve is
convex.
OM is the monopoly output, OQ the competitive output.
OM is greater than half OQ.

But complications are introduced into the comparison by the
existence of increasing and decreasing cost. The statement that
a monopolist will produce up to the point where marginal cost

[1] See p. 30.

is equal to marginal revenue is perfectly general; it applies equally to constant, decreasing, and increasing costs. But we have now discovered that marginal cost is not a simple notion. The a, β, and γ curves each show marginal cost in a different sense. Which of them shows the marginal cost which a monopolist will take into account? Before we can decide this question, we must consider whether the monopolist is obliged to pay rent to the factors which he employs. In some cases, as we shall see in a moment, it is unlikely that he will do so. If the monopolist pays the full rent for any scarce factor, then, on the assumption that the introduction of a single control in no way alters methods of production, the monopolist's average costs are the same for each output as average costs under competition; that is to say, they are the same as the competitive supply price for each output, and the marginal cost curve of the monopolist is marginal to the competitive supply curve. The competitive supply curve is β (average cost including rent) and the curve marginal to it is a (marginal cost including rent). When the demand and supply curves are straight lines, monopoly output will be half competitive output, whether the supply curve is rising or falling.

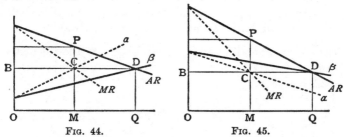

FIG. 44.   FIG. 45.

Let D be the point of competitive equilibrium.
Draw DB perpendicular to the y axis, cutting it in B, and cutting the marginal revenue curve in C. Then BC = CD.[1]
The a curve also cuts the marginal revenue curve in C.[2] The monopoly output (OM) is then equal to half the competitive output (OQ).[3]

This is true whatever the slope of the demand and supply curves. It is of course impossible that the supply curve under

---

[1] See p. 30.   [2] See p. 31.
[3] This result is already familiar; see Pigou, *Economics of Welfare*, p. 807.

L

decreasing cost should be a straight line throughout its length, for this would mean that after a certain output marginal cost became negative. There is no absurdity, however, in supposing it to be a straight line for the range of outputs necessary to the comparison.

If the supply curve is concave, and the demand curve is a straight line, then monopoly output is greater than half the competitive output whether the supply curve is rising or falling.

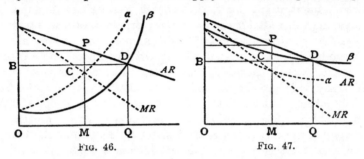

FIG. 46.   FIG. 47.

When the supply curve is rising, a will cut BD to the right of C, and when it is falling, to the left of C. In each case therefore it will cut MR below C and to the right of it. Therefore since BC = CD the monopoly output (OM) will be greater than half the competitive output (OQ).

Conversely, when the supply curve is convex, and the demand curve is a straight line, monopoly output will be less than half competitive output.

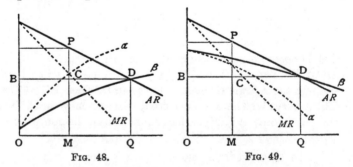

FIG. 48.   FIG. 49.

When the supply curve is rising, a will cut BD to the left of C, and when it is falling, to the right of C. Therefore in each case a will cut MR above C and to the left of it, and monopoly output (OM) will be less than half competitive output (OQ).

Similarly it can be seen that when the supply curve is a straight line (whether costs are rising, falling, or constant), monopoly output will be less than half competitive output for a concave demand curve, and it will be greater than half for a convex demand curve.

Thus we find that concavity of the supply curve and convexity of the demand curve lead to a high ratio of monopoly to competitive output. And convexity of the supply curve and concavity of the demand curve lead to a small ratio.

When the demand curve is concave and the supply curve convex, monopoly output must be less than half competitive output. When the demand curve is convex and the supply curve concave, monopoly output must be more than half competitive output. In this case price is falling at an increasing rate and cost rising at an increasing rate as output increases. It is therefore a case that is likely to occur in practice.[1]

When both the demand curve and the supply curve are concave, and when both are convex, monopoly output may be half, or more or less than half, competitive output.

In all these cases it is clear that monopoly output cannot be greater than competitive output. For outputs greater than the competitive amount the demand curve must lie below the supply curve (which represents average cost to the monopolist), so that any output greater than the competitive output would have to be sold at a loss.[2] At most the monopoly output may be equal to the competitive output. This may occur if either the demand or the supply curve after being sufficiently elastic becomes suddenly perfectly inelastic, as in the cases illustrated in Figs. 50 and 51.

These may be regarded as limiting cases of convexity of the demand curve and concavity of the supply curve, which each tend to produce a high ratio of monopoly to competitive output.

[1] In so far as any case in which monopolisation leaves the cost curves unchanged is ever likely to occur.

[2] See p. 33 where it is shown that for the output at which the average curves cut, the marginal revenue curve lies below the marginal cost curve, and consequently that the marginal revenue curve must cut the marginal cost curve from above at a smaller output.

Monopoly output would also be equal to competitive output if it so happened that the demand curve lay below the supply

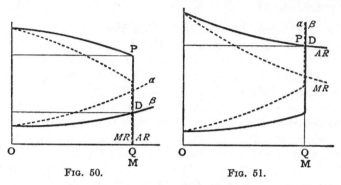

FIG. 50.   FIG. 51.

curve except at one point, where the two curves were tangential. There would then be only one output which could be produced without a loss,[1] and it must be this output which would be produced both under monopoly and under competition

Thus:

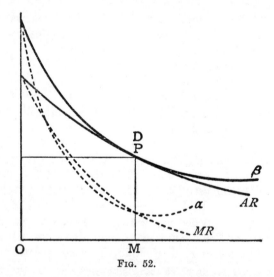

FIG. 52.

This may be regarded as the limiting case of the situation in

---

[1] Such a situation could only arise by chance for a competitive industry, but, as we saw above (p. 95), it is the ordinary situation of each individual firm in an industry which is earning normal profits.

which monopoly output must approach competitive output because the demand curve lies below the supply curve except for a small range of outputs, so that outputs outside this range could only be sold at a loss.

3

We have so far supposed that the monopolist is paying the full rent for the scarce factors which he employs. But this may not always be the case. If the scarce factor is land the monopolist will often omit rent from his calculations, and take account only of transfer costs, simply because he owns the land himself. Moreover, if the monopolist hires land but the land which he employs is owned by a large number of separate landlords, it is unlikely that he will be obliged to pay the full rent for it, since it will be possible for him to make a separate bargain with each landlord. The monopolist controls the whole demand for the land in its most profitable use. If it does not take service with him, it will have to earn a lower payment elsewhere. The monopolist therefore can offer to each landlord the transference earnings of the land, that is to say the payment which it could earn in its next best use; and, if the landlord rejects the monopolist's offer of the transference price for his piece of land, he will find that he can do no better by offering it to other producers, who must necessarily belong to some other industry for which the suitability of his land is not so great. It would be profitable to the monopolist on the other hand to pay for any individual site the full rent which it earns in his industry rather than to forgo the use of it. Thus for each piece of land there will be an upper and a lower limit to its earnings, which must lie somewhere between its full rent and its transference earnings. For land on the margin of transference the two limits coincide. The actual price which the monopolist will pay for each piece of land will depend upon his skill in bargaining relatively to the skill of the individual landlords.[1] In order to establish his reputation as a hard bargainer the monopolist may prefer to sacrifice the use of any site the owner of which resolutely stands out for a price greater than the transference earnings of his land, and by this means he may be able

[1] Cf. Pigou, *Economics of Welfare*, p. 280, for a discussion of the similar case of perfect price discrimination in selling.

so to weaken the resistance of the other landlords (who are not acting in concert) that he need pay no rent at all for the land that he employs. In other cases he will be obliged to pay part of the rent, but it seems on the whole improbable that he will ever be compelled to pay the full rent for all the land.

When the scarce factor is labour it will not be so easy for the monopolist to avoid paying rent. It is customary to pay all labour, of a given grade of efficiency from the point of view of the industry, at the same rate, and it may be troublesome and complicated to make separate bargains with individual workers.[1] Where unskilled labour is concerned, however, it may be possible to do so, and for the high-grade labour of salaried workers, since it is customary to make separate terms with each individual, the situation will be very similar to that of land, and the monopolist will often be able to acquire the services of each worker for no more than his transference earnings.

When the scarce factor is entrepreneurship, and the monopoly consists of a cartel formed by firms which were formerly competing, it will be the aim of the monopolist organisation to maximise the whole surplus which they receive, and the rent of entrepreneurship must clearly not be regarded as part of the expenses of production, but as part of the monopoly profit. Thus there will be many cases in which the monopolist pays no rent.

In order to discover monopoly output when the monopolist does not pay rent, it will be assumed that the transfer cost of individual productive units is independent of the scale of the industry.[2] We will first discuss the case in which there are no economies of large-scale industry.

In every case where the monopolist succeeds in avoiding the payment of the whole of the rent for any scarce factor that he employs, his marginal cost is the marginal cost to the industry excluding rent, and is shown by the γ curve. Now, as we have seen,[3] when there are no economies of large-scale industry, γ and

---

[1] But see p. 300, below, for the case in which men of different efficiency are paid the same daily wage.

[2] The relationship between the four cost curves shown in Section 4 of the last chapter will then obtain. For the sake of simplicity the assumption is retained in the rest of this chapter, but the comparisons can be made, when it is removed, by applying the results of Section 5 of the last chapter.

[3] See p. 135.

β coincide, for then average cost to the competitive industry is equal to marginal cost excluding rent. Marginal cost to the monopolist will therefore be shown by the β curve. If the monopolist pays part of the rent for any factor but not the whole of it, or if there are some scarce factors for which he pays the full rent, and others for which he pays none, his marginal cost will be somewhat greater than average cost to the competitive industry, but less than marginal cost including rent, and his marginal cost curve will lie somewhere between β and a. It is therefore clear that when the monopolist pays less than the full rent of any scarce factor the monopoly output will be a larger proportion of competitive output than when he does pay the full rent. For instance if the demand and supply curves are both straight lines he will produce more than half the competitive output. In the simple case where he pays no rent at all, so that his marginal costs are given by the β curve, it can further be seen that as long as the demand curve is a straight line he will produce more than half the competitive output whatever the shape of the supply curve. Thus:

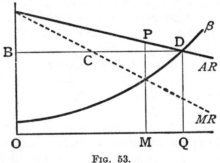

FIG. 53.

Since the demand curve is a straight line, BC = CD. But β must cut MR below C. Therefore OM is greater than half OQ.

We saw that in the cases where the monopolist pays the full rent (so that his marginal cost curve is marginal to the competitive supply curve), the ratio of monopoly output to competitive output for straight-line supply and demand curves is independent of their slope. In the case that we are now considering it can be seen that the ratio will tend to be greater the greater the elasticity of demand at the competitive point and the less the elasticity of supply.[1]

But even if the monopolist is paying no rent his output cannot exceed competitive output. At the point of competitive equilibrium the supply curve, which shows the monopolist's marginal cost, cuts the demand curve from below, so that for any output greater than the competitive amount, the price (and *a fortiori* the marginal revenue) must be less than marginal cost. In the limiting case, monopoly output may be equal to competitive output if the supply is perfectly inelastic for a sufficient range of prices.

4

We must now consider the case in which there are both scarce factors for which the monopolist does not pay the full rent and economies of large-scale industry, retaining the assumption that the transfer costs of individual productive units are independent of the scale of the industry. For the sake of simplicity let us suppose that the monopolist pays no rent at all. Then marginal costs are shown by the γ curve (marginal cost excluding rent) and the monopoly output will be determined by the intersection of γ with the marginal revenue curve.

The γ curve will lie below the β curve to an extent which depends upon the amount of the induced economies at each point, and the two curves do not stand in the average and marginal relation to each other as long as a scarce factor is present.

Since the marginal cost curve of the monopolist (γ) now lies below both the supply curve (β) and the curve marginal to the supply curve (a), it is clear that, if the demand is suf-

---

[1] The analysis of the case in which the monopolist pays no rent is of considerable importance, as it may be used to represent the case of short-period supply. In the short period the investment of capital in the industry, the number of entrepreneurs engaged in it, and the organisation of production, are all taken as given. The competitive supply curve is then the curve of marginal prime costs, and this is also the curve of marginal cost to the monopolist. The study of restriction of output in short-period conditions must therefore be made by means of the analysis, given above, in which the monopolist's marginal cost curve coincides with the competitive supply curve. Monopoly output will be that at which marginal prime cost is equal to marginal revenue, and the surplus above total prime costs is at a maximum; competitive output will be that at which marginal prime costs are equal to price, and the ratio between them will depend upon the elasticities of demand and supply.

ficiently elastic at the competitive point, monopoly output may be greater than competitive output (as in Fig. 55). This will

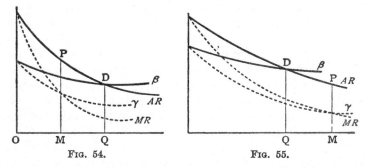

FIG. 54.   FIG. 55.

be more likely to occur the greater the elasticity of demand at the competitive point and the greater the amount of induced economies.[1]

5

It has now been shown that when the monopolist pays the full rent of the scarce factors, even if there are economies of large-scale industry, monopoly output cannot be greater than competitive output. And when there is a scarce factor for which the monopolist does not pay rent, but there are no economies, again monopoly output cannot be greater than competitive output. But if there are both economies and a scarce factor for which the monopolist does not pay the full rent, then it is possible for monopoly output to exceed competitive output. Neither condition is sufficient by itself, but both together may lead to a situation in which monopoly output is greater than competitive output. This conclusion may appear strange, but upon reflection it is seen to be consonant with common sense. When there are economies, but the monopolist pays rent, then his average cost is equal to the supply price, so that for any output greater than

---

[1] The monopoly output will be equal to the competitive output when the amount of induced economies is such that if there were no scarce factor (and therefore no rent for the competitive industry) the elasticity of supply would be equal to the elasticity of demand. If the amount of the economies is greater than this, monopoly output will exceed competitive output, and conversely, whatever the actual elasticity of supply. With a given amount of economies (shown by a given vertical distance between the γ and β curves) the monopoly output will approximate more closely to the competitive output the less the elasticity of supply.

the competitive output the price would be less than the average cost to the monopolist. And when the monopolist pays no rent, but there are no economies, the monopolist's marginal cost is equal to the supply price, so that for any output greater than the competitive output the price and, *a fortiori*, the marginal revenue would be less than marginal cost to the monopolist. But when there are both economies and a scarce factor for which rent is not paid, marginal and average cost to the monopolist are both less than the competitive supply price, and it is then possible that the monopolist will produce more than the competitive output.

Thus it is only when there is a scarce factor for which the full rent is not paid, and at the same time there are economies of large-scale industry, that it is possible that monopoly output may be greater than competitive output. In all other cases, as we have seen, monopoly output may (on extreme assumptions) be equal to competitive output, but it can never be greater.

CHAPTER 12

COMMENTARY ON THE COMPARISONS

1

THE comparisons of monopoly and competitive output which have been made in the last chapter make it possible to clear up a common confusion. It is often said that a monopolist will restrict output by less the greater is the elasticity of demand for his product, and the more rapid is the rate of decreasing cost, or that he will restrict output more the less the elasticity of demand and the more rapid the rate of increasing cost.[1] These propositions appear superficially plausible, for it is obvious that a monopolist gains more by restricting output the less is the elasticity of demand for his commodity, and the greater is the saving of cost due to a reduction of output. But the fact that they are fallacious at once becomes clear if we consider the case in which the demand and supply curves are straight lines. In that case, as we have seen, the extent to which the monopolist restricts output is exactly the same whatever the elasticity of demand or the rate of rising or falling cost. The fallacy lies in arguing that restriction will be carried furthest where it is most profitable to restrict at all. For instance, if there are two cases, in one of which the demand is more elastic than in the other, it is argued that because restriction will lead to a smaller monopoly net revenue in the case where the demand is more elastic, therefore the degree of restriction in that case will be less than in the case where the monopoly net revenue will be larger. But

[1] Cf. Marshall, *Industry and Trade*, p. 404; Taussig, *Principles*, pp. 200-204. In neither of the above passages are these fallacious propositions precisely set out, but each appears to suggest that its writer had these propositions in mind, and the impression which they make upon readers (for instance, undergraduates studying economics) is fairly represented by the fallacies set out in the text.

this is a false deduction. The profit which can be made from monopolising a commodity is certainly of the utmost importance, since, other things being equal, the greater the profit that can be made from the monopoly the more likely is a monopoly to be set up. But once the monopoly is set up, the degree of restriction will not be greater in one case than in another, merely because restriction is more profitable in one case than in another. The monopolist is conceived to choose the output which will give him the largest net revenue, and in each case he will restrict output to the point which in that particular case gives a larger net revenue than any other output; but there is no reason to suppose that the output at which the net revenue is a maximum, when he has hit upon it, will be the smallest in those cases in which the maximum net revenue is largest.

The comparisons set out in the last chapter have made it clear that the extent to which the monopolist restricts output cannot be related in any simple way to the elasticities of demand and of supply. For instance, if the monopolist pays the full rent of any scarce factors that he employs, so that his marginal cost curve is marginal to the competitive supply curve, and if the demand and supply curves are straight lines, then the ratio of monopoly to competitive output is always a half, whatever the slopes of the demand and supply curves may be. If the supply curve is a straight line, and the demand curve is concave, then the monopoly output will be a smaller proportion of competitive output the more rapidly costs are falling, or the more slowly costs are rising;[1] only if the demand curve is convex will it be true that monopoly output will be greater the more rapid the fall in costs. Similarly if the demand curve is a straight line, and the supply curve is convex, the monopoly output will be a smaller proportion of competitive output the greater the elasticity of demand; only if the supply curve is concave will it be true that monopoly output will be greater the greater the elasticity of demand.

The common view that the relation of monopoly to competitive output depends solely upon the elasticities of demand and supply is thus found to be mistaken, but the common fallacies are found to be true, as it were by accident, in certain special cases.

[1] Diagrams are not provided for these and the following propositions. The reader will find no difficulty in proving them for himself.

2

In place of these fallacious propositions a valid generalisation of the comparison can be found. We have seen that, with a given competitive output, monopoly output will tend to be reduced by concavity of the demand curve, and increased by concavity of the supply curve. This is to say, if the change in the slopes of the curves, as output is reduced, is in the direction that is favourable to the monopolist, he is encouraged to carry the reduction of output further. Thus, if the demand curve is concave, each successive reduction in output will lead to a greater and greater absolute rise in price, and this tends to increase the extent of the restriction of output. The effect of convexity in the supply curve is in the same direction, for with a convex supply curve each successive reduction in output leads to a smaller and smaller absolute rise in average cost under conditions of falling cost, and a greater and greater fall in cost under conditions of rising cost.

Conversely, if the demand curve is convex, so that each successive reduction in output leads to a smaller and smaller rise in price, or if the supply curve is concave, so that each successive reduction in output produces a greater and greater rise of cost under conditions of falling cost, or a smaller and smaller fall in cost under conditions of rising cost, the restriction in output will tend to be less. When the demand and supply curves are both straight lines, each successive reduction in output leads to the same rise in price, and the same rise or fall in cost, and the degree of restriction is independent of the slopes of the curves.

3

The foregoing propositions are only valid upon the assumption that the monopolist's average cost is the same as the competitive supply price for each output, so that the monopolist's marginal cost curve is marginal to the supply curve. These propositions are not true of the case in which there is a scarce factor for which the monopolist does not pay the full rent. We found that when no rent is paid monopoly output will tend to be a greater proportion of competitive output the greater is the elasticity of demand at the competitive point. In the limiting case, where the elasticity of demand is infinite, monopoly output is equal to competitive output if there are no economies of large-scale industry. The fallacious generalisation that monopoly output will be greater the greater the elasticity of demand thus fortuitously turns out to be correct, in this one case—in which the monopolist pays no rent. But the corresponding statement, that monopoly output is less the smaller the elasticity of supply, will be the reverse of the truth. If rent is not paid, and there are no economies of large-scale industry, the monopolist's marginal cost curve coincides with the competitive supply curve, and (with a given competitive output) the monopoly output will be larger the smaller is the elasticity of supply. In the limiting case, where supply is perfectly inelastic, monopoly output will be equal to competitive output.[1]

[1] Where there are both rent which is not paid and a given rate of induced economy of large-scale industry, monopoly output will be closer to competitive output the smaller the elasticity of supply. When monopoly output is less than competitive output, it will be greater the smaller is the elasticity of supply; and when monopoly output exceeds competitive output, it will be smaller the smaller is the elasticity of supply. When it is equal to competitive output, it will be independent of the elasticity of supply. (In each case the rate of induced economies is assumed to be given.) Cf. p. 153, note.

CHAPTER 13

1

THE effect of imposing a statutory maximum price upon a monopolist can be exhibited by means of our technical apparatus.[1]

When a maximum price is imposed, the demand (from the point of view of the monopolist) becomes perfectly elastic up to the amount of output which can be sold at that price. Beyond this amount the demand curve and the marginal revenue curve follow the same course as before. Thus:

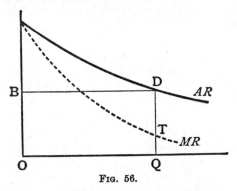

FIG. 56.

AR and *MR* are the original average and marginal curves. If OB (which equals QD) is the imposed price, OQ the

[1] Most of the following results are already well known (see Pigou, *Economics of Welfare*, chap. xxi. § 11, and Appendix III. § 23), but we shall find that by means of the marginal technique the inquiry can be carried a step further than it can reach when we are obliged to confine ourselves to straight-line curves.

* *This chapter is not of great importance for a reader who is not interested in purely technical questions.*

amount of output demanded at that price, and QT the
marginal revenue corresponding to the output OQ, then
the new average revenue curve will be given by BD, up
to the point D, and to the right of D will coincide with
AR; and the new marginal revenue curve will be given by
BDT, and to the right of T will coincide with MR.

The object of controlling price will be to obtain from the
monopolist the maximum possible output. This will be achieved,
when average costs are falling with increases of output, by
imposing the price which is given by the intersection of the
demand curve and his average cost curve. If any smaller price
were imposed it would be impossible for the monopolist to cover
his average costs, and no output at all would be produced. If
any greater price were imposed the monopolist would produce
whatever output could be sold at that price, unless the imposed
price were higher than the monopoly price, in which case the
restriction would have no effect, since the monopolist would prefer
to sell at the monopoly price. Thus the lowest effective price which
can be imposed is the price at which average cost is equal to
demand price, and it follows that this is the imposed price which
will produce the largest output.

If the conditions of demand and supply under competition
would be precisely the same as under monopoly the imposed
price which will obtain the largest output from the monopolist
would be the competitive price. The argument applies equally
well to the case of a monopoly considered in isolation, without
any reference to competition, but in the present discussion it will
be convenient to use the phrase "competitive output" to mean
the output at which average cost is equal to demand price, and
"competitive price" to mean the price at which that output will
be bought.

The case of an imposed price under conditions of falling cost
can be illustrated thus: [1]

β and a are the average and marginal cost curves, and AR
and MR the original average and marginal revenue curves.
QD is the imposed price.

---

[1] The following proof of the proposition that maximum output will be obtained
from the monopolist when the competitive price is imposed is not necessary,
but is included for the sake of consistency with what follows.

Then up to the output OQ the new average revenue curve is BD, and the new marginal revenue curve BDT. Beyond

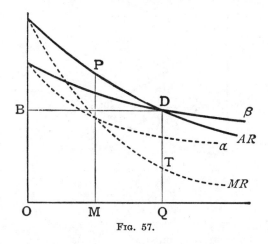

FIG. 57.

that output the new average and marginal revenue curves coincide with the old.

OM is the uncontrolled monopoly output, and MP the uncontrolled monopoly price.

OQ must be the output when DQ is the imposed price, since a (the marginal cost curve) must cut the new marginal revenue curve between D and T.

This follows from the fact that, at D, the slope of β (the average cost curve) is less than the slope of AR (the demand curve), so that the marginal cost of the output OQ must be greater than the marginal revenue, TQ.[1]

Under conditions of falling cost the competitive output can be evoked from a monopolist by fixing the competitive price as a maximum. But under increasing costs this device will not serve. If the competitive price is fixed the monopolist will produce less than the competitive output (assuming that he pays rent for the scarce factors), since he will produce only up to the point at which marginal cost is equal to the price. Thus: The new monopoly output will be that at which marginal cost is equal to the imposed price, that is (in the diagram) the output

---

[1] See p. 34.

at which a (the marginal cost curve) cuts the line BD. If a cuts
BD to the right of C the new monopoly output will be greater

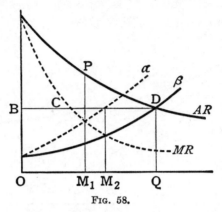

FIG. 58.

OB = QD = imposed price.
OM_1 = old monopoly output.
OM_2 = new monopoly output.
M_1P = old monopoly price.
MR cuts BD in C.

than the old. If it cuts BD to the left of C the new output will
be smaller than the old. Thus if the demand and cost curves are
straight lines (so that a cuts BD in C), the new monopoly output
will be the same as the old (and will be half the competitive
output). If, as in the illustration, the demand and cost curves
are concave, a must cut BD to the right of C, and the new
output will therefore be greater than the old. The new output,
though greater than the old, will still be less than the competitive
output. If the demand and cost curves are both convex, or if the
cost curves being concave the demand curve is sufficiently
convex, a will cut BD to the left of C, and the new output will
therefore be smaller than the old. Though the monopoly price
will have been lowered by the imposition of the maximum price,
the output will have been reduced.[1]

---

[1] These conditions (in which the new output is less than the old) are on the
whole less likely to be fulfilled than those in which the new output is larger.
Professor Pigou appears to have had this in mind when he says that if a price
is fixed between the monopoly and competitive price, the output will *probably*
be greater than the monopoly output. If monopoly output is reduced when the

Thus if the competitive price is imposed upon the monopolist when costs are rising, an output less than the competitive output will be produced, and, since at that price demand will exceed supply, it will be impossible to maintain the imposed price unless the controlling authority resorts to the rationing of consumers.

It remains to inquire what price would ensure the maximum output under conditions of rising cost. If the imposed price is less than the price at which the marginal cost curve cuts the demand curve the monopolist will produce that output whose marginal cost is equal to the price. If the imposed price is greater than this he will produce the output which can be sold at the imposed price, unless the imposed price is greater than the monopoly price, in which case it becomes ineffective.

Thus as the imposed price is reduced below the monopoly price the output will expand until that output is reached for which marginal cost is equal to demand price. Beyond this point a further reduction in price will reduce output, and after a certain point output might (in the conditions mentioned above) be reduced actually below the original monopoly output. The imposed price which will evoke the largest output is therefore the price at which marginal cost is equal to demand price.

In these cases of increasing cost it is assumed that the monopolist pays rent. If he does not, his marginal costs are equal to the competitive supply price, so that (just as in the case of decreasing cost) if the competitive price is imposed, the competitive output, which is the maximum possible output, will be produced. The monopolist, however, will retain the rent as a monopoly profit.

2

An ingenious though unpractical scheme[1] by which a monopolist would be led to produce the competitive output even under increasing costs (when rent is paid by the monopolist) could be arranged as follows: Fix the competitive price as a maximum. Then calculate the difference between marginal and

competitive price is imposed, then for a certain range of prices higher than this it would also be reduced. But the conditions in which this would occur are probably rare (*Economics of Welfare*, p. 807).

[1] It is believed that this device was first suggested by Mr. Robinson in an answer written in an examination.

average cost of the competitive output. Pay this sum as a subsidy per unit of output to the monopolist so that his average and marginal cost curves are lowered uniformly by this amount, and his marginal cost for the competitive output is equal to the average competitive cost. At the same time demand from the monopolist a lump-sum tax equal to the whole subsidy, as a condition of allowing him to produce any output at all. By this means the monopolist will be made to produce the competitive output and receive only the competitive profit.

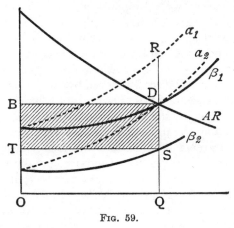

Fig. 59.

β_1 and a_1 are the average and marginal cost curves.
DQ = imposed price.
DR = subsidy per unit = SD.
β_2 and a_2 are the average and marginal cost curves after payment of the subsidy.
BDST = total amount of subsidy and tax.

The same result would be produced if, without an imposed price, the subsidy were equal to the difference between the marginal cost and the marginal revenue of the competitive output. This method of course could be applied equally to cases of decreasing cost. It would not be necessary for any money to change hands between the monopolist and the controlling authority. The authority could merely announce that the lump-sum tax will be required from the monopolist, but that a rebate (equal to the amount of the subsidy per unit) will be allowed for every unit of output. The monopolist will then find it profitable to produce the output at which the total amount of rebate that he earns completely wipes out the tax.

If demand and supply curves remained unchanged for sufficiently long and were sufficiently well known, this scheme might be practicable, but there is not likely to be much scope for applying it in actual cases.

CHAPTER 14

OBJECTIONS TO THE COMPARISONS

1

THERE are various objections to comparisons between monopoly and perfectly competitive output such as we have been making in the foregoing chapters. In the first place, there is a very common class of monopolies for which such a comparison is meaningless. In some industries, of which railways and the distribution of gas and electricity are familiar examples, the smallest practicable plant has a very large capacity output, and if the market is not sufficiently large to use one plant up to capacity, there is no possibility of competition. If by chance two firms were engaged in such an industry, they would either compete against each other so that neither was able to cover its costs, and the one with the least endurance would disappear, or they would form a combine. There is no possibility of long-period competitive equilibrium when the average costs of an individual firm fall with increases of output.

In the case of monopolies of this type, there can be no comparison with competitive output, since the circumstances of the case make competition impossible. The phrase "competitive output", however, may, as in the last chapter, be given the purely formal meaning of that output at which average costs (including normal profits) are equal to demand price.[1]

2

Supposing that the market is large enough to support a number of firms, so that it is possible to talk of a competitive

---

[1] It appears to be used in this sense by Professor Pigou, *Economics of Welfare*, p. 310.

* *Section 5 of this chapter contains some complexities which are not required for the succeeding argument except in Section 5 of Chapter 27.*

output, it is necessary to the comparison that the cost curves of the competitive industry are not altered by the formation of a monopoly.[1] It is natural to object that this will rarely be the case; that the expenses of a monopolist on advertising will be less; that firms within the industry can be allotted specialised tasks when they are under a single control; that selling costs will be less when marketing is done on a large scale; that cross-freights between one part of the market and another can be avoided; and so forth. In short, it is natural to suppose that when the industry is monopolised, its efficiency will be increased, and the cost curve of the commodity will be lowered.

This objection, however, is not valid. We have compared monopoly output, not with the output that would come about in an imperfect market, but with the perfectly competitive output. In a perfect market, competitive advertising would be unnecessary. If a very small reduction in price by one competitor would secure an indefinitely large increase in sales, it would be folly to spend money on advertisement. The only sort of advertisement which could take place would be aimed at increasing the aggregate sales of the commodity in question, and if this were undertaken by some corporate body acting on behalf of the competitive industry, it would also be profitable for the monopolist.

If the cost of production of individual plants could be lowered by specialisation, specialisation would come about in a perfect market. Suppose, for instance, that there are ten rolling mills, each of which keeps a set of rolls for making ten sizes of steel rails, and that none are used to capacity. A monopolist could allot to each mill one size, and save the expense involved by frequent changes and by maintaining surplus rolls. But in a perfect market any mill which specialised on a certain size could produce that size more cheaply than the rest, capture the whole market in that size, and force the other mills to specialise in the remaining sizes. This process would continue until each mill produced one size only, and the same result would come about as under monopoly. In a perfect market lateral disintegration of this type would be carried to the point

[1] It is further necessary to the comparisons that the demand curve should be the same under monopoly and under competition. But the demand curve which governs monopoly output may be influenced by prospective future sales in a way in which the demand curve governing competitive output is not (see p. 23).

at which there are no further economies to be had from specialisation.

Similarly, if there are economies from specialising upon particular processes in manufacture, vertical disintegration would come about under perfect competition. A specialist firm, such as the bleaching works in the cotton industry, or Morris's pressed steel works, would concentrate upon one process and supply the other producers with one particular service more cheaply than each could supply it for himself.[1]

If a large-scale sales organisation can deal more efficiently with the output of the whole industry than the separate sales departments of the separate firms, under perfect competition a system of independent merchants would grow up and an optimum sized sales unit would deal with the output of a number of producing firms. If there is a waste of transport cost because a more distant firm sells in a part of the market which could be more cheaply served by a firm nearer to it, perfect competition would ensure that this waste was eliminated, and each buyer would be served by the firm which could serve him most cheaply. In short, perfect competition would bring about all the economies which monopoly could introduce.[2]

The only exception to this rule is that when some firms possess trade secrets which enable them to produce more cheaply than others, there would be no tendency under competition for the secrets to be shared, while under monopoly the best methods known to any firm in the industry would be applied to the whole output. Thus when knowledge of methods is brought into account, there is some reason to expect the monopoly cost to be lower than competitive cost.

In respect of the rate at which new methods of production are introduced there are two opposite influences. On the one hand, the monopolist might find it worth while to carry out research to discover new methods, as well as applying those already known to the whole output. His motive for doing so is greater than the motive of any individual firm, and research

[1] Lateral and vertical disintegration in a perfect market are more fully discussed in the Appendix on Increasing and Diminishing Returns.

[2] Marshall (*Principles*, p. 484) appears to deal at one and the same time with a comparison between monopoly and competitive output which is only valid upon the assumption that competition is perfect, and with a lowering of cost by the monopolist which could only occur if competition were not perfect.

carried on by a centralised agency is more likely to yield results than the efforts of scattered experts. On the other hand, when an invention has been made, a competitive firm may find it worth while to make use of the new process, since the loss from the obsolescence of existing plant will fall mainly upon other firms, whereas a monopolist might prefer to delay the introduction of the new process until the old plant was worn out. It is therefore impossible to say *a priori* whether on balance the existence of monopoly is likely to hasten or to retard the introduction of new methods.

When rationalisation is under discussion, the argument is often advanced that a single control of an industry is desirable, not only from the point of view of the entrepreneurs concerned, who wish to increase their profits (or reduce their losses), but also from the point of view of society, for the reason that a single control would eliminate the wastes of competition, and lower the cost of production. But the wastes of competition are in reality the wastes of market imperfection, and perfect competition would eliminate them as well as monopoly. Rationalisation is not the cure for too much competition, but for too little.

Monopoly may be an easier and more certain cure to apply. In practice monopoly secures its economies by achieving more effectively than does imperfect competition the very organisation of production, for each output, that we should expect to find if competition were perfect. But the only point with which we are at present concerned is that monopoly cannot improve upon the organisation of industry which would come about under perfect competition (except by the dissemination of secret knowledge) however much it might improve on imperfect competition, and that for the purposes of our comparison, the cost curve under competition must be taken to show the most efficient organisation of industry which can be brought about with existing knowledge. The comparison between output under imperfect competition and output under monopoly is far more interesting from a practical point of view than the comparison which we have been making, but it cannot be made in the same general terms. The effect of monopolisation would depend on the degree and the kind of imperfection, and the competitive supply curve, used as the basis of comparison, would be different in each case.

3

It has already become plain how artificial and how far from reality the comparison of monopoly with competitive output must be. But there is a further difficulty, arising from the fact that if an industry is carried on under perfect competition the motive to form a monopoly is less than in an imperfect market. When the market is imperfect individual firms do not grow to their optimum size, so that even if there were no possibilities of specialisation between firms, production would still not be carried on in the most efficient way. Thus a monopolist could hope not only to raise the price of the commodity by restricting output, but also to lower costs by improving the organisation of the industry. Under imperfect competition there is a double motive for creating a monopoly, and under perfect competition only a single one. At the same time, a monopoly would be far more difficult to impose upon a perfectly competitive industry. The same conditions which make the market perfect, the absence of a preference on the part of groups of buyers (for whatever reason) for particular firms, also make entry into the industry easy, and as soon as the monopolist, after shutting down some firms, began to make more than normal profits, new firms would spring up to share in his gains. There is less motive for forming a monopoly, and a greater difficulty in maintaining it, in a perfect than in an imperfect market. Thus it is peculiarly unlikely that any actual case should ever present the opportunity of making a comparison between output under monopoly and under perfect competition.

4

Even, however, if all these objections have been met, and there is a perfectly competitive output with which to compare the monopoly output, we cannot yet be satisfied. Since the competitive firms, each producing a part of the output, are each of optimum size, the monopoly must be of much greater than optimum size. The monopoly organisation could allow production to be carried on in exactly the same way as would occur under competition for the same output, but under competition there would have been no organisation controlling the output. To ensure that the cost curve of the monopolist is the same as the cost curve under competition the agent which manages the industry must, therefore, have no cost and must have an indefinitely large capacity, so that it is not susceptible to the diminishing returns from a fixed unit òf entrepreneurship which, in the real world, often limit the size of individual firms.

This assumption is not perhaps so unreal as appears at first sight. When an industry is monopolised it is possible that its structure may remain unchanged except that some agency takes over the control of price, and allots to each unit its share in output. The cost of running this agency may be negligibly small. Each total output would then be produced in the same way and at the same cost as an output of that size would have been produced by a perfectly competitive industry. The firms which have become redundant (because the total output has been reduced) would be eliminated and those which remain would be unaltered. Each output would be produced in the most efficient way if it were divided between a number of separate units exactly corresponding to the firms which would have produced that output under perfectly competitive conditions. This leads to a formal difficulty, since the separate units in the industry have ceased to be firms upon our definition, and the men in charge of them have been degraded from the status of entrepreneur to the status of salaried labour. This is not a substantial objection, but it is further necessary to our comparison to assume that just that amount of cost of management must be incurred for each output as would have been incurred if that output had been produced under competition, and the entrepreneurs who are retained to produce it must each be paid the income which would have been necessary to attract them under competition, so that their salaries must be equal to normal profits apart from any share they may receive in the monopoly revenue.

5

It is only necessary to set out the conditions in which the comparison between monopoly and competitive output would be feasible in order to expose its unreality. But even if these conditions are fulfilled, there remains one further objection.

The comparisons were made upon the assumption that average cost to the monopolist and to the competitive industry are the same for any given output. And, even if all the more obvious objections to the comparisons can be met, the objection remains that this assumption can only be fulfilled in very peculiar cases.

In any ordinary case the cost curve under competition and under monopoly cannot be the same. Under perfect competition the supply of each factor to the individual firm is perfectly elastic, and each entrepreneur will employ that amount of each factor whose marginal productivity is equal to its price. To the individual firm the current rate of wages, of interest, or of rent, represents both the marginal and average cost for all amounts of each factor, whether or not their supply is perfectly elastic to the industry. Thus the factors will be combined together so that their marginal productivities are in the ratio of their prices.[1]

But if the supply of a factor is less than perfectly elastic to the competitive industry, the supply to the monopolist will also be less than perfectly elastic, and its average cost will rise as he employs more of it. He will regulate his use of it so that marginal cost to him is equal to marginal productivity, and the marginal cost to him of the factor will be greater than the average cost. The monopolist will employ factors so that their marginal productivities are in the ratio of their marginal costs to him, and only when they are all in perfectly elastic supply will their marginal costs be the same thing as their prices. By employing less, for instance, of labour, he may be able to lower the rate of wages he has to pay, and he will substitute capital for labour in circumstances where a competitive producer, for whom the wage is independent of the amount of labour he employs, would not find it profitable to do so. Thus the existence of scarce factors of production will prevent the ratio in which the factors are employed for each output from being the same under monopoly as under competition, and the cost curve of the commodity cannot be the same.

Similar considerations apply when one or other of the factors becomes cheaper when more is employed. If the monopolist knows that when he buys more machines from a subsidiary

[1] The argument of this and the succeeding paragraphs depends upon the analysis of monopsony which is set out at greater length in Books VI. and VII.

industry, all the machines which he buys will be cheaper, he is under a greater incentive to substitute capital for labour than are individual competitive producers, who would each individually receive only a negligible share in the induced economies resulting from their own purchase of the machinery.

The monopolist will alter the proportions in which the factors are employed wherever it is possible to do so in such a way as to lower his costs, and even when the more general objections to the comparisons have been disposed of it is only possible for the monopolist cost curves to be the same as the competitive cost curves when the proportions of the factors used for a given output are the same under monopoly and under competition. This condition might be fulfilled in various circumstances. It is possible, though not likely in the long period, that the proportions of the factors may be rigidly fixed by technical conditions.[1] For any given output it would then be impossible for the monopolist to deviate from the competitive proportions of the factors. This would entail not only that the proportions of labour, land, and capital engaged upon a given output were dictated by technical conditions and could not be varied, but also that the output of each "firm" (in the sense discussed in the last section) could not be altered, so that for a given output of the industry the number of "firms" could not be changed. This condition is unlikely to be fulfilled, since it can only be in very rare cases that the output of a firm is fixed by technical considerations. In any ordinary case, if the cost of other factors rises relatively to the cost of entrepreneurship as the competitive industry grows in size, the optimum output of the firm becomes smaller; that is to say, the proportion of entrepreneurship to other factors becomes greater. While if the cost of entrepreneurship becomes relatively greater, the optimum firm becomes larger. Similarly, if the supply price of entrepreneurs to the monopolist agency rises faster than that of other factors as more are employed, the monopolist will employ a smaller proportion of entrepreneurship to other factors than would be employed in each output under competition; he will organise his industry with larger "firms". And conversely when

---

[1] This may be expressed by saying that the marginal productivity of each factor falls infinitely rapidly if the amount is increased beyond the necessary proportions. See Hicks, "Marginal Productivity and the Principle of Variation", *Economica*, February 1932, p. 846, for a discussion of the assumption of fixed proportions.

the supply prices of other factors are rising faster than the price of entrepreneurship.

When technical conditions permit of variation, it is still possible that the proportions of the factors may be the same under monopoly and under competition. As we have already seen, if the supply of each factor to the industry is perfectly elastic the proportions are unchanged. The proportions would also be the same if the elasticity of supply of all the factors happened by chance to be the same.[1] In neither of these cases has the monopolist any motive for varying the proportions, which are not only the same as between monopoly and competition, but the same for each output. The marginal costs of the factors to the industry are then either equal to, or in the same ratio as, their average costs, so that the proportions of the factors under monopoly (regulated by their marginal costs) must be the same as the proportions under competition (regulated by their average costs). Finally, if the monopolist pays no rent for the scarce factors, the proportions will be the same, provided that there are no economies of large-scale industry, since the marginal cost of each factor to the monopolist will then be the same as its average cost to the competitive industry.

In all other cases the proportions of the factors in each output will be different under monopoly and under competition, and the monopolist's average cost curve will lie below the supply curve of the competitive industry. The comparisons which we have made, therefore, underestimate the monopoly output.[2]

The inaccuracy of our comparisons will be greater the greater is the difference between average cost under monopoly and

---

[1] See p. 242, below, for the proof of this proposition.

[2] In order to make accurate comparisons we must look behind the cost curves and study the supply curve of each factor. For example, when the supply curves of all the factors are straight lines with differing elasticities, and there are no economies, the supply curve of the commodity will be convex, and if the demand curve is a straight line the monopoly output, as shown by the uncorrected comparison, would appear to be less than half the competitive output. But we have just seen that the uncorrected comparisons are likely to underestimate the monopoly output, and in these conditions an accurate comparison would show that monopoly output will be exactly half the competitive output. Similarly, if the supply curve of the commodity is a straight line the uncorrected comparison would show that monopoly output is half competitive output (if the demand curve is a straight line). But in this case the supply curves of the factors must be on balance concave, and monopoly output must be more than half competitive output (cf. p. 278, note, below).

under competition. They will therefore be more inaccurate the greater the technical possibilities of variation of the proportions of the factors, and the greater the divergence between the elasticities of supply of the separate factors, that is to say, the greater the scope for improvement upon the competitive costs.

These complications, as well as the more general objections to the comparison of monopoly and competitive output, apply in the main only to long-period cases. In the short period the technique of production cannot be much altered, and we may suppose that in general the monopolist's short-period marginal cost curve will coincide with the supply curve under perfect competition. The comparison can then be accurately made by means of the method set out in Chapter 11.[1]

6

The discovery that costs under monopoly are lower than under competition considerably enlarges the class of cases in which monopoly output may exceed competitive output. When the competitive supply curve is falling, the monopoly marginal cost curve will lie both below the supply curve and below the marginal cost curve of the competitive industry, and it is clear that if the demand for the commodity is sufficiently elastic, monopoly output will be greater than competitive output. When the supply curve is rising, it is only possible for the monopolist's marginal cost curve to lie below the supply curve when there are sufficient economies of large-scale industry.[2] When this is the case monopoly output will be greater than competitive output if the demand is sufficiently elastic.

The conclusions of Chapter 13 must also be modified in the light of this result. Under conditions of falling supply price it will be possible to evoke from the monopolist an output larger than the competitive output by imposing as a maximum the price for which the demand price is equal to the monopolist's average cost. Under conditions of rising supply price an output greater than the competitive amount will be evoked merely by the imposition of a maximum price, without recourse to the device of a subsidy and tax, provided that the monopolist's marginal cost curve lies below the competitive supply curve;

[1] See p. 152, note.   [2] See p. 278, below.

but the monopolist will still be earning a surplus profit. In general the output evoked by an imposed price will be greater than that shown by the analysis of the last chapter, which is only exact for those cases in which the proportions of the factors are the same under monopoly as under competition.

BOOK V
PRICE DISCRIMINATION

CHAPTER 15

PRICE DISCRIMINATION

1

It often happens that a monopolist finds it possible and profitable to sell a single commodity at different prices to different buyers. This can occur when he is selling in several markets which are divided from one another in such a way that goods which are sold in the cheaper market cannot be bought from the monopolist and resold in the dearer market; and when customers in the dearer market cannot transfer themselves into the cheaper market to get the benefit of the lower price. The act of selling the same article, produced under a single control, at different prices to different buyers is known as *price discrimination*.

Under conditions of perfect competition price discrimination could not exist even if the market could be easily divided into separate parts. In each section of the market the demand would be perfectly elastic, and every seller would prefer to sell his whole output in that section of the market in which he could obtain the highest price. The attempt to do so, of course, would drive the price down to the competitive level, and there would be only one price throughout the whole market. So long as the market is perfect it is only if all sellers are combined or are acting in agreement that they can take advantage of the barriers between one part of a market and another to charge different prices for the same thing.

* *The argument of the rest of the book does not depend, except at a few points, on this and the following chapter. The analysis of the latter part of Section 2 of this chapter and of the special case dealt with in Section 3 is somewhat complicated, though it contains no essential difficulty. The argument of Sections 5 and 7, giving the comparison of simple with discriminating monopoly, is extremely intricate. The reader is advised to revive his acquaintance with the geometry of Chapter 2 before studying the formal analysis in this chapter.*

But if there is some degree of market imperfection there can be some degree of discrimination. The market is imperfect because customers will not move readily from one seller to another, and if it is possible for an individual seller to divide his market into separate parts, price discrimination becomes practicable. But since under ordinary competitive conditions the demand curves for the individual sellers are likely to be very elastic, price discrimination will not usually lead to any very great differences in the prices charged to different buyers by any one seller.

When a single seller is not subject to close competition, or when there is an agreement between rival sellers, price discrimination is more likely to occur. The most usual case is in the sale of direct personal services, where there is no possibility of a transfer from one market to another. For instance surgeons commonly grade the fee for an operation according to the wealth of the patient. This practice is maintained by a tradition among doctors, and would break down if they chose to compete among themselves by underbidding one another in the fees charged to rich patients. Or discrimination may occur when the markets in which a monopolist is selling are divided from each other geographically or by tariff barriers, so that there would be a considerable expense in transferring goods from a cheaper market to be resold in a dearer market; when this type of discrimination leads to a concern selling at a lower price in an export market and a higher price at home it is commonly described as "dumping". Or discrimination may occur when several groups of buyers require the same service in connection with clearly differentiated commodities. Thus a railway can charge different rates for the transport of cotton goods and of coal without any fear that bales of cotton will be turned into loads of coal in order to enjoy a cheaper rate.

There is probably also a good deal of rather haphazard discrimination wherever goods are sold on special orders, so that the individual buyer has no means of knowing what price is being charged to other buyers for a similar commodity.

Even when there is no natural barrier between groups of customers there are various devices by which the market may be broken up so as to make price discrimination possible. Various brands of a certain article which in fact are almost exactly alike may be sold as different qualities under names and labels which induce rich and snobbish buyers to divide themselves from poorer buyers; and in this way the market is split up, and the monopolist can sell what is substantially the same thing at several prices. The device of making the same thing appear in different guises will also serve to save the monopolist from the reproaches of injustice between customers which sometimes put difficulties in the way of price discrimination.

2

In some cases the demand in one market will depend upon the price that is being charged in another market. The case of first- and third-class railway fares, analysed by Edgeworth,[1] is of this nature. In the following argument we shall only consider cases in which the demand curve in each separate market is independent of the prices charged in the other markets.

An analysis of price discrimination can then be built up from the analysis already given for simple monopoly when only one price can be charged for a single commodity. If it is possible for a monopolist to sell the same commodity in separate markets it will clearly be to his advantage to charge different prices in the different markets, provided that the elasticities of demand in the separate markets are not equal. For if he charges the same price in each market he will find that, at that price, the marginal revenue obtained by selling an increment of output in each market separately is greater in some markets than in others. He can therefore increase his profit by selling less in those markets where the elasticity of demand is less and the marginal revenue smaller, and selling more in those markets where the elasticity of demand is higher and the marginal revenue greater. He will therefore adjust his sales in such a way that the marginal revenue obtained from selling an additional unit of output in any one market is the same for all the markets. And his profits will be at a maximum when the marginal revenue in each market is equal to the marginal cost of the whole output.[2] The method by which prices will be determined can be shown by the following method.

[1] *Papers Relating to Political Economy*, vol. i. p. 174.
[2] Professor Pigou does not make use of this method, but he is evidently aware of the underlying fact, though he expresses it in a somewhat obscure mathematical form (*Economics of Welfare*, p. 302, note 1).

Suppose that there are two markets, I and II, in which the conditions of demand are different. With the same system of axes, draw the demand curves (D_1 and D_2) of the two markets with the corresponding marginal revenue curves, and sum them laterally, so as to obtain an aggregate demand curve showing the total amount that would be sold at each price if the price were the same in both markets, and an aggregate marginal revenue curve showing the amount of sales that would correspond to each value of the marginal revenue if the marginal revenue were the same in both markets. This curve will show the marginal revenue obtained by the discriminating monopolist.

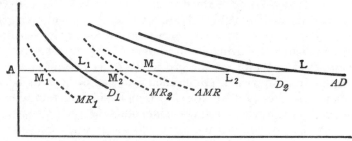

FIG. 60.

This construction can be exhibited thus:

Draw any line AL parallel to the x axis, to cut D_1 in L_1, D_2 in L_2, and the aggregate demand curve (AD) in ،.
Let it cut MR_1 in M_1, MR_2 in M_2, and the aggregate marginal revenue curve (AMR) in M.
Then $AL = AL_1 + AL_2$, and $AM = AM_1 + AM_2$.

The monopoly output under price discrimination is determined by the intersection of the monopolist's marginal cost curve with the aggregate marginal revenue curve. This total output is made up of the amounts sold in the two markets, in each of which marginal revenue is equal to the marginal cost of the whole output. The price in each market will be the demand price for the amount of output sold there.[1]

[1] Professor Yntema makes use of this construction (see "The Influence of Dumping on Monopoly Price", *Journal of Political Economy*, December 1928), but he confines himself to establishing with its aid a proposition which can be proved without resort to any such complicated apparatus; see below, p. 205, note.

OM is the total output, and is equal to $OM_1 + OM_2$.
MC is the marginal cost of the output OM.

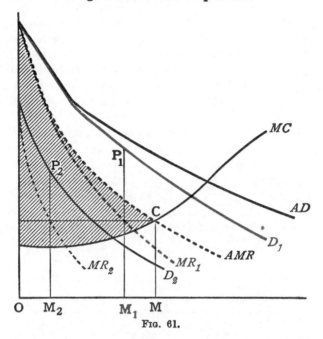

FIG. 61.

OM_1 is sold at the price M_1P_1 in market I. OM_2 is sold at the
price M_2P_2 in market II. The shaded area shows the monopoly revenue, which is equal to the area lying under the
aggregate marginal revenue curve (total revenue) *minus*
the area lying under the marginal cost curve (total costs).

In Fig. 61 marginal costs are rising, but whether marginal
costs are constant, rising, or falling, output will be determined
by the point at which the aggregate marginal revenue curve
cuts the marginal cost curve, and the amount sold in each
market will be the amount for which marginal revenue is equal
to the marginal cost of the whole output.[1]

[1] The points at which the separate marginal revenue curves cut the marginal
cost curve have no significance, since these points (except when costs happen
to be constant) do not show the marginal cost of the whole output which is
actually being produced.

3

A special case of price discrimination will be found when a
producer is selling in two markets, one of which is perfectly
competitive, so that the demand for his product is perfectly
elastic there, while in the other he has a monopoly. This might
occur if one market was his home country, and the other a
foreign country where his produce was in competition with local
rivals.

Let market I be the sheltered home market, and market II
the foreign competitive market. In market II the marginal
revenue is equal to the competitive price. The monopolist will
therefore regulate his sales both so that the marginal revenue
in market I is equal to the price in market II, for it is only at
that point that the marginal revenues in the two markets are
equal, and so that the marginal cost of the whole output is equal
to the price in market II.

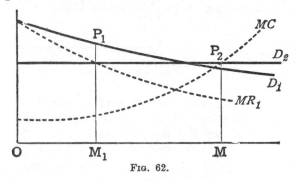

FIG. 62.

In Fig. 62 the total output, OM, is given by the point of
intersection, P_2, of the perfectly elastic demand curve, D_2,
of market II, with the marginal cost curve, MC, which
must be rising if equilibrium is to be attained.

MP_2 is the price and marginal revenue in market II, and
the output in market I, OM_1, is such that the marginal
revenue there, given by MR_1, is equal to MP_2.

The output sold in market II is the difference, M_1M, between OM_1 and OM.

If the competitive price in market II is lowered, the total

output will be reduced, for M will move to the left, and marginal cost will be lowered. The output in market I will be increased, for M_1 will move to the right. And the amount sold in market II (M_1M) will be reduced. If the price in market II fell below the level at which the marginal revenue curve, MR_1, of market I cuts the marginal cost curve, no output would be sold in the unsheltered market.

4

The existence of price discrimination, as we have seen, depends on a difference between the elasticities of the demands in the markets in which it is possible to sell. If the demand curves of the separate markets were iso-elastic,[1] so that at any price the elasticity of demand was the same in each market, then the same price would be charged in all of them; for when the marginal revenues were equal in each market, the prices would then also be equal, and the result would be the same as though the market was not divisible. This would occur, for example, if the demand curves of individual buyers were all identical. One market might contain more buyers than another, so that one demand curve was simply an enlargement of the other. The same result would be produced if the demand curves of individuals were of various shapes, but each market was made up of the same proportions of individual demands of various types. If the only practicable subdivisions of a market were such that the demand curves in each were iso-elastic, there would be no advantage from price discrimination. It might be possible for a village barber to charge a differential price for shaving red-haired clients, but if the red-haired members of the village had the same wealth and the same desire to be shaved as the rest of the inhabitants, the barber would find it profitable to charge them the same price as the rest.

The profitability of the monopoly will depend upon the manner in which the market is broken up. In many cases the division into sub-markets will be arbitrarily dictated by circumstance; for instance geographical or tariff barriers may divide the markets. But it may often happen that even when the monopolist can fix only a small number of different prices he

[1] See p. 43.

can influence to some extent the manner in which buyers are distributed between the markets in which the different prices rule. In the rate-schedules of railway companies the types of goods which are to be charged at various rates are grouped together at the will of the company. Moreover, when the monopolist divides up his market by the introduction of various "brands" of the same article, he will attempt to divide the customers from each other, so as to be able to charge a higher price for the higher class "brands" of the article. In this way the markets will be divided up in a manner which is partly under the control of the monopolist.

It is therefore necessary to inquire in what way a monopolist would divide his market if he were perfectly free to do so in the manner most profitable to himself. Let us suppose that the monopolist is in possession of some device which enables him to separate buyers from each other at will, and let us suppose that he is at first charging a single monopoly price throughout the market, and then proceeds to divide it up by successive stages. The total demand of the market is made up of the demands of individual buyers, and if at the single monopoly price the elasticities of the demands of individuals are all the same there is nothing to be gained by discrimination, and the market will not be divided. But if the elasticities of demand are different he will first divide all individual buyers into two classes such that the highest elasticity of demand in the one class is less than the least elasticity of demand in the other class. To the first class he will raise the price, and to the second class he will lower it. Now if at the new prices the elasticities of demand of all individual buyers within each class are the same there can be no gain from further subdivision. But if they are not alike each sub-market will be split into two on the same principle as before, the parts will again be subdivided, and so forth, until the point is reached at which each sub-market consists of a single buyer, or a group of buyers whose elasticities of demand are the same. As long as any two individual buyers with different elasticities of demand are being charged the same price the monopolist can increase his gains by selling to each of them at a different price, if it is possible to do so.[1]

---

[1] This treatment of the matter is somewhat different from that given by Professor Pigou (*Economics of Welfare*, pp. 279-82). He envisages the mono-

In most cases, of course, it will not be possible for the monopolist to divide the market at will, and there will be an arbitrary
element in the possible barriers between individual buyers which
will prevent him from achieving the most profitable division of
the market.[1] But however the market is divided, once the
division has been achieved the sub-markets will be arranged in
ascending order of their elasticities, the highest price being
charged in the least elastic market, and the lowest price in the
most elastic market.[2]

polist as dividing, not the individual buyers, but the separate units of the
commodity, between the different markets, but he does not make it clear how
this can be done.

[1] Even if the monopolist is able to charge a separate price to each buyer he
will not necessarily have achieved what Professor Pigou describes as "discrimination of the first degree". For discrimination of the first degree (which
may be called *perfect discrimination*) is only achieved when it is possible to sell
each separate unit of output at a different price (*loc. cit.* p. 279), and this
condition will not be fulfilled if each separate buyer varies the amount of his
purchases with the price that he is charged. Perfect discrimination could only
occur if each consumer bought only one unit of the product and was forced to
pay a price which represented his maximum offer for it (prisoners of war might
have been held to ransom on this principle in mediaeval times, and so may the
victims of kidnappers in modern America). Or if the monopolist knew the
average price which each buyer would give for that quantity of output whose
marginal cost to the monopolist is equal to its marginal utility to the buyer, and
made to each buyer an all-or-none offer of that amount at that price; as long as
the total sum which he was forced to pay did not exceed his estimate of the
total utility of that amount of the commodity, the buyer would prefer to
purchase rather than to go without, so that the price per unit charged to each
buyer would represent the average utility of the amount which he purchased.
(For the meaning of average and marginal utility see p. 211, below.)

Professor Pigou's discrimination of the "second degree would obtain if a
monopolist were able to make n separate prices, in such wise that all units with
a demand price greater than x were sold at a price x, all with a demand price
less than x and greater than y at a price y, and so on" (*loc. cit.* p. 279). This
could only be achieved if each individual buyer had a perfectly inelastic demand
for the commodity below a certain maximum price, above which he would buy
none at all.

[2] Professor Pigou states that "it is not, indeed, true, as is sometimes supposed, that the relative rates [prices] charged to different markets will depend
. . . simply upon the comparative elasticities (in respect of some unspecified
amount of output) of the demands of these markets" (*loc. cit.* p. 302). But it
is true that the prices will depend on, and be in the same order as, the elasticities
of demand in the separate markets at the prices charged in these markets.
This follows from the formula, $\text{Price} = \dfrac{\text{Marginal Revenue}}{1 - 1/\epsilon}$, where ϵ is the elasticity
of demand; for the marginal revenue is the same in each market. Professor
Pigou, in a footnote to the above passage, finds the price in each market for
straight-line demand curves by considering "the demand price of the unit that
is most keenly demanded", overlooking the fact that this highest demand
price can be deduced (for a straight line) from the value of the elasticity of
demand at any given price.

In order to discover the profitability of a monopoly it is convenient to know the average revenue obtained from selling various amounts of output. When the monopolist can charge only one price this is a simple matter. The demand curve for the commodity provides us with the average revenue curve of the monopolist. When various prices are charged the average revenue from each output is the average of the prices charged, weighted according to the amounts of output sold at each price. We have seen how to obtain the marginal revenue curve, under discrimination, by summing the amounts of output for which, at each value of the marginal revenue, the marginal revenues in all the sub-markets would be equal. From this aggregate marginal revenue curve it will also be possible to discover the average revenue corresponding to each output. The total revenue is shown, at each output, by the area lying under the marginal revenue curve.[1] Thus we have only to divide this area by the amount of output to discover the average revenue.[2]

5

Our next task must be to discuss the comparison between monopoly output when only one price can be charged for a commodity (the simple monopoly output) and output under price discrimination (the discriminating monopoly output).[3] Let

---

[1] Cf. Fig. 61, p. 183.

[2] This involves the difficulty (see p. 29) that in order to derive average from marginal revenue it is necessary to know the whole course of the marginal curve back to the y axis. But the change in monopoly net revenue due to an increase of output will be shown by the change in the area lying between the marginal cost curve and the marginal revenue curve.

[3] When discrimination is perfect the comparison is simple. Under perfect discrimination each unit of output is sold at a separate price. Each additional unit sold therefore adds to revenue an amount equal to the price for which it is sold: the demand curve of the commodity is therefore the marginal revenue curve of the monopolist. It follows that perfectly discriminating output will be that at which the marginal cost curve cuts the demand curve, while simple monopoly output is that at which the marginal cost curve cuts the simple marginal revenue curve, which is marginal to the demand curve. The relations between simple monopoly output and perfectly discriminating monopoly output can therefore be derived quite simply from our knowledge of the relations between marginal and average curves. For instance, when marginal costs are constant perfectly discriminating output will be more or less than twice as great as simple monopoly output according as the demand curve is concave or convex. Further, the comparison between perfectly competitive output and perfectly discriminating monopoly output can easily be made in those cases where it is legitimate to assume that the average cost curve is the same under monopoly

us consider a case in which the aggregate demand for a commodity is composed of the demands of two separate markets, so that under price discrimination it is possible to sell the commodity at two prices. Suppose that a monopolist is selling his commodity at a single price, and that he then discovers that discrimination between the two markets is possible, everything else remaining the same.[1] He must now decide in what way it will be profitable to alter the price in the two markets. If the simple monopoly output is small the power to introduce price discrimination may have no effect at all. For it may happen that above a certain price there are buyers in only one market, and if the simple monopoly price is so high that only members of the stronger market will buy it is possible that the power to discriminate will be ineffective merely because the marginal revenue in the weaker market is too small to make it worth while for the discriminating monopolist to sell any output there. In such a case the weaker market is not served at all, either under discrimination or under simple monopoly, and the only buyers are members of the stronger market. There will thus be only one price even when discrimination is possible, and the power to discriminate will not alter the situation in any way.

Within the region in which only the stronger market is served the price and output will be the same whether discrimination is possible or not. But as soon as the marginal revenue in the stronger market is equal to the highest price at which any output will be bought in the weaker market it will begin to be profitable for the discriminating monopolist to sell some output there, although the simple monopoly price is still most profitably fixed at a level at which only the members of the stronger

and under competition. Perfectly discriminating output will be greater or less than perfectly competitive output according as average costs are falling or rising. It will be equal to competitive output when average costs are constant; or when the discriminating monopolist pays no rent and there are no economies of large-scale industry, since marginal cost to the monopolist is then equal to average cost under competition. The average revenue of the perfectly discriminating monopolist can be derived directly from the demand curve and will coincide with the curve of average utility to the consumers.

[1] The introduction of discrimination is likely to alter cost slightly—there may be extra book-keeping expenses or additional cost for the attractive labels of the "high quality" brand of the commodity—but for the sake of simplicity this factor in the problem may be ignored. The complication which it introduces into the analysis presents no fundamental difficulty.

market can afford to buy. The effect of discrimination will then be to increase output.[1]

If it is profitable to fix the simple monopoly price at a level at which members of the weaker market can buy, both markets will be served under simple monopoly as well as under discrimination. Then, if at the simple monopoly price the elasticities of demand are different in the two separate markets, the marginal revenue obtained by selling a unit of output in the market in which the elasticity of demand is lower will be less than the marginal revenue obtained by selling a unit of output in the more elastic market; and it will pay, when discrimination becomes possible, to cut down output and raise price in the less elastic market and to increase output and lower price in the more elastic market until the marginal revenue in each is the same. Output in one market is increased and in the other reduced, and it remains to discover whether the total output will increase or diminish when discrimination is introduced, or whether it will remain unchanged.

It is possible to establish the fact that total output under discrimination will be greater or less than under simple monopoly according as the more elastic of the demand curves in the separate markets is more or less concave than the less elastic demand curve; and that the total output will be the same if the demand curves are straight lines, or indeed in any other case in which the concavities are equal. This can be proved[2] as follows:

Let MP be the simple monopoly price and OM the simple monopoly output, made up of outputs OM_1 and OM_2 sold in the two separate markets.

Let AP be the tangent to the aggregate demand curve (AD) at P. Draw PF perpendicular to the y axis to cut it in F, and to cut the two separate demand curves (D_1 and D_2) in P_1 and P_2.

Let the tangents to D_1 and D_2 at P_1 and P_2 cut the y axis

---

[1] The increase is less than, equal to, or greater than the amount of the commodity sold in the weaker market according as marginal costs are rising, constant, or falling (see p. 195, below).

[2] I am indebted to Mr. M. H. A. Newman, of St. John's College, Cambridge, for some mathematical analysis connected with this proof. The problem finally yielded to geometrical treatment, but Mr. Newman's analysis was of great assistance in clearing some difficulties from the ground.

in A_1 and A_2. Let AC, A_1C_1, and A_2C_2 be the correspondents[1] to the demand curves at P, P_1, and P_2, cutting the

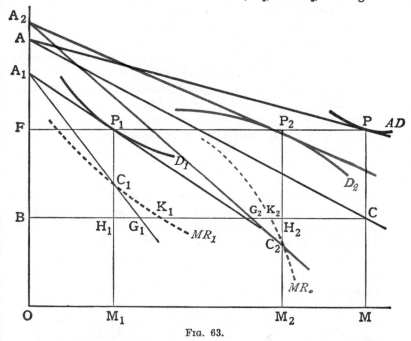

FIG. 63.

perpendiculars to the x axis through P, P_1, and P_2 in C, C_1, and C_2.

Now the aggregate demand curve (AD) is obtained by summing the separate demand curves (D_1 and D_2) and in the same way the tangent AP represents the (lateral) sum[2] of the tangents A_1P_1 and A_2P_2. It follows that AC (the correspondent to the aggregate demand curve at P) is the sum of the two correspondents A_1C_1 and A_2C_2; for at any ordinate the abscissa of each correspondent is half the abscissa of the tangent.

(Thus, for the ordinate OF, A_1C_1 bisects FP_1, A_2C_2 bisects

[1] For the definition of a correspondent see p. 32.
[2] This can easily be seen by considering a chord of the aggregate curve between any two prices. The chord of the aggregate demand curve is the sum of the chords of the two separate demand curves between the same two prices. The tangent at any price is the limiting position of the chord as the two given prices converge.

FP_2, and AC bisects FP. But FP is the sum of FP_1 and FP_2. Similarly for any other ordinate. Therefore AC is equal to the (lateral) sum of A_1C_1 and A_2C_2.)

Now draw BC perpendicular to the y axis to cut P_1M_1 and P_2M_2 in H_1 and H_2, and to cut A_1C_1 and A_2C_2 in G_1 and G_2. It can now be proved that H_1G_1 is equal to H_2G_2.

For $BH_1 = FP_1$, $BH_2 = FP_2$, and $BC = FP$.

∴ $BH_1 + BH_2 = FP_1 + FP_2 = FP$, since AD is the (lateral) sum of D_1 and D_2.

∴ $BH_1 + BH_2 = BC$.

But $BG_1 + BG_2 = BC$, since AC is the (lateral) sum of A_1C_1 and A_2C_2.

∴ $H_1G_1 - G_2H_2 = 0$.

It follows at once that if the demand curves are straight lines, so that they coincide with their tangents, discriminating monopoly output is equal to simple monopoly output. For when the monopolist finds himself able to discriminate and equates the marginal revenue in each market, given by the curves MR_1 and MR_2 (which in this case coincide with A_1G_1 and A_2G_2), with the marginal cost of the total output (which is equal to the marginal revenue, MC, of the simple monopolist), he will increase output in one market from OM_1, or BH_1, to BG_1, and reduce it in the other, from OM_2, or BH_2, to BG_2, by equal amounts, H_1G_1 and G_2H_2, so that the total output is unchanged.

Since the total output is the same under discrimination when the demand curves are straight lines as it is under simple monopoly, it makes no difference whether marginal costs are rising, falling, or constant; the total output and the marginal cost are unchanged by the introduction of discrimination, though the prices, the outputs in the individual markets, and the profit of the monopolist are altered.[1]

We must now consider the case in which the demand curves are not straight lines. If the separate demand curve of one market is concave, as is D_1 in Fig. 63, its marginal revenue curve, MR_1, must cut FP to the left of the correspondent,[2] and since it passes through C_1 it must cut BC outside H_1G_1. It

---

[1] The fact that output under discrimination is the same as under a single price for straight-line demand curves (provided that some output is sold in each market under the single price) was established by Professor Pigou (*op. cit.* p. 809).   [2] See p. 40.

follows that when the more elastic demand curve is concave (as in the diagram) the increase in output in the separate market that results from discrimination will be greater than when the demand curve is a straight line. And when the less elastic curve is concave the decrease in output will be greater than for a straight line. If the demand curve is convex, as is D_2 in Fig. 63, the marginal revenue curve must cut BC between G_2 and H_2,[1] and the increase or reduction in output in the separate market will be less than for a straight line.

Thus if the more elastic demand curve is concave and the less elastic curve is a straight line or convex, the increase in output in the market in which output is increased will be greater than the reduction of output in the other market (as in the case illustrated), and the total output will be greater under discrimination than under simple monopoly. And if the less elastic demand curve is concave, and the more elastic a straight line or convex, then the total output under discrimination will be less than under simple monopoly. If both are concave or both convex it is obvious that the result must depend upon whether or not the more elastic demand curve is, in some sense, "more concave" than the less elastic demand curve. The relevant property of the curve, which makes it in this sense more or less "concave", is the rate of change of the slope (at the simple monopoly price) multiplied by the elasticity (at the simple monopoly price) multiplied by the square of the simple monopolist's output in the separate market.[2] This property may be described as the "adjusted concavity" of the demand curve.

---

[1] See p. 40.

[2] The mathematics required to elucidate the exact nature of the "adjusted concavity" which determines whether discrimination increases or diminishes output is troublesome unless the assumption is made that the distances H_1C_1, H_2C_2 are small, *i.e.* that the elasticities of the two demands are not very different. In this case the arcs C_1K_1 and C_2K_2 of the marginal revenue curves can be regarded as straight lines.

Now $H_1G_1 = G_2H_2$.

It follows that $H_1K_1 \gtrless K_2H_2$, according as $\dfrac{H_1K_1}{H_1G_1} > \dfrac{K_2H_2}{G_2H_2}$,

i.e. according as $\dfrac{\text{slope of marginal revenue curve at } C_1}{\text{slope of correspondent at } C_1} \lessgtr \dfrac{\text{slope of marginal revenue curve at } C_2}{\text{slope of correspondent at } C_2}$.

Now if $y = f(x)$ is the equation of a demand curve, the slope of the correspondent is $2f'(x)$ (p. 30), the equation of the marginal revenue curve is

O

If the "adjusted concavities" of the two demand curves are equal, total output will be unchanged by discrimination, straight-line demand curves being a special case of two demand curves of the same concavity.[1]

It might at first sight appear that the above argument is only valid on the assumption that marginal cost is the same under simple and under discriminating monopoly. When the output is altered by the introduction of price discrimination the marginal

$y = f(x) + xf'(x)$, the slope of the marginal revenue curve is $2f'(x) + xf''(x)$, and the elasticity of demand is $\dfrac{-f(\dot{x})}{xf'(x)}$. Let $y = f_1(x)$ be the equation of the more elastic demand curve and $y = f_2(x)$ of the less elastic demand curve, x_1 and x_2 be the outputs at the simple monopoly price, and ϵ_1 and ϵ_2 the elasticities of demand at the simple monopoly price. Then it follows that output is increased or diminished by discrimination according as $\dfrac{2f'_1(x_1) + x_1 f''_1(x_1)}{2f'_1(x_1)} \begin{smallmatrix}<\\>\end{smallmatrix}$

$$\dfrac{2f'_2(x_2) + x_2 f''_2(x_2)}{2f'_2(x_2)};$$

i.e. according as $\epsilon_1 x_1^2 f''_1(x_1) \gtrless \epsilon_2 x_2^2 f''_2(x_2)$, for $f_1(x_1) = f_2(x_2)$.

For a concave demand curve $f''(x)$ is positive, and for a convex demand curve it is negative; while ϵ is always positive. It is to be remembered that the suffix 1 refers to the more elastic market (where the price is lowered) and the suffix 2 to the less elastic market (where the price is raised). There follows at once the proposition—proved quite generally in the text—that if the one curve is concave or a straight line and the other straight line or convex, output is increased or diminished by discrimination according as the former curve is the more elastic or the less elastic. If both curves are concave, output is increased or diminished according as $\epsilon x^2 f''(x)$ is greater for the more elastic or for the less elastic curve, and if both curves are convex, as $\epsilon x^2 f''(x)$ is numerically greater for the less elastic or for the more elastic curve.

The entry of the term x^2 (the square of the simple monopolist's output in the individual market) into the expression for the "adjusted concavity" can be utilised to deduce some general conclusions. If both curves are concave and the more elastic market is sufficiently larger than the less elastic market (*i.e.* if $f''_1(x_1)$ and $f''_2(x_2)$ are both positive and x_1 is sufficiently greater than x_2), output is increased by discrimination; while if the less elastic market is sufficiently larger than the more elastic market, output is reduced. If both curves are convex, the reverse propositions are true.

If the simplifying assumption, that H_1C_1 and H_2C_2 are small, is removed a more complicated treatment of the same general nature would be required. I am indebted to Mr. Kahn for this mathematical analysis.

[1] All these results can of course be generalised to apply to a case in which there are more than two markets. All markets can be divided into two classes, those in which the elasticity of demand at the simple monopoly price is greater (and in which the discriminating monopolist lowers the price) and those in which it is less (and in which he raises the price). If the demand curves in all markets are straight lines, the output is the same under discrimination and under simple monopoly. If they are not straight lines, the result will depend upon whether the more elastic group of demand curves is more or less concave on balance than the less elastic group.

cost may be altered. It is true that when output would be increased by discrimination the increase will be carried less far if
marginal costs are rising; and if output would be reduced by
discrimination it will be reduced by less if marginal costs are
falling (so that the cost of a smaller output is greater than of a
larger output). But the alteration in marginal cost cannot be
sufficient to prevent the change in output, for if it were so the
alteration in marginal cost would not occur. Moreover, if marginal cost is falling, an increase in output due to discrimination
will be enhanced; and if marginal costs are rising, a decrease in
output will be enhanced. If the increase in output due to price
discrimination is sufficiently great and if marginal cost is falling
sufficiently rapidly, the effect of discrimination may be to lower
the price in both markets.[1]

If the effect of discrimination is to leave the total output unchanged, it will make no difference whether costs are rising,
falling, or constant.

6

We must now consider a wholly different type of case in
which the total output is unaffected by the introduction of the
power to discriminate. This is the case in which the power to
discriminate is not exercised, because the elasticity of demand
at the simple monopoly price is the same in the two markets.
The marginal revenues in the two markets are then the same,
and there is nothing to be gained by discrimination. In such a
case the price and output in each market are unaltered, and the
monopolist continues to sell the same total output at the same
single price as before.

7

It is now possible to trace the relationship between the aggregate marginal revenue curve of the discriminating monopolist
and the marginal revenue curve of the simple monopolist
(which may be called the simple marginal revenue curve), and
between the average revenue curve of the discriminating
monopolist[2] and the aggregate demand curve, which is the
average revenue curve of the simple monopolist. The relations
between the outputs under simple and discriminating monopoly

[1] See p. 205, below.   [2] See p. 188.

will depend on the position of the marginal cost curve. If it cuts the two marginal revenue curves where the aggregate marginal revenue curve lies below the simple marginal revenue curve, output will be smaller under discrimination. If it cuts them where the aggregate marginal revenue curve is the higher, output will be larger under discrimination. If it cuts them where they cut each other (or where they coincide), the output will be the same.

When marginal cost is high and output consequently small it may happen, as we have seen,[1] that the power to discriminate will be ineffective because neither the simple monopolist nor the discriminating monopolist makes any sales in the weaker market. For small outputs, therefore, (O to OM_1 in Fig. 64) the two marginal revenue curves must coincide, since both are given by the marginal revenue curve of the stronger market, and the average revenue curve of the discriminating monopolist must coincide with the aggregate demand curve, since both are given by the demand curve of the stronger market.

At the point at which the marginal revenue in the stronger market is equal to the highest price at which any member of the weaker market will buy (given by the point where the demand curve in that market cuts the y axis) it begins to be profitable for the discriminating monopolist to sell in the weaker market, and at this point there is a kink[2] in the aggregate marginal revenue curve which suddenly changes its slope and diverges from the simple marginal revenue curve (the horizontal distance between them measuring the amount of output sold in the weaker market under discrimination) and the discriminating monopolist's average revenue curve will diverge from the aggregate demand curve.

Meanwhile the simple monopolist would be selling only in the stronger market, and the simple marginal revenue curve will continue to coincide with the marginal revenue curve in the stronger market. At the price at which the demand curve in the weaker market leaves the y axis there is a kink in the aggregate demand curve, since at this price there suddenly sets in an addition to sales because members of the weaker market now begin to buy. Vertically below this kink in the aggregate demand curve the simple marginal revenue curve will rise discontinuously, and below this point (beyond which there are sales in both markets even under simple monopoly) it may lie either above the aggregate marginal revenue curve or below it (as in the diagram), according to the relative concavities of the separate demand curves. The following diagram illustrates the situation described above.

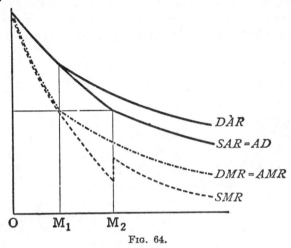

FIG. 64.

DAR is the average revenue curve of the discriminating monopolist.

AD or SAR is the aggregate demand curve (which is the simple monopolist's average revenue curve).

AMR or DMR is the aggregate marginal revenue curve (which is the marginal revenue curve of the discriminating monopolist).

SMR is the simple monopolist's marginal revenue curve.

For outputs less than OM_1 output and price are unaffected by the possibility of discrimination, since it is not profitable to sell in the weaker market. Between OM_1 and OM_2 only the discriminating monopolist sells in the weaker market,[1]

---

[1] The fact that over the range OM_1 to OM_2 output under price discrimination is necessarily greater than under simple monopoly is consistent with the rule that output will be increased by discrimination when the more elastic demand curve is the more concave. At the simple monopoly price the demand curve of the weaker market coincides with the y axis (since no output is sold there at that price) and at some lower price it leaves the y axis. This may be regarded as the extreme degree of concavity, so that the demand curve in the other market cannot fail to be less concave.

and beyond OM_2 there will be sales in both markets even by the simple monopolist.

If the conditions are such that the simple monopoly price would be fixed at a level at which some output would be sold in each market it is clear that if the demand curve in one market is consistently more elastic than in the other, there is always something to be gained by discrimination, and the discriminating monopolist's average revenue curve must consistently lie

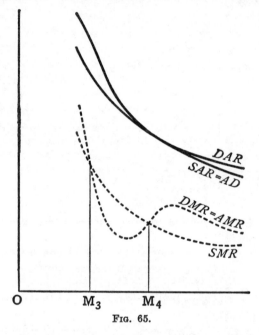

Fig. 65.

above the aggregate demand curve. And if, in addition, the more elastic of the separate demand curves is consistently the more concave, the discriminating marginal revenue curve must consistently lie above the simple marginal revenue curve.

But if the more elastic demand curve is not consistently more concave (relatively to the less elastic curve) a point will come at which the concavities of the two curves are the same.[1] At this point (the output OM_3 in Fig. 65) the discriminating

[1] It is impossible that the more elastic curve should be consistently less concave; see p. 200, note, below.

marginal revenue curve must cut the simple marginal revenue curve, and beyond this point it must lie below the simple marginal revenue curve, so long as the more elastic of the two separate demand curves is the less concave. The two marginal revenue curves may cross and recross in this way, according to the relative concavities of the two separate demand curves, while the average revenue under discrimination is always greater than the average revenue under a single price, that is to say, while the discriminating monopolist's average revenue curve always lies above the aggregate demand curve.

But if one of the separate demand curves does not remain consistently more elastic than the other, the one which is more elastic at first becoming relatively less and less elastic as it falls, then a point will come at which the elasticities of the two curves are the same. At this point, since the price is the same whether discrimination is possible or not, the average revenue must be the same under discrimination as under simple monopoly. Both for smaller and for greater outputs (for which the elasticities of the separate demand curves are unequal) the average revenue is greater under discrimination. It follows that at this point (the output OM_4 in Fig. 65), at which the separate demand curves are iso-elastic, the average revenue curve of the discriminating monopolist must be tangential to the aggregate demand curve. For a slightly smaller output the elasticity of the discriminating average revenue curve must be less than that of the aggregate demand curve, and for a slightly greater output its elasticity must be greater. It follows that the discriminating marginal revenue curve, which cuts the simple marginal revenue curve at the output at which the two average curves are tangential, must lie below it for slightly smaller outputs and above it for slightly greater outputs. Thus the discriminating marginal revenue curve may lie below the simple marginal revenue curve for some outputs.

It is impossible, however, that it should do so consistently. This can easily be proved. The total revenue in each case is shown by the area lying under the marginal revenue curves, and it is impossible that the total revenue under discrimination should be less than the total revenue under simple monopoly, since at worst the discriminating monopolist can leave the simple monopoly price unchanged. Now if the discriminating

marginal revenue curve were to lie consistently below the simple
marginal revenue curve, the area below it would be less than the
area below the simple marginal revenue curve. But this we see
to be impossible. It follows that if the discriminating marginal
revenue curve lies below the simple marginal revenue curve for
any range of outputs there must have been some preceding
range of outputs at which it lay above.[1] Moreover for the range
of outputs over which it lies below, the excess of total revenue
under discrimination over total revenue under simple monopoly,
which is given by the difference in the areas lying below the two
curves, falls with every increase of output; it is therefore tending
towards a point at which the two will be equal. Thus if the discriminating marginal revenue curve lies below the simple marginal revenue curve for any range of outputs, there is likely to
be a succeeding range of outputs over which it will lie above.[2]
And it has just been shown that there must be a previous range
of outputs over which it will lie below. It follows that there is a
larger range of outputs over which the discriminating marginal
revenue is the higher than over which the simple marginal
revenue curve is the higher.[3]

---

[1] This result can easily be interpreted in terms of relative concavities, though
a precise mathematical proof would be difficult. What we have to show is that
if at any price the more elastic curve is less concave, there must be some higher
price where it becomes more concave. Now so long as the more elastic curve
remains less concave, it approaches the y axis more rapidly than the less elastic
curve. But it cannot cross the y axis. It follows that, in order to avoid doing so,
it must eventually become more concave than the less elastic curve, or alternatively it strikes the y axis and is infinitely concave at the point of impact.
Moreover, the longer it defers becoming more concave, the greater its relative
concavity has in the end to become. In other words, the longer the range over
which the discriminating marginal revenue curve lies below the simple marginal
revenue curve, the greater must have been the previous divergence between the
two curves in the opposite sense.

[2] This fact may be explained as follows. The output under discriminating
monopoly can only be less than under simple monopoly if the less elastic of the
two demand curves is the more concave. But for the more concave curve the
elasticity will fall more slowly, as the price falls, than for the less concave curve.
As the price falls, therefore, the difference between the elasticities of the two
curves grows less and less. As they pass through the point at which they are
iso-elastic their positions are reversed, and beyond this point the more concave
curve is the more elastic. It is possible, however, that they may not reach the
iso-elastic point towards which they tend until they have become inelastic, so
that the marginal revenue is negative. In this case the discriminating marginal
revenue curve will continue to lie below the simple marginal revenue curve, and
will approach towards it, but will fail to cut it before it has passed below the
x axis.

[3] The case in which the two separate demand curves are straight lines was

The above analysis suggests that on the whole it is more likely that the introduction of price discrimination will increase output than that it will reduce it.[1] Moreover there is some reason, beside these purely formal considerations, to suppose that cases in which the less elastic demand curve is more convex than the more elastic demand curve (so that price discrimination will increase output) are likely to be common. The monopolist (as we have seen) will, whenever possible, divide up the separate markets in such a way that they are as nearly homogeneous as possible,[2] so as to get the maximum benefit from the power to discriminate. Now the demand of each individual buyer for any commodity is likely to be satiable—that is to say, for each individual buyer there is likely to be a certain

worked out (by a different method) by Professor Pigou (*Economics of Welfare*, p. 809). The case of straight lines may be illustrated thus:

This represents a special case of the situation illustrated in Fig. 64 above. As we then saw, the aggregate demand curve must contain a kink at the price at which the lower demand curve cuts the y axis. When the two separate demand curves are straight lines the simple marginal revenue curve which rises vertically below this kink coincides with the aggregate marginal revenue curve for all outputs beyond that (OM_2) at which the kink occurs. The difference between the two revenues (which is shown by the difference in the areas lying below the

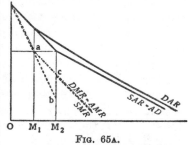

Fig. 65A.

two marginal revenue curves) is independent of the output (so long as the simple monopoly price is at a level at which there are some sales in the weaker market), and is equal to the triangle abc. The average revenue curve of the discriminating monopolist is therefore asymptotic to the aggregate demand curve.

[1] Professor Pigou states that in conditions in which there would be some sales in each market under a single price "there is no adequate ground for expecting either that output under discriminating monopoly . . . will exceed, or that it will fall short of, output under simple monopoly" (*op. cit.*, p. 286). But he was led to this conclusion because his precise analysis deals only with straight-line demand curves and does not enable him to isolate the conditions in which discrimination will increase or reduce output.

In a passage which appears inconsistent with this one, he reasons that because perfect discrimination must increase output ordinary discrimination is likely to increase output (*loc. cit.* p. 287), and he argues that it will be more likely to do so the larger are the number of separate markets in which the monopolist can sell. But, as we have seen, the result depends not upon the number of markets but upon the relative concavities of the separate demand curves.

[2] See p. 186.

price at which he will buy as much of the commodity as he requires, so that any reduction below this price will not tempt him to buy much more. Thus a market composed of individual buyers who are all closely similar is likely to have a more or less definite saturation point, below which the demand is highly inelastic. If the separate markets are of this type, then for any market in which the simple monopoly price is below the saturation price the demand curve will be both highly inelastic and highly convex, while for any market in which the simple monopoly price lies above the saturation price the demand curve will be more elastic and less convex. When the markets are of this type, therefore, the introduction of discrimination is likely to increase output.

On the other hand, the "adjusted concavity" of the demand curve of the separate market tends, as we have seen,[1] to be numerically greater the larger is the amount of output sold in that market under simple monopoly. Now the more elastic market may often be composed of a large number of poor buyers and the less elastic market of a small number of rich buyers. The amount of output sold in the more elastic market may therefore be considerably larger than in the less elastic market, and if the demand curves are convex, this is likely to result in a reduction of the total output when discrimination is introduced. Only if the demand curve in the more elastic market is concave will the fact that it is larger than the less elastic market strengthen the presumption that output will be increased by discrimination.

[1] See p. 193.

CHAPTER 16

THE MORAL OF PRICE DISCRIMINATION

1

IT is now possible to inquire how far price discrimination is harmful or advantageous to the customers of the monopolist and to society as a whole. First of all, it is clear, since average revenue is greater under price discrimination than under simple monopoly, that there may be cases in which no output would be produced at all if price discrimination were not possible.[1] If the average cost curve of a certain product lay above the demand curve for it throughout its length no profit could be made by producing it under any one-price system. But if the average cost curve, though above the demand curve, lay at some point below the average revenue curve under price discrimination, a profit could be made and some output would be produced provided that discrimination was possible.[2] It may happen, for instance, that a railway would not be built, or a country doctor would not set up in practice, if discrimination were forbidden. It is clearly desirable that price discrimination should be permitted in such cases, for the average revenue of the monopolist cannot be greater than average utility to the consumers.[3] If

---

[1] Cf. *Economics of Welfare*, p. 287.

[2] Professor Pigou (*op. cit.* p. 808) has worked out the conditions of this problem under perfect discrimination (see p. 187, note). Under perfect discrimination the marginal revenue curve is given directly by the demand curve, and Professor Pigou points out that if the demand curve lies below the marginal cost curve throughout its length no output would be produced even under perfect discrimination. And he shows that the more rapid the rate of fall of average cost the more likely is the demand curve to lie above the marginal cost curve for a sufficient distance to ensure that some output will be produced: to ensure, in our terms, that the monopolist's average revenue curve at some point shall be cut by the average cost curve.

[3] For the purposes of discussions of this type it is necessary to attach some meaning to utility as a measure of economic welfare. See p. 214, below.

average revenue is greater than average cost, average utility will also be greater, and the investment will lead to a gain to society.

But this fact must not be considered to justify (from the point of view of the community) price discrimination on the part of a concern in which very long-lived investment (such as the permanent way of a railway) has been made in the past and which discovers that, owing to a decline in demand, normal profits can only be made in the present if price discrimination is possible. From the point of view of society it is only necessary that the concern should make sufficient profit to maintain the efficiency of the plant, and not a profit which would have been sufficient to justify the original investment.

2

When some output would be produced even if discrimination were forbidden, it is only possible to say definitely whether price discrimination is damaging to the interests of the customers, as compared with a single price monopoly, if we identify ourselves with one or other group of customers. As compared with simple monopoly, discrimination must always be disadvantageous to those buyers for whom the price is raised, and advantageous to those for whom the price is reduced, and it is impossible to set the gains of one group against the losses of the other. But we may have some reason to prefer the interests of one group above those of the other. For instance, members of the more elastic markets (for whom price is reduced) may be poorer than members of the less elastic markets, and we may consider a gain to poorer buyers more important than a loss to richer buyers. In this case price discrimination must always be considered beneficial. On the other hand, the less elastic market may be at home and the more elastic market abroad, so that the interests of the members of the stronger market are considered more important than the interests of the weaker market.

But in this case price discrimination need not always be disadvantageous, for, as we have seen,[1] when the conditions are such that output under discriminating monopoly is larger than under simple monopoly then, if marginal costs are falling, dis-

[1] See p. 195.

crimination may actually be beneficial to the members of the less elastic market, since the marginal cost of the total output will be reduced, and the price which they are required to pay may be lowered. It must be lowered (provided that marginal costs are falling) if the conditions are such that the simple monopolist would sell no output in the weaker market. For then output is necessarily increased by the introduction of discrimination, and consequently marginal cost is reduced; but for the simple monopolist marginal cost is equal to marginal revenue in the stronger market; hence it follows that marginal revenue, and consequently price, in the stronger market are necessarily reduced by the introduction of discrimination.[1]

We have seen that the condition in which output will be much increased by discrimination is that the demand curve in the more elastic market shall be highly concave. This is probably a common case where the more elastic market is an export market in which the exported goods are in competition with those produced locally. It will often happen that only a small amount can be exported at relatively high prices but that as the price of the exported goods approaches and falls below the price of the local rival goods the demand for them increases very rapidly —in short the demand curve is highly concave.[2] Thus there are likely to be many cases in which the "dumping" of a commodity (that is, selling at a lower price in the export market

---

[1] Professor Pigou (*op. cit.* p. 286) points out that discrimination may sometimes be beneficial to the members of the stronger market, but he only considers the case in which no output at all would be sold in the weaker market under simple monopoly. Professor Pigou's analysis is limited to this case because he is only able to reach exact results for the case in which the separate demand curves are straight lines. When no output would be sold in the weaker market under simple monopoly, the introduction of discrimination will leave the price in the stronger market unchanged if marginal costs are constant, and raise it if marginal costs are rising; cf. Pigou (*op. cit.* p. 810, note. But Professor Pigou's statement is ambiguous, for he talks of supply price in place of marginal cost). Professor Viner (*Dumping*, p. 103) states, without proof, that the price in the stronger market will always be unchanged and challenges his readers to find a case in which it will be altered. This challenge was taken up by Professor Yntema (*loc. cit.*) who reaches the same conclusions as Professor Pigou, by a method in some respects similar to that employed in the last chapter; cf. p. 182, note. Neither Professor Viner nor Professor Yntema seem to have been aware of Professor Pigou's simple treatment of this problem.

[2] As we have seen, in the limiting case there is a certain price above which no output at all can be sold in the weaker market, and the demand curve takes on the limiting degree of concavity (p. 197). The case considered above, in which price in the stronger market must necessarily fall if marginal costs are falling, is thus seen to be an extreme example of the general case.

than in the home market) is likely to reduce its home price, provided that marginal costs are falling with increases of output.

It is sometimes argued (for instance by railway officials anxious to justify the practice of discrimination[1]) that the members of the high-price markets must in any case benefit from the fact that other markets are served at a lower price. The argument runs as follows: If a single price were charged the output sold in the weaker markets would be less; a larger share of the total cost of the concern would then have to be borne by the stronger markets alone, and the price charged to them would therefore be higher than when discrimination occurred. This argument would be valid if the monopolist was limited to earning a certain fixed profit, although the conditions of demand were such that he could make a larger profit. But so long as the monopolist acts upon the principle of maximising his profits (as he is assumed to do throughout the analysis of this book), discrimination can only benefit members of the high-price markets in the situation described above.

From the point of view of society as a whole it is impossible to say whether price discrimination is desirable or not. It is obviously wasteful, from the point of view of society, if any commodity fails to be produced up to the point where its marginal utility (shown by its demand price[2]) is equal to its marginal cost. But under simple monopoly marginal revenue is equal to marginal cost; monopoly output is therefore undesirably small. From one point of view, therefore, price discrimination must be held to be superior to simple monopoly in all those cases in which it leads to an increase of output, and, as we have seen, these cases are likely to be the more common. But against this advantage must be set the fact that price discrimination leads to a maldistribution of resources as between different uses,[3] a subject which would take us too far afield to discuss. Before it is possible to say whether discrimination is desirable or not, it is therefore necessary to weigh up the benefit from the increase in output against this disadvantage. In those cases in which discrimination will decrease output it is undesirable on both counts.

[1] *E.g. Report on Rail and Road Transport*, 1932, p. 12.
[2] See below, p. 214 and p. 318, for a further discussion of this point.
[3] See *Economics of Welfare*, pp. 284-85 and 288-89, for the exposition of this subject.

3

One further point remains to be considered. In Chapter **13**
we discussed the question of price control, but we assumed that
only a single price could be imposed. We must now consider
whether it would be preferable to impose a system of discriminating prices.

Under a single price the maximum output will be achieved,
when average costs are falling, if the imposed price is that at
which demand price and average cost are equal. This, however,
involves a waste, since there would be a considerable range of
output, beyond that at which demand price was equal to average
cost, over which demand price exceeded marginal cost; and since
demand price is presumed to measure marginal utility, it is
desirable that this additional output should be produced. This
waste could be partly eliminated and a larger output could be
achieved if it were possible to impose discriminating prices. The
average revenue under uncontrolled price discrimination is
greater than under uncontrolled simple monopoly, and the
largest possible output will be that for which the average
revenue of a discriminating monopolist would be equal to his
average cost. With any given system of markets, in order to
induce the monopolist to produce the maximum possible output, it is necessary to impose a system of prices such that the
marginal revenues in all markets are equal, and such that
average total revenue is equal to average cost. The required
output will then be produced. No larger output could be sold
without involving the monopolist in a loss.[1]

This method would ensure that the largest possible output
should be produced, but it is subject to the general objection to
price discrimination referred to above. It might therefore be
considered desirable to sacrifice some part of the increase in
output which could be obtained by this method, and to indulge

---

[1] The difference between average revenue under discrimination and under
simple monopoly will be greatest in those cases in which the difference between
output under discrimination and under simple monopoly is greatest. The same
conditions, therefore, which make discriminating output large as compared to
simple monopoly output (relative concavity of the more elastic demand curve)
will make the output obtainable by the above method large relatively to the
output obtained by a single imposed price.

in a smaller degree of price discrimination, but some degree of discrimination will almost certainly be desirable.[1]

[1] Professor Pigou, having established the fact that perfect competition is generally preferable to discriminating monopoly, proceeds to argue (*Economics of Welfare*, chap. xviii.) that it is desirable that railway rates should be fixed at the level appropriate to simple competition, which, as he shows, would entirely eliminate price discrimination. But his argument is extremely obscure. Under competition price is equal both to average and to marginal cost for the individual concern. It would only be possible to impose such a price upon a railway if it so happened that it was working just at its optimum capacity, so that average cost was at a minimum and equal to marginal cost. But, as Professor Pigou himself points out, railways are very likely to be working under falling average costs, and when average cost for the individual concern is falling there is no such competitive price, since marginal cost must be less than average cost. Professor Pigou may, however, be interpreted to mean that it is desirable to impose the price at which demand price is equal to average cost. This, as we have seen, will involve a waste of output which might be secured by the method here suggested, which appears to have been overlooked by Professor Pigou. In order to justify price discrimination in favour of the weaker markets he introduces the fact that demand price may not be as great as the marginal social utility of the commodity, for instance when cheap workmen's tickets enable workers to live healthily in the country (*loc. cit.* p. 314). But in order to establish the fact that there is a waste of potential output it is only necessary to consider that, for a greater output than that which would come about under a single imposed price, the demand price (which is taken to measure marginal utility) is greater than the marginal cost.

BOOK VI
MONOPSONY

P

CHAPTER 17

A DIGRESSION ON THE BUYER

1

So far we have looked at the initial problem, Why does that banana cost a penny? through the eyes of the seller. We have considered the question, Why did that man take a penny for a banana? in forms of ever-increasing complexity. We must now open the second question, Why did the other man give a penny for a banana? Here we are immediately faced with one of the most awkward of the fundamental questions of economic analysis. It is usual to describe the quality in commodities which causes them to be bought or otherwise acquired as *utility*, but no perfectly satisfactory definition of utility has ever been found. The attempt to define it has generally originated in a desire to justify the use of a marginal utility curve. The use of the curve, and the apparently sensible results obtained from using it, precede the definition. The spectacle of successive economists erecting card-house definitions and of successive critics blowing them down (leaving the curve itself unaffected) has tempted the present writer to build a definition in which the cards are already lying flat.

Utility is the quality which makes commodities desirable to buyers. The *marginal utility* of a given commodity is the addition to the total utility obtained by a single buyer, when a unit addition [1] is made to the amount of this commodity which he buys.

The fundamental assumption of economic analysis is that every individual acts in a sensible manner, and it is sensible for the individual to balance marginal cost against marginal gain.

---

[1] See p. 122, note.

It follows that when a given marginal cost is being incurred by a buyer in purchasing a commodity the marginal utility of the commodity to him is equal to its marginal cost.

Now this account of utility is based on a circular argument. The house of cards is already lying flat.

The point can be illustrated thus: Take as a definition of sensible conduct: conduct that leads to survival. Then a man who looks to the right and to the left when crossing a street is a sensible man. A man who allows himself to be run over by a bus is not sensible. But a man who wishes to commit suicide is sensible, upon a less restricted definition of common sense, when he allows a bus to kill him (for common sense, as the phrase is used in this book, must be understood to entail an absence of ethical prejudices). The analysis based on this definition of common sense is therefore not capable of giving a completely satisfactory account of the actions of all pedestrians, but it covers a sufficiently high proportion of all cases to make it of practical interest.

Or take as a definition of sensible conduct: conduct which leads to the maximisation of money gains. Then a man who balances marginal money cost against marginal money receipts is sensible. A man who fails to do so is not sensible. A man who has a good reason for not doing so (for instance, that he prefers lying in bed to making money) is sensible upon a less restricted definition of common sense, and the cases to which an analysis based upon the economist's definition of common sense does not apply satisfactorily are a far higher proportion of all cases than the proportion of suicides to all pedestrians. But even so, the economist's definition of sensible conduct may be held to give results of some practical interest. Both definitions of common sense are temporary expedients which allow an analysis to develop to a certain length, and which may be removed when the analysis becomes capable of dealing with a more general and more complicated definition of common sense. But when we come to analyse the conduct of buyers who buy commodities, not for the sake of money gain, but for the sake of owning and consuming the commodities, we have no objective criterion of common sense, such as survival or money gain. Utility is the criterion, and the notion of utility already involves the definition of common sense.

This difficulty would be of no importance if a behaviourist technique of experiment were available to discover actual curves for typical individual buyers, showing the marginal costs incurred in the purchase of all amounts of an actual commodity. The utility of any given amount of a commodity, to a given buyer, would then be the integral of the curve, and it would be unnecessary to inquire whether the buyer was sensible or not. But, although such an experimental technique could be imagined, it certainly does not exist. A technique of *Gedanken Experimente* may be used to eke out the meagre equipment of behaviourist psychology. A series of questions may be put by the analytical economist to himself: How many bananas would I buy in a week if the price were a halfpenny? How many would I buy if my income were £500 a year? How many would I buy if oranges were seven for sixpence? How many would I buy if I saw a poster saying Eat More Fruit as I went to my office by tube? How many would I buy if it were a hot summer? How many would I buy if my next-door neighbour owned a Persian cat? These questions enable the economist to give a rough, imperfect, and admittedly treacherous account of his own marginal utility curve for bananas. By assuming that other people have much the same psychology as himself he can, by an act of blind faith, admit the existence of a definite marginal utility curve for bananas for individuals other than himself. And he can continue to make use of marginal utility curves with a pacified— though not quite contented—professional conscience. It would be possible to apply the same method to the cost curve. Marginal cost might be defined as that which is equated to marginal revenue, and total cost might be regarded as the integral of a marginal cost curve drawn up by behaviouristic methods of investigation. Such a marginal cost curve would diverge from the marginal cost curves which we have been employing in the case of sellers who were not sensible or who had some good reason for not wishing to maximise their money gains. There is thus no essential asymmetry between the marginal cost curve and the marginal utility curve. But since the principle of maximising money gains provides a convenient objective criterion of common sense, it appears more profitable to assume that all sellers are sensible and all endeavour to maximise their money gains. It is then possible to use an objective conception of marginal cost, the definition of which does not involve a circular argument, and this policy has been pursued throughout our analysis of selling.

The marginal utility curve is the weakest link in the chain of the marginal analysis of value. But it is not a very important link. There is no reason to despair of an experimental method for discovering demand curves showing the amounts of a commodity that will be bought at various prices in a given market in a given time, and it is with demand curves of this nature that the first part of this book was concerned. The first part of this book would survive the complete destruction of the notion of marginal utility.[1]

When we are concerned with a demand curve, which is looked at objectively by the seller, there is no need to inquire into the nature of utility. And when we are concerned with the analysis of the decisions of the individual buyer a marginal utility curve discovered by behaviouristic methods and a purely formal definition of utility will serve our turn. There is no part, therefore, of the analysis of value which requires a knowledge of the real nature of utility. Only in the departments of Public Finance and the Economics of Welfare is the real nature of utility of importance. For these departments of economic analysis it is necessary to have some definition of sensible conduct, which involves the notion that buyers act in their own economic interests, for which no objective criterion has yet been found. In the department of the analysis of value the circularity involved in the definition of utility is only a minor blemish. But in the departments of analysis which involve the conception of economic welfare the circularity of the definition of utility is certainly a stumbling-block. If buyers are not sensible, or if they have good reasons for not pursuing their economic interests, the utility of a commodity to a buyer, represented by the integral of his marginal utility curve, will not provide a quantitative measurement of the economic welfare, in any interesting sense, derived by him from the consumption of the commodity. Thus even if a behaviouristic marginal utility curve could be discovered it would not be of service in the analysis of economic welfare, unless it

---

[1] This fragment of philosophy was taught me by the marginal technique of analysis. But I am indebted to a philosopher, Mr. R. B. Braithwaite, of King's College, Cambridge, for assistance in formulating it.

were possible to discover that all buyers are sensible upon some relevant definition of common sense.

The notion of *consumer's surplus*, the difference between the total utility of any given amount of a commodity consumed by a buyer, and its total cost, has therefore no real or interesting meaning until a relevant definition of common sense has been found. A purely formal conception of consumer's surplus, derived geometrically from the marginal utility curve, is used in the following analysis. In the following chapter it is assumed that the marginal utility curve for a buyer can be drawn, either by behaviouristic investigation or by *Gedanken Experimente*. Once the curve has been drawn up there is no further need to inquire into its nature, and the analysis can take its course.

None of these objections applies to the analysis of the decisions of a buyer of a factor of production. Factors of production are not bought for their own sake, but for the sake of earning money income by selling the commodities which they produce. The principle of maximising money gains will therefore once more provide an objective criterion of common sense, and it is only necessary to assume that the buyer is sensible in order to be able to proceed with the analysis of buying. The treacherous notion of utility is therefore only required for the purposes of the chapter which follows. The analysis of Book VII., which deals with the decisions of buyers of factors of production, is free from the difficulties which beset the analysis of the buying of commodities.

2

It is necessary to find a name for the individual buyer which will correspond to the name *monopolist* for the individual seller. In the following pages an individual buyer is referred to as a *monopsonist*.[1]

The criterion of perfect competition among sellers is that the demand curve for the individual seller should be perfectly elastic; similarly the criterion for perfect competition among buyers is that the supply curve to the individual buyer should be perfectly elastic. This is the case in an ordinary competitive

---

[1] The older phrase "monopoly buyer" is illogical, and is associated with a conception of monopsony corresponding to the conception of monopoly discussed on p. 5. I am indebted to Mr. B. L. Hallward, of Peterhouse, Cambridge, for the word *monopsony*, which is derived from ὀψωνεῖν, to go marketing.

market. A buyer can walk into a shop and buy as much as he pleases at the current price. If he offers less he can buy nothing, and if he offered a little more he would engross the whole supply. Perfect competition among sellers requires two conditions, that the number of sellers shall be large, and that the customers shall all have the same preference (or the same indifference) between one firm and its rivals. Similarly perfect competition among buyers requires that the numbers of buyers composing a market shall be large, so that a change in the amount purchased by any one of them has a negligible effect upon the total purchases of the market, and that sellers are indifferent as to whom they provide with their wares. The second condition will not always be fulfilled—some firms will give special terms to certain customers either from sentiment, family connection, gratitude, or a "lively expectation of benefits to come"—but it is clearly more frequently fulfilled in the real world than are the conditions of a perfect market from the point of view of sellers.[1] So long as competition among buyers is perfect, marginal utility must be equal, for each buyer, to the price of the commodity. For price is equal to marginal cost to the buyer, and marginal utility is defined as some quantity which is equated to marginal cost. But the marginal utility curve for a buyer is not a demand curve. It does not represent a list of the amounts of a commodity which will be bought at various prices; it represents the amounts which will be bought at various marginal costs to the buyer. So long as the supply of the commodity is perfectly elastic to the buyer the marginal utility of each amount of it will be equal to its price (since its price is equal to its marginal cost). It is therefore formally correct to describe the marginal utility curve of a buyer as his demand curve upon the assumption that the competition among buyers is perfect, just as, under perfect sellers' competition, where marginal cost is equal to price, the marginal cost curve of a seller is the supply curve of his output. When competition among buyers is known to be perfect the demand curve of the market may be taken to represent the marginal utility curve of the buyers as a group. The total amount purchased is divided between the buyers in such a way that the marginal

---

[1] Moreover, the supply to an individual buyer may be perfectly elastic, even though the market is not perfect, since there are often a large number of buyers to each seller, so that the relevant amount of purchases for any one buyer can be had at a constant price.

utility of the amount purchased by each one of them is equal to the price.[1]

We saw in Chapter 7 that it is impossible to draw up the supply curve of a commodity produced by a number of sellers without first postulating the conditions of demand for the individual sellers. Similarly it is impossible to draw up the demand curve for a commodity purchased by a number of buyers without postulating the conditions of supply to the individual buyers. But to postulate that competition among buyers is perfect is far more realistic than to postulate that competition among sellers is perfect, since the number of buyers in any ordinary market is large relatively to the number of sellers. In the following chapter, therefore, we shall only consider the case of a single buyer on the one side and a perfectly competitive market of buyers on the other, and ignore the problem of an imperfectly competitive market of buyers.

[1] Even if all the problems connected with the definition of utility are assumed to be solved, the difficulty remains that the marginal utilities of different buyers composing a market are not measured on the same scale (see Marshall, *Principles*, p. 128), because the utility of money, in which the utility of the commodity is measured, will be different for buyers who differ in respect of relevant social and psychological characteristics, or in respect of their money income. But it is convenient for some problems to regard the demand curve of a market as a collective marginal utility curve, and provided it is recognised that marginal utility is a purely formal conception which may be, in some circumstances, devoid of any real or interesting meaning, it appears legitimate to make use of it.

CHAPTER 18

1

THE principle underlying the analysis of the decisions of a buyer as to how much of a commodity to buy is that he will equate marginal utility to marginal cost. As we have seen, this statement is no more than a tautology. If the supply of the commodity to him is perfectly elastic he will equate marginal utility to price. This will occur, first, if he is one of a large number of buyers, so that a change in his purchases has a negligible effect upon the total output of the commodity, and consequently a negligible effect upon its price; or, second, if the commodity is sold under conditions of constant supply price, so that even if a change in his purchases produces a significant change in output it causes no change in price.

Examples of a buying agency whose purchases represent the whole or a large proportion of the output of a commodity produced by a competitive [1] industry are found when the consumers of a certain commodity are organised, or when a socialist government regulates imports, or when a certain individual happens to have a taste for some commodity which no one else requires. An everyday example occurs when an individual orders note-paper with his address printed on it. In such cases, if the commodity is not produced under constant supply price, marginal utility will not be equal to price. The amount purchased will be regulated so that marginal utility is equal to marginal cost. The price will be the supply price of that amount of the commodity, which may be either greater or less than its marginal cost to the buyer.

---

[1] The case of a monopsonist buying from a monopolist (usually called "bilateral monopoly") is not discussed in this book.

2

Our next task is to consider the change in the amount of a commodity purchased when the market changes from an indefinitely large number of competing buyers to a single buying agency. This may be described as the comparison between competitive and monopsony buying, just as the corresponding comparison for selling was called the comparison between competitive and monopoly output.

The present comparison is not subject to the formidable objections which were raised against the earlier comparison. The chief objections sprang from the fact that in order to give a definite basis to the comparison it was necessary to postulate conditions of perfect competition, which are rarely to be found in the real world. It is true that the demand curve only has an unambiguous meaning when buying is perfectly competitive, but this state of affairs is the rule rather than the exception in most ordinary markets, since there are usually a large number of buyers to each seller. The basis of our comparison, therefore, the competitive demand curve, can be used without hesitation. It is easy to imagine a group of buyers at first acting independently of each other, and then forming an agreement to act in concert without causing any change in the demand curve, which may be taken to represent the marginal utility curve of the monopsonist organisation,[1] or any change in the conditions of supply of the commodity which they consume.[2] We can therefore set out the comparison between the amounts of a commodity that would be bought under competition and under monopsony when the marginal utility curve and supply curve are the same in the two cases, without being obliged to make the reservation that in practice they never will be the same.

The comparison will be in some respects similar to the comparison between monopoly and competition. A monopsonist has to pay the supply price of the output of the commodity which he

---

[1] See p. 216.

[2] It is important to notice, however, that a monopsonist organisation will reproduce the conditions of a perfect market. It will therefore enforce reorganisation upon an imperfectly competitive industry, in such a way as to ensure that any given output is produced in the most efficient manner.

buys, but he will regulate his purchases in such a way that marginal cost is equal to marginal utility; while under competition it is the price, or average cost to the buyer, which is equal to marginal utility. It follows that under constant supply price, when average and marginal cost are equal, the amount purchased under monopsony will be the same as under competition. But when an industry is working under increasing or diminishing supply price, marginal cost to the monopsonist will not be equal to the price of the commodity.

Under increasing supply price, since each additional purchase which the monopsonist makes raises the price which he must pay, the marginal cost to him is greater than the supply price of the commodity. Supply price is average cost to the monopsonist, but he will regulate his purchases by reference to marginal cost.

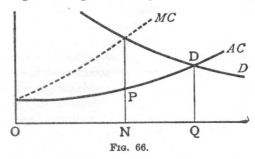

FIG. 66.

MC is the marginal cost curve to the industry, and this is the marginal cost curve from the point of view of the monopsonist.

AC is the average cost curve of the industry, or the supply curve.

The monopsonist will buy that output (ON) at which marginal utility (or competitive demand price) is equal to marginal cost, and he will pay NP, the supply price for that output, which is less than the competitive price (QD).

If the curves are straight lines, it can be seen that he will buy something more than half the competitive amount. If his demand were perfectly elastic (a case which it is hard to conceive), and the supply curve was a straight line, he would buy exactly half the competitive amount.

If the industry is working under decreasing supply price, he will find that every increase in his purchases lowers the supply price,[1] and marginal cost to him, which is the same thing as marginal cost to the industry, will be less than the supply price. He will therefore buy more than the competitive amount. Thus:

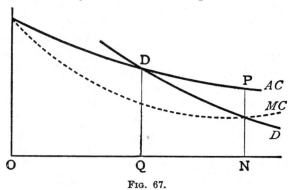

Fɪɢ. 67.

ON will exceed OQ, and NP, the monopsony price, will be less than QD, the competitive price.

ON may exceed OQ without limit, and with a given supply curve it will be greater the less the slope of the demand curve. It will approach more closely to the competitive amount the greater the slope of the demand curve.

If the demand of the monopsonist is perfectly inelastic (as might occur over the relevant range of prices) he will purchase the competitive amount at the competitive price.

3

An interesting special case of monopsony can be illustrated by the example of note-paper printed from a special die. This introduces a type of relationship between marginal and average curves which we examined in Chapter 2.[2] A certain cost has to be incurred for the die, and once the die has been made the

---

[1] Under conditions of decreasing supply price the monopsonist cannot proceed merely by declaring the price at which he will buy, for an unconditional offer of a certain price would call out an indefinitely large output from the industry. The monopsonist (who is conceived to know the course of the supply curve of the commodity) must decide upon the output that he will buy, and allot it between the different sellers.

[2] See p. 39.

marginal cost of printing more paper will be constant. Thus marginal cost is constant and average cost for successive amounts will consist of this constant cost of printing and paper, *plus* an ever diminishing share in the fixed cost of the die. The average curve will be of the form of a rectangular hyperbola to which the marginal curve is an asymptote.

The householder who buys note-paper must incur the cost of the die even if he requires only one sheet, and when it has been made the marginal cost of all amounts of note-paper will remain constant. Thus if we ignore the general costs of the stationer and consider this one transaction in isolation, we see that the householder will order that amount of note-paper (ON in Fig. 68) at which marginal utility is equal to the cost per unit of paper and printing, but he will have to pay the average cost (NP) including the total cost of the die.

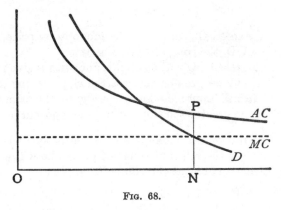

Fig. 68.

Let us now compare this householder with an undergraduate who buys note-paper with a college crest, of which there are a number of purchasers and sellers. Let us suppose that the demand curves for note-paper of the undergraduate and of the householder are exactly alike, and that the cost of the die and the paper are the same in each case. The price of paper to the undergraduate will be less than to the householder, since his die is used more fully. But the marginal cost of paper to the house-holder (which regulates the amount that he purchases) will be less than the price to the undergraduate (which regulates the purchases of the undergraduate), since this price must cover the average cost of the die, in addition to the cost of paper and printing.

We thus reach the curious conclusion that the householder will buy more paper than the undergraduate, although he pays a higher price. This trivial example illustrates a principle which may be of importance when goods, for instance a type of machine which is only used by one manufacturing firm, are customarily bought on special orders.

4

The analysis of monopsony is usually made in a way similar to the conventional analysis of monopoly. The monopsonist is conceived to maximise his consumer's surplus[1] in the same way as the monopolist maximises his net revenue. Thus:

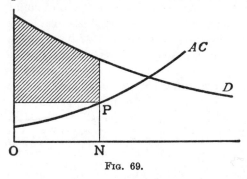

Fɪɢ. 69.

At the output ON, bought at its supply price NP, the consumer's surplus is represented by the shaded area. When this area is at a maximum ON will represent the most profitable amount for the monopsonist to purchase.

This method gives the same result as the analysis set forth above, for clearly consumer's surplus is at a maximum when marginal cost and marginal utility are equal. If purchases were pushed beyond this point, marginal cost would exceed marginal utility, and the surplus would be reduced, while if purchases were reduced below this point, the loss of utility would be greater than the saving in cost.[2]

[1] See p. 215.
[2] If the demand curve is known throughout its length, consumer's surplus can

5

Just as we have price discrimination for a monopolist, so we may have price discrimination for a monopsonist. This would occur when groups of sellers can be dealt with separately, just as seller's discrimination can occur when buyers can be divided into separate markets. The monopsonist will buy from each source of supply in such a way that the marginal costs to him of the outputs bought from each source are equal to each other and to the marginal utility of the whole amount purchased, in just the same way as the monopolist will sell in each separate market such an amount that the marginal revenues are equal in each market and equal to the marginal cost of the whole output.[1] The possibility of discriminating with advantage will depend upon a difference in the elasticities of supply from various sources, that is, the elasticities of the average cost curves of each group of sellers. If the elasticity of supply from each source is the same, the amount purchased from each source under simple monopsony (when there is only one price) will be such as to equalise the marginal cost of each separate output, and there will be no advantage from discriminating. When the elasticities

be shown in a manner similar to rent (see p. 136, note). From the demand curve, which represents marginal utility, the average utility curve (*AU*) can be de-

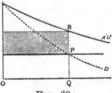

FIG. 69A.

rived. Then, under perfect competition, if the price is PQ the amount (OQ) will be bought for which marginal utility is equal to PQ, while the average utility (RQ) is greater than the price. Consumer's surplus (the shaded area in the figure) is thus shown as the difference between marginal and average utility (PR) multiplied by the amount bought.

This presentation of consumer's surplus does not, of course, remove any of the fundamental difficulties involved in the conception. Average utility cannot be known directly, but can only be inferred from marginal utility. Thus it is necessary to know the demand prices for all quantities between zero and the amount actually consumed before we can discover the consumer's surplus which the commodity yields at a given price, and since it is almost always impossible to discover the whole course of the demand curve for a commodity from zero it is impossible to discover the consumer's surplus which it yields. In any case consumers' surplus is here regarded as a purely formal conception (see p. 215) which may be devoid of any interesting meaning as a measure of the economic welfare derived by the buyer from the commodity.

[1] The cost of production in each group is assumed to be independent of the amount bought from the other groups. This assumption is similar to that made in the analysis of price discrimination: that each market is independent of the price charged in the others.

are different the amount bought from the less elastic sources of supply will be reduced below what would have been bought from those sources under simple monopsony, and the price to them will be lowered.[1] The amount bought from the more elastic sources will be increased, and price to them will be raised. The analysis is in every way symmetrical with the analysis of discrimination under monopoly, and the comparison between simple and discriminating monopsony output can be made by means of the same technique. Further, as soon as the marginal cost curve to the discriminating monopsonist has been discovered it is a simple matter to compare the amount bought under discriminating monopsony with the amount bought under competitive conditions.

The extent to which discrimination will be possible will depend upon the number of separate sources into which the total supply can be divided and upon the conditions of supply from each source. Perfect discrimination would be achieved if each unit of the commodity were bought at a different price. This would be possible if each separate seller of the commodity owned one indivisible unit of it, or if it were practicable to deal with each seller by making an all-or-none offer for that amount of the commodity whose marginal cost to the seller is equal to its marginal utility to the monopsonist, at a price equal to its average cost.[2] The monopsonist would then be able to purchase each unit of output at its minimum supply price, and would avoid

---

[1] It is assumed that the supply curve from each source is rising. If the supply curve from any source is falling for all amounts of output the monopsonist will buy only from that source, except in so far as it is profitable to buy a small amount of output from some other source where costs are rising (or falling more slowly) but are lower for a range of small outputs.

[2] Perfect discrimination in selling or "discrimination of the first degree" (p. 187) requires a similar condition: that the buyer should only buy one indivisible unit of the commodity or that he should be made an all-or-none offer of a certain amount at a price equal to the average utility. Now it is obviously far more likely that the owner of a factor of production, the purchase of which is the most common case of monopsony, should have a perfectly inelastic supply (above a certain supply price) than that the buyer of a commodity should have a perfectly inelastic demand (below a certain maximum demand price). Moreover, under customary methods of selling it is more often feasible for a single buyer to deal with each of a number of sellers separately than for a single seller to deal with each of a number of buyers separately, and the resentment of a seller at being presented with an all-or-none offer for a certain amount of output is likely to be less than the resentment of a buyer at receiving a similar offer to buy a certain amount of output. Perfect discrimination under monopsony is therefore more likely to be practicable than perfect discrimination under monopoly.

Q

the payment of the whole of what, under competitive conditions, would be the rents earned by the factors employed in producing the commodity.

The comparison between purchases under perfectly discriminating monopsony, simple monopsony, and perfect competition can easily be made (assuming that the demand curve is the same in each case) when the commodity is produced by an industry working under increasing supply price, without economies of large-scale industry.[1]

The monopsonist under perfect discrimination will purchase that amount of the commodity at which supply price is equal to demand price. The supply price to competitive buyers is the price per unit which they must pay for each amount. As the amount bought increases the supply price rises, and each unit of the greater amount must be paid for at the higher price. But under perfect discrimination the monopsonist does not increase the price which he gives for each unit of the whole amount when he increases the amount that he buys. He pays for the additional unit at a higher price without affecting the price of the rest. Thus the marginal cost to him of each amount is equal to the supply price of that amount. The simple monopsonist will equate marginal utility with marginal cost to the industry, and this, under increasing cost, will be greater than supply price.

> *SMC* is the curve of marginal costs to the simple monopsonist.
>
> *DMC* is the supply curve. It represents both marginal costs to the perfectly discriminating monopsonist and average costs to the simple monopsonist.
>
> *DAC* is the average cost curve of the discriminating monopsonist.
>
> *DMC* is marginal to *DAC*, while *SMC* is marginal to *DMC*.

The perfectly discriminating monopsonist will thus buy the competitive amount of output (ON′ = OQ) and the simple

---

[1] The existence of economies of large-scale industry would invalidate the condition that the cost in each source of supply shall be independent of the amount bought from other sources, and the analysis of a case in which there are economies of large-scale industry would require a different technique from that set out above. It is further necessary to the comparison set out above that the existence of perfectly discriminating monopsony should not alter in any way the organisation of the industry.

monopsonist will buy ON, which is less than the competitive amount, at the price NP. The perfectly discriminating monop-

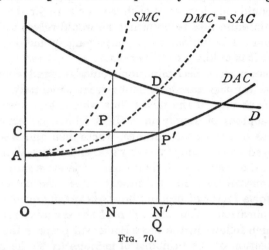

FIG. 70.

sonist will pay the prices ranging from OA and QD, so that his average cost is QP', the average of the supply prices of all outputs up to OQ. His total cost is equal to the area OADQ, or to the rectangle OCP'Q.

6

The most important cases of monopsony will occur in connection with monopoly. A monopolist must necessarily be a monopsonist of the factors which he employs. Discriminating monopsony is likely to occur when the monopolist employs a non-homogeneous factor of production. In the case of land it is easy to imagine perfect discrimination to occur, since it is customary for a separate bargain to be made for each piece of land according to its quality. Thus a monopolist would have the opportunity of acquiring the land which he needs at its transfer price, and when he increases the amount that he employs, the fact that he is extending his "margin of cultivation" may have no effect on the rent payable for land that he has already acquired. In short, he may keep for himself the rent of land in his industry. This, as we have already seen, has an important effect on monopoly output.[1]

[1] See p. 151.

Where there was an imperfectly elastic supply of labour to an individual employer perfect discrimination might also occur, but this could only happen if each worker were hired separately at that minimum rate below which he would refuse the offer of employment. Discrimination in employing labour is likely to occur, but it is unlikely to be perfect.

Less than perfect discrimination would be found where it was impossible for the monopsonist to treat separately with the seller of each unit of the factor, but where there were several separate sources of supply in each of which the elasticity of supply was different; for instance, where men and women can be employed on the same type of work, and where all men have to be paid the same rate, and all women the same rate, but men and women can be paid at different rates. The nature of the demand for a factor of production, however, involves considerable complications. The discussion of the demand curve for a factor which follows in the next Book will prepare the way for the application of the principle of monopsony to the purchase of factors of production.

CHAPTER 19

RELATIONSHIP OF MONOPSONY AND MONOPOLY TO PERFECT COMPETITION

THE principle of monopsony of factors of production is to some extent latent in the analysis of monopoly. Under increasing cost the monopolist takes into account the whole increment to the costs of the industry as the output of his commodity increases, which is the same thing as to say that he takes into account the fact that when he increases his purchases of one or other of the factors of production he raises the supply price of the factor against himself. Under decreasing cost he takes into account the whole of the economies induced by each increase in output; that is to say, he takes into account the fact that when he increases his purchases of one or other of the factors its efficiency is increased and its efficiency cost lowered.

In short, when we say that a monopolist regulates his output by the marginal cost to him of the output, we have already implied that he is a monopsonist in respect of the factors of production which he uses. The principle of monopoly thus involves the principle of monopsony and we were implicitly introducing the principle of monopsony when we were engaged in the analysis of monopoly.

The principle of monopsony entails that when the supply curve of a commodity is not perfectly elastic from the point of view of a single buyer (whether it be an individual or a group acting in concert), the buyer will equate marginal utility with marginal cost, and will pay for the commodity at the appropriate supply price. Yet this is exactly what each individual buyer does in conditions of competition. Each buyer equates marginal utility to him with marginal cost to him; the only difference is that the marginal cost to him of the commodity is simply the ruling price, so that price, marginal cost to him, and marginal utility are all equal.

The principle of monopoly entails that the monopolist will equate marginal revenue to marginal cost, yet this, again, is exactly what is done by competitive producers. The only difference is that for each competitive producer marginal revenue is simply the current price of the commodity, so that price, marginal revenue to him, and marginal cost are all equal.

Thus the common-sense rule that the individual will equate marginal gains (whether of utility or revenue) with marginal cost, applies equally to monopsony, to monopoly, and to perfect competition.

This principle, though sufficiently obvious in itself, is of the utmost importance in economic analysis. The assumption constantly made, tacitly or openly, in most economic text-books, of perfectly competitive conditions, has tended to obscure its workings. When we say, for instance, that price is equal to marginal cost, or that marginal net productivity of labour is equal to wages, or that marginal utility is equal to price, we are tacitly assuming perfectly competitive conditions. It is true that under conditions of competitive selling marginal cost is equal to price, but the fundamental fact (itself merely a matter of common sense) is that marginal revenue to the individual seller is equal to marginal cost to the individual seller. It is only because marginal revenue to the individual happens to coincide with price in competitive conditions that it is true to say that price is equal to marginal cost. In the same way, the wage will only be equal to marginal net productivity (the demand price for labour) if the supply of labour happens to be perfectly elastic, and price will only be equal to the marginal utility of the individual buyer if supply happens to be perfectly elastic. The cases which arise in perfect competition are only special cases of the general rule that the individual will equate marginal cost to him with marginal gain.

It is remarkable to what an extent concentration on "monopoly net revenue" has concealed the similarity of the forces determining competitive and monopoly value, so that while monopoly provides the most clear and striking examples of the working of the marginal principle it has always been treated as an exceptional case to which the marginal analysis could not be applied. It is the object of the treatment suggested in this book to break down the hard and fast distinction between the analysis suitable to competition and the analysis suitable to monopoly, and to show that the same system of ideas is equally applicable to monopoly, monopsony, and perfect competition.

When (for the sake of illustration) we suppose that a perfectly competitive industry is monopolised, the demand and cost curves remaining unchanged, the essential point is that the unit of control has altered. Marginal cost or marginal gain exert no influence unless they are marginal cost and marginal gain to some definite decision-making entity, whether an individual buyer, a firm, or a group acting in concert. Under competition, the unit of control is the firm, and it is marginal gain and marginal cost to the firm which govern output. When a monopoly is formed and the firms begin to act in concert, it is marginal gain and marginal cost to the whole group which determines output. It is only because marginal cost or marginal revenue is different for the whole group and for the separate individuals that monopoly output differs from competitive output. The mechanism by which it is determined is the same in each case.

BOOK VII

THE DEMAND FOR A FACTOR OF PRODUCTION

CHAPTER 20

A DIGRESSION ON MARGINAL NET PRODUCTIVITY

1

IN order to continue the analysis of monopsony it is necessary to examine the nature of the demand curve for a factor of production. Labour will serve as an example of a factor, and in order to simplify the discussion we will assume that all men are alike, so that a "man" represents an efficiency unit[1] of labour.

The discussion must perforce be carried on in a manner even more abstract and far from reality (since the reality is even more complicated) than the discussion of the competitive supply curve. It is necessary to deal with the problem first of all in its most abstract terms before it is possible to evolve an analysis capable of dealing with the intricacies of actual cases.

For an individual unit of control there is no such thing as a demand curve,[2] but it is convenient to call the wage at which a given number of men would be employed if the supply of labour were perfectly elastic at that wage, the "demand price" for that number of men, and to call the curve connecting the demand price (in this sense) and the number of men the "demand curve" for labour.

We have hitherto been chiefly concerned with the supply curve of a commodity. Our present task is to discover the demand curve for labour. The demand curve for any one factor of production will depend upon the demand curve for the commodity, the technical conditions of production, and the supply curves of the other factors of production. Our method of procedure must therefore be to consider any given number of men, and then, assuming the demand curve for the commodity and

---

[1] In the language of the Appendix this is not an *efficiency unit* but a *corrected natural unit;*   [2] See p. 216.

the supply curves of the other factors to be known, to find the demand price for that amount of labour, that is to say, the wage at which that number of men will be employed. But first it is necessary to equip ourselves with certain definitions.

It is commonly said that "wages tend to equal the marginal net productivity of labour", and that for a given number of men the marginal productivity of that number represents the demand price for them. This notion of "marginal net productivity", however, is not a simple one, and before we can proceed we must examine it more closely.

The term "marginal" only has meaning from the point of view of some definite individual or group of interests. There is no such thing as the marginal utility of bananas, as such. There is only the marginal utility of a given quantity of bananas to a given individual buyer, or group of buyers. In the same way there is no such thing as the marginal productivity of a given group of workers as such. There is only their marginal productivity to a given employer, or group of employers.

Our definitions therefore will yield different results according to whether they are applied from the point of view of a firm, selling in a perfect or an imperfect market, of a competitive industry or of a monopolistic combination of firms.

The definitions are here set down in their most general form for any group of producers, whether they constitute a unit of control or not.

2

The *marginal physical productivity* of labour is the increment of output caused by employing an additional unit of labour with a fixed expenditure on other factors. For convenience we will suppose that capital and entrepreneurship are the only factors other than labour, so that the marginal physical product of labour is the addition to output caused by employing one more man with the same amount of capital and entrepreneurship measured in terms of total cost. When we are studying long-period conditions the other factors are conceived to be adapted in such a way as to give in each case the maximum efficiency with the number of men actually employed;[1] and for

---

[1] See Robertson, *Economic Fragments*, p. 47. Marginal productivity in the short period, when the other factors are fixed not only in amount but in form, will be very different from marginal productivity in the long period.

our present problem the notion of a change in the form of other factors of given total value, to adapt them to an increased amount of labour, need not present any fundamental difficulty.

When there are economies of large-scale industry, the marginal physical productivity of labour to a competitive industry will be greater than to the individual firms, since an increment of employment given by one firm will enhance the efficiency of the others.

Marginal productivity[1] is the increment of value of the total output caused by employing an additional man, the total value of other factors remaining unchanged. That is to say, it is the marginal physical productivity multiplied by the marginal revenue to the unit or group under consideration. When the demand for the commodity is perfectly elastic (for instance, when we are considering a firm in conditions of perfect competition), marginal revenue is equal to price, and therefore marginal productivity is equal to the value of the marginal physical product. When the demand is not perfectly elastic, marginal revenue is less than price, and marginal productivity is less than the value of the marginal physical product.

The demand for a commodity produced by an industry composed of a number of firms must always be less elastic than the demand for the output of any one firm.[2] Marginal revenue must therefore be less to the industry than to the firm and marginal productivity to the industry must consequently be less than marginal productivity to the firm. The difference between them is most clearly seen in a perfectly competitive industry where the demand for the commodity is inelastic. The marginal physical product is the same from either point of view (unless there are economies of large-scale industry). Now to find marginal productivity to the firm we must multiply the physical product by the marginal revenue to the firm, which is equal to the price of the commodity; to find marginal productivity for the industry we must multiply by the marginal revenue to the industry, and when the demand is inelastic, marginal revenue to the industry is negative. Thus marginal productivity to a firm in a perfectly competitive industry will always be positive (until

---

[1] This and other similar terms have been used in a variety of senses by different writers. These definitions apply to the senses in which they will be used in the following chapters.

[2] See p. 51.

the output is reached at which the price of the commodity is zero), but marginal productivity to the industry as a whole will be negative if the demand for the commodity is inelastic.

3

Is it marginal productivity, thus defined, which tends to be equal to wages? When the group under consideration is a unit of control, whether a single firm, selling in a perfect or imperfect market, a monopolised industry, or any other unit, then it is clear that there must be some relationship between marginal productivity and the cost of labour. The marginal productivity of any amount of labour is the increment of value of output to any group caused by employing an additional man, with a constant expenditure on other factors. It is therefore clear that the marginal productivity of labour to any unit of control must be equal to the marginal cost of labour to that unit; for if marginal productivity were greater than the marginal cost of labour, it would pay to increase the number of men employed, and if it were less, it would pay to diminish the number employed. This is merely an application of the general rule that every buyer will regulate his purchases in such a way that marginal gain to him is equal to marginal cost to him. Thus the marginal productivity and the marginal cost of labour must be equal to any unit of control, but it is only when the market for labour is perfect, so that the marginal cost of labour to the firm is equal to the wage, that marginal productivity to the firm is equal to the wage. If the demand for the commodity as well as the supply of labour are perfectly elastic for the unit of control, the wage is equal to the marginal physical product of labour valued at the price of the commodity.

4

So far we are upon familiar ground, but our set of definitions is not yet complete, and some new terms must be introduced. We have so far only considered the case in which the amount of labour is increased, the expenditure on other factors remaining unchanged; but when the number of men employed is increased, other factors will in most cases also be increased. The manner in which the adjustment of factors to each other is brought about will be considered in a moment. We must first set out the terms required to describe the case in which other factors, as well as labour, are changed in amount. The following definitions are, once more, perfectly general, and apply to any group, whether it is a unit of control or not. A given amount of labour is now conceived to be working with that amount of the other factors which would actually be employed with that amount of labour.

Average gross productivity is the average value of output per man. It is the total value of output divided by the number of men employed.

Marginal gross productivity is the increment of value of output caused by employing an additional man with the appropriate addition to other factors. It bears to average gross productivity the ordinary relationship of marginal to average value.

Average net productivity is the average value of output per man less the average cost of other factors employed per man.

Marginal net productivity is the marginal net increment of value of output caused by employing an additional man. It is the marginal gross productivity caused by employing an additional man with the appropriate addition to other factors, less the addition to the cost of other factors. It bears the ordinary marginal relationship to average net productivity.

5

The relationship between marginal net productivity and marginal productivity must now be examined, and we must therefore consider what regulates the "appropriate" addition of other factors as the number of men increases.

For a given unit of control the marginal productivity of capital (which for convenience may be taken to stand for all other factors), working with a given number of men, must be equal to the marginal cost of capital to that unit. Let us suppose that the wage is such that a certain given number of men are being employed. Then, if we know the demand curve for the commodity, the technical conditions, and the cost curve of capital to the unit of control, we know how much capital will be employed with those men. It will be such that (in the given conditions) the marginal productivity of capital is equal to its marginal cost, the marginal physical productivity of capital being determined by the technique of industry.[1]

Now, when both labour and capital are increased in the appropriate proportions, what is the relationship between the marginal productivity and the marginal net productivity of labour? Suppose that there is a small increase in the number of men employed by a unit of control and that the appropriate change is made in capital (which stands for all other factors). It follows from the definition of marginal net productivity that the total increment of value of output is equal to the marginal net productivity of labour multiplied by the increase in labour *plus* the increment in the cost of capital. But the same final position can be reached by another route. The same increase in labour and capital can be imagined to occur in two stages. First increase labour, the amount of capital remaining unchanged, and then increase capital, the amount of labour remaining unchanged. In each case, the factor which remains unchanged in amount is assumed to be suitably adapted in form. The increment in value of output brought about by this means is then equal to the marginal productivity of labour multiplied by the increase in labour *plus* the marginal productivity of capital multiplied by the increase in capital.

If the changes in capital and labour are small,[2] the total change in value of output is the same whether the two factors are increased simultaneously or one at a time. Thus:

Increment in value of output = (marginal net productivity of labour) × (increment of labour) + (increment in cost of capital);

---

[1] In some cases it will be impossible to vary the proportions of labour and capital employed, so that with a given number of men there is a fixed amount of capital. In such a case any increase in the amount of capital employed beyond the necessary amount would cause the marginal physical productivity of capital to fall to zero or become negative. If the proportions are variable, the amount of capital employed with a given number of men would, of course, alter if the demand curve for the commodity altered, or if the supply curve of capital altered, but given these curves, the amount of capital employed with any given number of men can be determined, and in order to discover it, it is not necessary to know the wage which would ensure that this number of men should be employed.

[2] If the changes in amount of the factors are not small, the change in their marginal productivities will not be negligible, and it would not be accurate to say that the change in the value of output is the change in each factor multiplied by its marginal productivity.

and

increment in value of output = (marginal productivity of labour) × (increment of labour) + (marginal productivity of capital) × (increment of capital).

As we have seen, the marginal productivity of capital is equal to its marginal cost to the unit of control. The marginal productivity of capital multiplied by the increment of capital is therefore equal to the increment in cost of capital. That is to say, the additional output due to the increase in capital is exactly equal to the additional cost of the capital. Hence it can be seen from the above equations that the marginal net productivity of labour is equal to the marginal productivity of labour. This proposition is, of course, only true for a unit of control.

6

In the foregoing analysis we have taken "labour" to stand for the factor of production whose cost is not given, and for whose demand price we are searching, and "capital" to stand for the other factors whose conditions of supply are known. We have considered the manner in which the proportions of other factors are adjusted to a given amount of labour. Our definitions can also be applied to the description of the manner in which a given output of the commodity is produced when the conditions of supply of all factors (including "labour") are known.

Any unit of control, producing a given output, is assumed to keep its costs of production at a minimum. This will be achieved when the marginal cost of each factor to the unit of control is equal to its marginal productivity. The marginal productivities of the various factors will then bear the same ratio to each other as their marginal costs. The marginal productivity of a unit of money laid out upon each factor is the same, and nothing can be gained by employing more of one and less of another.

In a competitive industry the unit of control is the individual firm. It is therefore the marginal productivities of the factors to the firm which are in the ratio of their marginal costs to the firm. When the supply of the factors is perfectly elastic to the individual firms it follows that the marginal productivities of the factors must be in the ratio of their prices, for the price of any

R

factor is then equal to its marginal cost to the firm. But if the industry as a whole were the unit of control, for instance if the industry were to come into the hands of a monopolist (everything else remaining unchanged), the monopolist would make it his business to equate, for each output, the marginal cost to the whole industry of each factor with its marginal productivity to the industry, so that the marginal productivities of the factors would be in the ratio of their marginal costs to the industry.

It follows that the proportions of the factors used in producing a given output will only be the same under monopoly and under competition when the average costs of the factors to the competitive industry (that is, their prices) are in the same ratio as their marginal costs to the monopolised industry. This would occur if all factors were in perfectly elastic supply to the industry, so that the average cost of each was the same as its marginal cost; or if the only factors not in perfectly elastic supply are scarce factors for which the monopolist pays no rent, so that the marginal cost of a given amount of the factor to the monopolist was equal to average cost to the competitive industry;[1] or, when rent is paid, if all factors were subject to rising or falling supply price at such rates that their marginal costs happened to be in the same ratio as their average costs—in other words, if the elasticity of supply of each were the same.[2] In all other cases the ratios of the marginal costs and of the average costs will be different, so that (unless the proportions of factors are rigidly fixed by technical conditions) the monopolist, in producing a given output, will economise his use of those factors whose marginal cost is rising more rapidly (or which give less economies) and increase his use of those factors whose marginal cost is rising less rapidly (or which give greater economies), and the proportions of the factors will be different from what they are under competition.

This conclusion was anticipated in Chapter 14, when we were discussing the relationship of monopoly and competitive cost curves.

[1] See p. 151.

[2] When the elasticities of supply of all the factors are equal the ratio of average to marginal cost is the same for each (see p. 36). It follows that the ratio of the prices is equal to the ratio of the marginal costs.

CHAPTER 21

THE DEMAND FOR LABOUR OF THE INDIVIDUAL EMPLOYER

1

WE may now attempt to construct the demand curve for labour of a single unit of control, using the term demand curve in the illogical but convenient sense of the curve showing the amount of labour that would be employed at any given wage if the supply of labour to the unit of control were perfectly elastic at that wage. The unit of control is assumed to consist of a single unit of entrepreneurship, that is to say, it is a single firm. It may form part of an industry in which competition is perfect, or is imperfect, or it may be an isolated monopoly. The cost of entrepreneurship is assumed to be independent of output,[1] and consequently of the number of men employed. With each number of men, as we have seen, there is a certain amount of capital which will be employed, such that its marginal productivity to the firm is equal to its marginal cost to the firm. Capital must now be taken to stand for all factors other than labour and entrepreneurship. The case of a firm which is part of a perfectly competitive industry is merely a particular example of a unit of control, but it will be easier, for our present purpose, to treat it separately before giving the general case.

2

Suppose that the demand for the output of a firm is perfectly elastic, and the supply of capital to the firm is perfectly elastic. The amount of capital employed with each number of men will then be such that its marginal productivity is equal to its price.

Supposing each number of men to be working with the appropriate amount of capital, draw a curve of average gross pro-

---

[1] See p. 17.

ductivity, measuring the number of men along the x axis and the average value of output per man along the y axis. If there are no technical economies (to the firm) of large-scale production, the amount of capital employed per man and the gross output per man will be constant until that output is reached at which diseconomies of large-scale management begin to be felt. These diseconomies may of course arise however small the number of men employed, so that the gross productivity curve falls throughout its length. But it is only in a very simple type of production that there will be no economies of large scale to the firm. More usually the gross productivity curve will at first rise and then fall. It will rise at first because if more men and more capital are employed by a single firm, their efficiency will be improved by specialisation; and after reaching a maximum point it will begin to fall since the unit of management is limited and it is assumed that an indefinitely large output cannot be produced by one firm without loss of efficiency.[1] This decline in output per head as the firm increases in size occurs because either the organisation of the business becomes less efficient or if efficiency is to be maintained, the proportion of administrative staff to directly productive workers has to be increased.[2]

From this gross productivity curve, which shows the value of the output per head for any number of men employed, subtract the cost of the other factors per man, employed with that number of men, so as to obtain the average net productivity curve. The amount of capital may be the same for all numbers of men, or it may vary, according to the technical conditions. In many cases it will increase as the number of men increases, but where there is a large minimum investment in plant, as in the case of a railway, it may fall as the number of men increases. We have taken "capital" to stand for all other factors (except entrepreneurship). In so far as the other factors consist of raw material, the amount employed per man will vary in the same way as gross productivity per man. The amount of land per man will in some cases increase and in some cases diminish as the number of men (and machines) increases. In every case, since the price of the commodity and the costs of the factors are

---

[1] Unless this is the case it is impossible that competition should be perfect; see p. 95.

[2] Cf. Robinson, *Structure of Competitive Industry*, chap. iii.

assumed to remain constant as the number of men changes, the variation in the proportion of labour to other factors with changes in the number of men is determined solely by the technical conditions of production. The average cost per man of the entrepreneur must fall as the number of men increases. Since (upon our definition of a firm) the cost of entrepreneurship is independent of the number of men employed the cost per man will be indefinitely great for a very small number of men and will fall continuously as the number of men increases. Thus the average net productivity curve will begin by rising, even when the gross productivity curve is at first constant or falling. It will reach a maximum and then fall.

Next draw the curve marginal to the average net productivity curve. This curve shows the marginal net productivity of each number of men working with the appropriate amount of other factors. It shows at each point the increment of value caused by employing an additional man, with the appropriate addition to other factors (marginal gross productivity) less the marginal increment of cost of other factors. Since there is no addition to cost of entrepreneurship when an additional man is employed it will be independent of the cost of entrepreneurship. Moreover, as we have seen, it will show the marginal productivity [1] of each amount of labour when it is working with the appropriate amount of the other factors.

It is clear that the curve of marginal net productivity must represent the demand curve for labour of the individual firm (under the given conditions of price of product and of cost of capital). With a given supply curve of labour to the individual firm, it will pay the firm to employ that number of men whose marginal net productivity, shown by this curve, is equal to the marginal cost of labour to the firm (which will be equal to the wage when the supply of labour to the individual firm is perfectly elastic). If more men are employed, more is added to the wages bill than to the value of output (after allowing for other costs), and if fewer are employed, it would be possible by employing more to add more to the value of output (after allowing for other costs) than to the wages bill. The marginal net productivity curve, then, is the demand curve for labour which we set out to find.

[1] See p. 241.

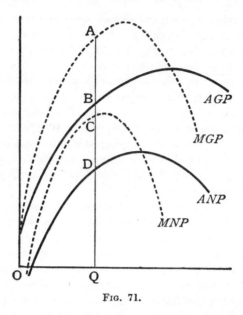

FIG. 71.

AGP is the curve of average gross productivity per man.
MGP is the curve of marginal gross productivity.
ANP is the curve of average net productivity per man.
MNP is the curve of marginal net productivity.
For any number of men OQ, AC (*MGP* – *MNP*) is the marginal increment of other costs; and BD (*AGP* – *ANP*) is the average cost per man of other factors.

3

When the unit of control for which we are constructing the demand curve for labour is not selling its commodity and buying the other factors under conditions of perfect competition, it is not possible to assume that the prices of the commodity and of the factors are independent of the number of men employed. As the number of men employed by the firm increases the output of the commodity increases and its price falls; the amounts of the other factors alter, and their prices may change. But when competition is not perfect the curves are drawn up upon the same principle as when competition is perfect, and the marginal net productivity curve is the demand curve for labour whether competition is perfect or not, although the curve of marginal net productivity itself will alter with the degree of competition. The amount of capital will be determined, for any amount of labour, in such a way that the marginal cost of capital to the unit of control is equal to its marginal productivity, so that average gross productivity per man is determined by the technique of production, the supply curve of capital, and the demand curve for the commodity. Average net productivity is then obtained by subtracting the average of other costs per man from average gross productivity.

So long as physical productivity per man is constant, the gross productivity curve of the individual firm will fall with the fall in the price of the commodity which occurs as the number of men, and consequently the output of the commodity, increases. A rise in physical productivity (due to technical economies) may offset this effect, but in any case the productivity curves (which measure the output in terms of value) will rise less rapidly and fall more rapidly the less elastic is the individual demand curve of the firm. Further, as the output of the firm increases and the price of the commodity falls, the marginal productivity to the firm of a given amount of capital per man will tend to fall, even though the marginal physical productivity may be constant. Therefore if the proportions of labour to capital are not rigidly fixed the amount of capital employed per man will tend to rise less rapidly or fall more rapidly, as the number of men increases, than it would if the demand for the product of the individual firm were perfectly elastic, and the gross productivity curve of labour will tend to rise less rapidly, or fall more rapidly, for two reasons, both because of the fall in price, and because of the fall in physical productivity due to the reduction in the amount of capital per man. If the supply of capital to the individual unit is less than perfectly elastic, the amount of capital per man will be still further reduced because of the rise in cost of capital when more is employed. If no variation in the proportions is possible, the gross productivity curve will be unaffected by the rise in the cost of capital, but the net productivity curve will fall faster (or rise less fast) than would be the case if the supply of capital to the firm were perfectly elastic.

4

For any unit of control, whether it is selling in a perfect market or not, the demand curve for labour is shown by the curve of marginal net productivity. The unit will be in equilibrium (as far as the number of men employed is concerned) when the marginal cost of labour is equal to marginal net productivity, but if the unit in question forms part of a competitive industry (whether the market is perfect or not), we must further consider in what conditions the industry will be in equilibrium when there is free entry of firms. The condition for equilibrium of the industry is that the firms in it should be making normal profits, that is to say, that the entrepreneur should receive neither more nor less than his normal reward, which is allowed for in calculating the cost of factors other than labour in drawing up the average net productivity curve.

Now if the wage is equal to the average net productivity of labour, the entrepreneur will be receiving his normal reward, and the total value of the output will be equal to its total cost of production (including the cost of entrepreneurship). If the wage is less than this, the total value of output will be greater than its cost. The difference between the wage and the average net productivity of labour, multiplied by the number of men employed, will represent a surplus profit over and above the normal cost of the entrepreneur. Similarly, if the wage is greater than the average productivity, the value of the output will be less than the full costs of production, and the entrepreneur will receive less than his normal reward. Only when the wage is equal to average productivity is the value of the product exactly equal to full costs of production, no more and no less.

Fig. 72.) *ANP* and *MNP* are the curves of average and marginal net productivity to the firm.

If the supply of labour is perfectly elastic at a wage OC, the number of men (OQ) will be employed whose marginal net productivity (QE) is equal to OC. Their average net productivity, QD, is greater than the wage, and there is a surplus above normal profits (CEDB) equal to ED (the difference between marginal and average net productivity) multiplied by OQ (the number of men employed).

Thus for full equilibrium it is necessary that the marginal cost of labour should be equal to marginal net productivity, and

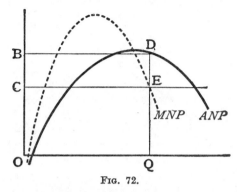

FIG. 72.

the average cost of labour (the wage) should be equal to average net productivity. When the supply of labour to the individual unit is perfectly elastic the marginal and average costs of labour are equal, and the double condition of equilibrium can only be fulfilled when the wage is equal to the value at which the marginal and average net productivity curves cut, that is to say, to the maximum value of average net productivity.[1]

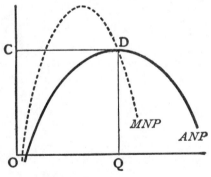

FIG. 73.

At the wage OC, OQ men are employed and the wage is equal to both marginal and average net productivity (QD).

When the supply of labour to the individual firm is less than perfectly elastic,[2] the conditions of full equilibrium with normal

[1] See p. 28.   [2] See Chapter 26.

profits are fulfilled when the supply curve of labour is a tangent
to the average net productivity curve.

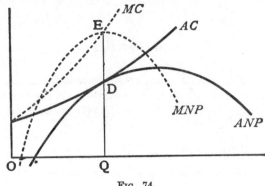

For the number of men at which the average curves are
tangential, the marginal curves will cut.[1] Thus for that number
of men the wage is equal to average net productivity, the marginal cost of labour is equal to marginal net productivity, and
full equilibrium is obtained. In equilibrium OQ men will be
employed at the wage QD.

5

The method by which full equilibrium is established (in
a competitive industry into which there is free entry) has
already been discussed.[2] The same process can be described in
terms of the demand curve for labour and the cost of labour
to the individual firm. If the wage is less than average net productivity surplus profits are earned and new firms are attracted
into the industry. The output of the commodity is increased,
and the demand curves for the individual firms are lowered.
Consequently the average net productivity curves are lowered,
and equilibrium is established when the average net productivity
curve is tangential to the average cost curve of labour. When the
supply of labour to the firm is perfectly elastic the two curves
will be tangential at the maximum point on the net productivity
curve, and when the supply is less than perfectly elastic, to the
left of the maximum point.[3] The manner in which the curves

[1] See p. 33.   [2] See p. 94.
[3] When we are discussing the supply curve of a commodity we assume the

alter as new firms enter the industry will also be influenced by
the existence of economies, or by a rise in the cost of other
factors, from the point of view of the industry as a whole. These
are discussed in the next chapter. Unless the supply of labour
is perfectly elastic to the industry as a whole, the effect of the
entry of new firms will be to raise the cost of labour to all firms
as well as to lower the demand curve for the commodity of each
individual firm, and as equilibrium is re-established the wage
will rise to meet the average productivity curve of the firm at
the same time as the average productivity curve falls to meet
the wage.

6

When a perfectly competitive industry is in full equilibrium,
each firm produces such an output that the average cost of production per unit of output is at a minimum,[1] and we now see
that the number of men employed by each firm is such that
average net productivity per man is at a maximum. It follows
that for a firm of optimum size (that is, with minimum costs
of production) the number of men employed is the number for
which average net productivity per man is at a maximum. To
secure that profits shall be normal the price of the commodity
must be equal to the minimum cost of production and the wage
must be equal to the maximum average net productivity. Thus
the wage and the price must be so adjusted that, at a certain
wage, the minimum cost of production is equal to the price, and
at that price, maximum net productivity is equal to this wage.

When the market for the commodity is not perfect, the firms,
in full equilibrium, will be of less than optimum size,[2] and it will

supply curves of all factors to be given. When we are discussing the demand
curve for labour we assume the supply curves of factors other than labour and
the demand curve for the commodity to be given. A very close analogy can be
found between the two. If the demand for the commodity is perfectly elastic
for the firm full equilibrium is established when price is equal to the minimum
average cost of the firm. Similarly when the supply of labour to the firm is
perfectly elastic equilibrium is established when the wage is equal to the
maximum average net productivity of labour to the firm. When the demand
for the commodity is not perfectly elastic equilibrium is established when the
demand curve and the average cost curve are tangential, and similarly when
the supply of labour is not perfectly elastic equilibrium is established when the
supply curve of labour is tangential to the average net productivity curve.

[1] For a discussion of the meaning of minimum cost when all entrepreneurs
in the industry are not alike, see p. 125.
[2] See p. 97.

no longer be true that the number of men whose average net productivity is a maximum will be the number that would be employed by a firm which is of optimum size at the given wage.[1]

[1] The formal proof of this is as follows:

For any output—

Average gross productivity (per man) = average net productivity (per man) + average other costs (per man).

Costs (per man) = wages (per man) + average other costs (per man).

Subtracting—

Costs (per man) – average gross productivity (per man) = wages (per man) – average net productivity (per man).

$$\therefore \quad \frac{\text{costs (per man)}}{\text{average gross productivity (per man)}}$$
$$= 1 + \frac{\text{wages (per man)} - \text{average net productivity (per man)}}{\text{average gross productivity (per man)}},$$

i.e. costs per unit of proceeds
$$= 1 + \frac{\text{wages (per man)} - \text{average net productivity (per man)}}{\text{average gross productivity (per man)}}.$$

It is now to be supposed that the supply of labour is perfectly elastic at a wage equal to the maximum value of average net productivity. It follows that for the output at which average net productivity is a maximum, cost per unit of proceeds is a minimum, and if, in addition, the demand for the commodity of the individual firm is perfectly elastic, cost per unit of output, *i.e.* average cost of production, is a minimum and the firm is of optimum size. But if the demand is not perfectly elastic the firm will be of less than optimum size.

CHAPTER 22

THE DEMAND CURVE FOR LABOUR OF AN INDUSTRY

1

It is now possible to discuss the nature of the demand curve for labour of a perfectly competitive industry in which profits are normal. Wages, as we have seen, must be equal to average net productivity for each firm, and since average net productivity, unlike marginal net productivity, is the same to the industry as to the firms, it is the curve of average net productivity to the industry which gives the demand curve for labour.

For each number of men there will be a certain output, and this output will be sold at a certain price. With this number of men and this price there is a certain wage at which the industry will be in equilibrium. When this wage rules the firms will be of optimum size, and the number of firms will be such that the appropriate output can be produced at the given price and at the given wage under equilibrium conditions. The wage will be equal to the average net productivity of the number of men employed. This wage represents the demand price for this number of men. The analogy between the competitive demand curve for labour and the competitive supply curve of the commodity is very close. The demand curve for labour shows the average net productivity of labour in just the same way as the supply curve of a commodity shows the average cost of production (including rents and normal profits).

At each point on a perfectly competitive industry's demand curve for labour the marginal net productivity and the average net productivity of labour are equal to the individual firms, in the same way as, at each point on the competitive supply curve,

---

* In this chapter the analysis contained in Section 6 is somewhat intricate, and is not required in the succeeding argument.

the average and marginal costs of a unit of output are equal to the individual firms. Marginal and average productivity of labour are not equal from the point of view of the industry, any more than average and marginal cost are equal to the industry under conditions of decreasing cost. For with every increase in the number of men employed by the industry, the output will increase and the price of the commodity will fall; and the addition to the value of output caused by employing one more man, looked at from the point of view of the firm, will be the marginal physical product multiplied by the price of the commodity (which is the marginal revenue to the firm), while looked at from the point of view of the industry it will be the marginal physical product multiplied by marginal revenue to the industry. The first, in equilibrium, is equal to both marginal and average net productivity from the point of view of the individual firm, and to average net productivity from the point of view of the industry. The second is equal to marginal productivity from the point of view of the industry.[1] Thus the familiar proposition that wages under competitive conditions tend to equal the marginal net productivity of labour must be interpreted to mean that wages tend to equal the value of the marginal physical product from the point of view of the individual employer (provided that he is both selling his product and buying his labour in a perfect market), and it should be supplemented by the statement that so long as there is free entry into the trade, the marginal net productivity of labour to the individual employer will tend to equal average net productivity, which is the same to the individual as to the industry.

2

The industry's demand curve for labour is given by the curve of average net productivity. It may be directly derived by drawing the gross productivity curve of labour for the industry, and then subtracting from it at each point the cost of the other factors employed per man. We have already seen that the amount of capital employed with each number of men is such that the marginal productivity of capital, to the individual firm,

---

[1] For the firm, but not for the industry, marginal productivity and marginal net productivity are equal; see p. 241.

is equal to the marginal cost of capital to the firm. The number of entrepreneurs will be such that the individual firms earn normal profits. We take the conditions of supply of the factors other than labour, and the conditions of demand for the commodity, to be given.

Let us first examine the case in which the supply of the other factors to the industry is perfectly elastic, and there are no economies of large-scale industry. As the number of men increases, output increases and the price of the commodity falls, and consequently less of other factors will tend to be employed per man. The gross productivity curve of labour will therefore fall somewhat more steeply than the demand curve for the product. But it may be that technical conditions make substitution impossible, and that the amount of other factors employed per man remains constant for all numbers of men.[1] If it is impossible for the amount of other factors employed per man to vary (and if there are no economies of large-scale industry or rise in the cost of other factors), the gross physical productivity of labour is the same for all numbers of men, and the average gross productivity curve is merely a replica of the demand curve for the commodity. The net productivity curve can be obtained by lowering it by a constant amount, representing the cost per man of other factors. For any given number of men the slope of the two curves will be the same, but the elasticity of the lower curve will be less. Thus the elasticity of demand for labour is less than the elasticity of demand for the product when no substitution is possible.

This result follows from the principle of joint demand.[2] A given proportionate reduction of wages will cause a smaller proportionate reduction in total costs, so that a given proportionate fall of wages causes a smaller increase in employment than the same proportionate fall in the price of the commodity. In the same way the demand for petrol is less elastic than the demand for car-miles, and the demand for bricks is less elastic than the demand for houses. When no substitution is possible the elasticity of demand for labour will be equal to the elasticity of demand for the commodity multiplied by the pro-

---

[1] This is an improbable condition (see p. 173) but one which gives a useful datum line for the subsequent inquiry.

[2] Marshall, *Principles*, p. 385.

portion of total costs represented by wages. The smaller the proportion of labour cost to total cost the greater will be the difference between the elasticity of demand for the commodity and the elasticity of demand for labour.

3

When the amount of capital per man is not rigidly fixed by technical conditions and there are no economies of large-scale industry there will be a tendency to employ less capital per man as the number of men increases and the price of the product falls. The elasticity of demand for labour will tend to be greater than when the proportions cannot be altered, for a reduction in wages will increase the output of the commodity, and at the same time (owing to the reduction in physical productivity per man due to the reduction in the amount of capital per man) it will increase the number of men producing a given output.

4

The proportions of the factors will always be such that their marginal physical productivities are in the same ratio as their prices (under perfect competition).[1] The degree to which substitution of factors is possible can best be measured by considering the change in the ratio of the factors which occurs when the relative prices alter. For instance, if the price of capital remains unchanged and the price of labour falls there will be such a reduction in the amount of capital employed per man as will raise the ratio of the marginal physical productivity of capital to that of labour in the same proportion as the price of labour has been reduced. It appears appropriate to call the proportionate change in the ratio of the amounts of the factors employed divided by the proportionate change in the ratio of their prices[2] to which it is due, the *elasticity of substitution*, by analogy with elasticity of demand or of supply.[3] The elasticity of substitution is determined by the technical conditions of production. When the proportions of the

---

[1] See p. 241.

[2] This interpretation of the elasticity of substitution applies only under conditions of perfect competition; see below, p. 330, note.

[3] See Foreword, p. vii.

factors are rigidly fixed no change in the ratio of labour to capital can be made however great the fall in wages, and the elasticity of substitution is zero. If the smallest fall in wages (the cost of capital remaining the same) were to cause the whole output to be produced by labour alone, the elasticity of substitution would be infinite.

The conclusion reached in the last section may therefore be expressed by saying that the elasticity of demand for labour will be greater the greater is the elasticity of substitution.

5

We will next consider the case in which the supply of capital to the industry as a whole is less than perfectly elastic, and the technical conditions impose a fixed amount of capital per man. It is clear that (with a given demand curve for the commodity) the demand curve for labour will be less elastic when the cost of capital rises as more men are employed, than it would be if the supply of capital were perfectly elastic. The gross productivity curve will not be affected by the change in the cost of capital (since the physical amount of capital per man is fixed), but the amount to be subtracted from the gross curve as cost of capital will increase as the number of men increases, and the demand curve for labour will fall more steeply than the demand curve for the product. It will thus be less elastic for two reasons, both because it is lower, and because it is more sloping. That is to say, a given fall in the cost of labour represents a smaller proportionate fall in the cost of the commodity not only because labour is not the whole of cost, but also because every increase in the amount of labour employed entails a greater average cost for the other factors that must be employed with it.

6

So far our results are familiar from Marshall's analysis of joint demand. In his well-known illustration of the demand for plasterers' labour he lays it down that the demand for one factor of production will be less elastic the less elastic is the demand for the commodity; that the demand for the factor will be more elastic when substitution is possible than when it is

s

not; that it will be less elastic the smaller is the proportion of total costs represented by this factor; and that it will be less elastic the less elastic is the supply of other factors.

The last two propositions are true, as we have seen, if substitution is not possible, but Marshall appears to have overlooked the complications which are introduced into them when substitution is possible.[1]

To deal with these complications it is necessary to consider the effect of a change in wages upon the aggregate amount of capital employed in the industry. When wages are reduced output will be increased. But the amount of labour employed per unit of output will also be increased. There are therefore two opposite influences on the aggregate amount of capital employed. In so far as output increases there will be a tendency for the amount of capital to increase, but in so far as the amount of labour employed per unit of output increases, there will be a tendency for the amount of capital to be reduced. Now the increase in output will be greater the greater the elasticity of demand for the commodity, and the increase in the amount of labour employed per unit of output will be greater the greater the elasticity of substitution. It can be proved that when these two elasticities are equal the two contending influences will counter-balance each other, and there will be no change, as a result of the fall in wages, in the amount of capital employed. If the elasticity of substitution is greater than the elasticity of demand for the commodity the amount of capital employed will be reduced when the amount of labour is increased (as a result of the fall in wages), and if the elasticity of substitution is less than the elasticity of demand the amount of capital will be increased as the amount of labour increases.[2] Those pro-

---

[1] See *Principles*, p. 853.

[2] It is necessary to consider the effect of a small fall in wages upon the amount of capital employed (taking labour and capital to be the only factors employed in producing the commodity). The following proof establishes the fact that a fall in the price of labour increases or reduces the demand price for a given amount of capital according as η, the elasticity of substitution, is less or greater than ϵ, the elasticity of demand for the commodity. To prove that the demand price for a given amount of capital will rise is equivalent to proving that the amount of capital employed will increase, and conversely.

Let the price of labour in the first position be l, and in the second position $l - \Delta l$. When the price of labour falls more labour will be employed with a given amount of capital. Let the amount of labour employed per unit of capital in the first position be L, and in the second position $L + \Delta L$. With more labour the

positions can be illustrated most simply by considering the two extreme cases. When the elasticity of demand for the commodity

gross productivity of the given amount of capital will be greater. Let G be the gross productivity per unit of capital in the first position, and $G + \Delta G$ in the second position. Let the net productivity per unit of the given amount of capital (which is equal to the demand price for it) be N in the first position and $N + \Delta N$ in the second position. It is required to prove that ΔN will be equal to zero when the elasticity of substitution is equal to the elasticity of demand for the commodity. Now average net productivity is unchanged (so that ΔN is zero) when the increase in gross productivity is equal to the increase in the cost of labour. But

$$N = G - Ll \text{ (by definition)}$$

and
$$N + \Delta N = (G + \Delta G) - (L + \Delta L)(l - \Delta l).$$
$$\therefore \Delta N = \Delta G - (l\Delta L - L\Delta l - \Delta L\Delta l).$$

Since Δl is small ΔL will also be small, and $\Delta L\Delta l$ can be neglected.

$$\therefore \Delta N = 0 \text{ when } \Delta G = l\Delta L - L\Delta l.$$

Now ΔG (the change in gross productivity) is equal to ΔL (the change in the amount of labour per unit of capital), multiplied by the marginal productivity of labour to the industry, and l is equal to the marginal productivity of labour to the firm. On the assumption (made in the text) that there are no economies of large-scale industry, marginal productivity to the firm is greater than marginal productivity to the industry in the ratio of price to marginal revenue (p. 237).

$$\therefore \Delta G = l\Delta L \cdot \frac{M}{A}, \text{ where M is marginal revenue and A is the price of the com-}$$

modity.
$$\therefore \Delta N = 0$$

when
$$l\Delta L \cdot \frac{M}{A} = l\Delta L - L\Delta l;$$

that is, when
$$\frac{A - M}{A} = \frac{\Delta l}{l} \cdot \frac{L}{\Delta L}.$$

Now $\frac{A - M}{A} = \frac{1}{\epsilon}$ (see p. 36). And when the price of capital does not alter it

follows from the definition of the elasticity of substitution (η) that $\frac{\Delta l}{l} \cdot \frac{L}{\Delta L} = \frac{1}{\eta}$.

Therefore we can write the above proposition thus:

$$\Delta N = 0 \text{ when } \frac{1}{\epsilon} = \frac{1}{\eta}.$$
$$\therefore \Delta N = 0 \text{ when } \epsilon = \eta,$$

which was required to be proved.

It can be seen that ΔN will be positive or negative according as η is less or greater than ϵ.

It follows that the amount of capital employed will increase or diminish, as a result of a small fall of wages, according as the elasticity of substitution is less or greater than the elasticity of demand for the commodity. Similarly, a fall in the price of capital will increase or diminish the amount of labour employed according as the elasticity of substitution is less or greater than the elasticity of demand for the commodity. And conversely for a rise in the price of capital.

From this proof it is possible to deduce the rider that a fall in the supply curve of capital will raise the demand curve for labour if η is less than ϵ, and lower it if η is greater than ϵ. Conversely for a rise in the supply curve of capital.

is zero there will be no change in output, and the amount of capital must be decreased as the amount of labour increases; and when the elasticity of substitution is equal to zero there is no change in the proportions of labour and capital, and the amount of capital must increase as the output increases. The change in the amount of capital, in either direction, will be greater the greater the divergence between the two elasticities.

Now the change in the proportion of labour to capital is determined by the elasticity of substitution and by the change in the prices of labour and capital. It can be seen that, when the conditions are such that the aggregate amount of capital remains constant, the elasticity of demand for labour is equal to the elasticity of substitution. When the conditions are such that the amount of capital increases as a result of a fall in wages (that is, when the elasticity of substitution is less than the elasticity of demand for the commodity), the elasticity of demand for labour is greater than the elasticity of substitution, since the proportionate increase in the amount of labour employed must then be greater than the proportionate change in the proportions of the factors. And when the conditions are such that the amount of capital is reduced (that is, when the elasticity of substitution is greater than the elasticity of demand for the commodity) the elasticity of demand for labour will be less than the elasticity of substitution. The greater the change in the amount of capital induced by the fall in wages the greater will be the difference between the elasticity of demand for labour and the elasticity of substitution.

We must now consider Marshall's proposition that the elasticity of demand for labour will be less the smaller the proportion of labour to capital (which stands for all other factors). In order to isolate the effect upon the demand for labour of the proportions of the factors let us consider the case in which the supply of capital is perfectly elastic, so that its price does not alter with the amount employed. The greater the proportion of labour to capital the greater will be the proportionate change in the aggregate amount of capital due to a given fall in wages. In the conditions in which the amount of capital increases it will increase by more the greater the proportion of labour; and in the conditions in which the amount of capital decreases it will decrease by more the greater the proportion of labour. Thus, when the elasticity of demand for the commodity is greater than the elasticity of substitution (so that the amount of capital increases) the elasticity of demand for labour will be greater the greater the proportion of labour. And when the elasticity of substitution is greater than the elasticity of demand for the commodity (so that the amount of capital decreases) the elasticity of demand for labour will be less the greater the proportion of labour.

Marshall's proposition, therefore, that the elasticity of demand for labour is greater the greater the proportion of labour to capital, is only true in the case in which the aggregate amount of capital increases when wages fall; that is, in the case in which the elasticity of substitution is less than the elasticity of demand for the commodity. The case, examined above, in which the proportions of the factors are fixed (so that the elasticity of substitution is zero) is the extreme case. Marshall's proposition is not correct in the case in which the elasticity of substitution is equal to the elasticity of demand for the commodity, for then the elasticity of demand for labour is independent of the proportions in which the factors are employed (being equal to the elasticity of substitution), and it is the reverse of correct when the elasticity of substitution is greater than the elasticity of demand for the commodity, for then the elasticity of demand for labour is less the greater the proportion of labour to capital.[1]

We must next consider Marshall's proposition that the elasticity of demand for labour will be less the smaller the elasticity of supply of capital. To examine this point it is necessary to consider the effect of a change in the price of capital upon the demand for labour. We have seen that a fall in wages will increase or diminish the amount of capital employed according as the elasticity of substitution is less or greater than the elasticity of demand for the commodity.[2] By the same proof it can be seen that a rise in the price of capital will diminish or increase the amount of labour employed according as which of the two elasticities is greater.

Now if the supply of capital is less than perfectly elastic, an increase in the amount of capital employed will raise its price.

---

[1] I am indebted to Mr. J. R. Hicks in this passage, for I had not considered this case until I saw his analysis of it in the Appendix to his *Theory of Wages*
[2] See p. 258, note.

But, as we have seen, the amount of capital will only increase (as a result of a fall in wages) if the elasticity of demand for the commodity is greater than the elasticity of substitution, and when that same condition is fulfilled the rise in the price of capital will check the increase in the amount of labour employed. In this case, therefore, the less elastic is the supply of capital the less elastic will be the demand for labour. Conversely, when the amount of capital is reduced the price of capital will fall. The amount of capital will only fall (as a result of a fall in wages) if the elasticity of substitution is greater than the elasticity of demand for the commodity, and, when that condition is fulfilled, the fall in the price of capital will check the increase in the amount of labour employed. Hence, once more, the demand for labour will be less elastic the less elastic is the supply of capital. Thus, in either case, Marshall's proposition is correct. It is only incorrect when the two elasticities are equal, so that the amount of capital does not alter. In that case the elasticity of demand for labour is independent of the elasticity of supply of capital (and is equal to the elasticity of substitution), for since the amount of capital does not alter, its price is unchanged whatever its elasticity of supply. The effect of the elasticity of supply of capital upon the elasticity of demand for labour will be greater the greater the divergence between the elasticity of substitution and the elasticity of demand for the commodity, and the effect will be nil when the two elasticities are equal.[1]

7

We have so far assumed that there are no economies of large-scale industry. If economies are of the simplest type, for instance if the industry uses a certain kind of machine which becomes cheaper as the industry expands (because the machine-making

---

[1] I am once more indebted to Mr. Hicks, as the consideration of his results led me to remove an error from my argument. But Mr. Hicks himself appears to be in error in his analysis of this case. He points out that when the elasticity of demand for the commodity is only slightly greater than the elasticity of substitution the elasticity of demand for labour is almost independent of the proportions of the factors. But he fails to notice that, in those conditions, it is equally true that the elasticity of demand for labour is almost independent of the elasticity of supply of capital (*loc. cit.* p. 246). The explanation of this oversight appears to be that he has failed to notice that in his equation (3) (*loc. cit.* p. 245) the square term, which contains $(\eta - \sigma)$, is equal to zero when the elasticity of demand for the commodity and the elasticity of substitution are equal.

industry is producing under conditions of falling supply price), the effect is the same as though the cost of capital fell as the industry increased in size. The case is then exactly symmetrical (in the opposite sense) with the case in which the cost of capital rises as more is employed, and we may say that the elasticity of demand for labour will be greater the smaller the elasticity of the falling supply curve of capital.

When the economies of large scale are of a more complicated type, associated with changes in productive technique, they cannot so easily be fitted into our system. It is argued, however, in the Appendix on Increasing and Diminishing Returns that it is possible to represent economies of any type by a falling supply curve of capital. Every type of economy can thus be treated in terms of the simplest type, where a certain machine becomes cheaper as the industry expands. Thus the proposition that economies of large scale tend to make the demand curve for labour more elastic is of perfectly general application.

So far we had found that when substitution of factors is not possible the elasticity of demand for labour must be less than the elasticity of demand for the commodity (unless no factors other than labour are employed). But it has now become clear that if there are economies of large-scale industry it is possible that the demand for labour should have an elasticity as great or even greater than the elasticity of demand for the commodity, even though there is no substitution. If a given proportionate reduction in wages brings about an equal proportionate reduction in other costs (by increasing output, and so leading to economies) the elasticity of demand for labour will be as great as the elasticity of demand for the commodity. And with a greater degree of economies the elasticity of demand for labour will be greater than the elasticity of demand for the commodity, so that if the elasticity of demand for the commodity is large, it may be possible that the demand curve for labour may have an infinite elasticity or even be rising. Economies of large-scale industry sufficiently great to ensure a rising demand curve for labour are perhaps improbable, but they are not theoretically impossible. If substitution is possible the elasticity of demand for labour will be greater than when it is not, and the likelihood of a rising demand curve is increased.

If the demand curve for labour is rising, obviously no equili-

brium is possible unless the supply curve for labour is also rising.
If the economies of large-scale industry were so great as to give
a rising demand curve for labour, and the supply of labour was
perfectly elastic, it would mean that the supply curve of the
commodity was falling faster than the demand curve for it, and
no equilibrium would be possible until an output was reached at
which the demand curve became less elastic than the supply
curve. But as the demand curve for the commodity became less
elastic, so would the demand curve for labour, and at the point
of equilibrium the demand curve for labour would be falling.

BOOK VIII

THE COMPARISON OF MONOPOLY AND COMPETITIVE DEMAND FOR LABOUR

CHAPTER 23

COMPARISONS OF MONOPOLY AND COMPETITIVE DEMAND FOR LABOUR

1

In earlier chapters we set out to compare the output of an industry under conditions, on the one hand, of perfect competition, and on the other, of a single monopoly. A similar comparison can be made between monopoly and competitive demand for labour.

We found that the assumptions which are necessary to make a valid comparison between monopoly and competitive output are open to various objections,[1] and many of these objections apply to the comparison of monopoly and competitive demand for labour with equal force. Once more the comparison must be regarded rather as an exercise in the use of the technique than as an inquiry likely to be of practical importance in itself.

We found, moreover, a final objection which showed not that the comparison is impossible (provided that the other objections can be met), but that the technique which we had used was too simple. Except in certain cases the proportions of the factors used under monopoly and under competition in producing a given output will not be the same. When the proportions are different average cost to the monopolist will be less than average cost to the competitive industry, and the results which we obtain by assuming that the monopolist's marginal cost curve bears the ordinary marginal relationship to the competitive average cost curve (the supply curve) are not valid unless the proportions of the factors are the same, at any given output,

[1] See Chapter 14.

* This and the following chapter are to be regarded mainly as an exercise in the use of the technique.

under monopoly and under competition. The comparisons set out in Chapters 11 and 12 underestimate the monopolist's output when the proportions of factors are variable, and in order to make valid comparisons it is necessary to go behind the supply curve of the commodity and examine the supply curves of the factors of production.[1]

2

In the present comparison we shall follow the same procedure as in the comparison of monopoly and competitive output. We shall first make the comparison which would be valid upon the assumption that the factors of production are used in the same proportions (for any given output) under monopoly and under competition,[2] and examine the cases in which this assumption is not fulfilled in the next chapter.

If the proportions of the factors producing any output are the same under monopoly and under competition, it follows that with any given number of men the monopolist employs the same amount of capital (which stands for all other factors) as would be employed under competition. The amount of capital per man may vary with the number of men, but for each number of men it is the same under monopoly and under competition. The gross productivity curve of the industry is therefore the same in either case, the cost of capital per man is the same (provided that the monopolist pays rent for any scarce factor), and the marginal and average net productivity curves are the same. The demand curve for labour of the industry under competition is given by the average net productivity curve; under monopoly, since the industry is a unit of control, the demand curve[3] is given by the marginal net productivity curve of the industry. The monopolist's demand curve for labour is thus marginal to the competitive demand curve.

This fact is a result of the working of the general principle that the individual buyer will balance marginal gain against marginal cost. If a competitive industry is imagined to come into the hands of a monopolist (everything else remaining un-

[1] See p. 174, note.

[2] As we shall see in the next chapter, this assumption is even less likely to be fulfilled for the purposes of the present comparison than it was for the earlier comparison.

[3] Demand curve being used in the sense discussed on p. 235.

changed), the identity of the individual buyer whose interests must be taken into account immediately changes, the centre of gravity shifts, as it were, from the firm to the industry, and the demand for labour will be regulated by marginal gain to the industry as a whole instead of being regulated by marginal gain to the individual firm. Marginal gain to the industry as a whole is the net increment of value caused by employing an additional unit of labour, and this, in the case that we are considering, is the same as the marginal net productivity of labour to the competitive industry, while marginal gain to the firm is the value of the increment of output caused by employing an additional unit of labour, and this is equal to the average net productivity of labour.

Since the monopolist's demand curve is marginal to the competitive demand curve the comparison between monopoly and competitive demands for labour can be made by means of the same geometrical apparatus as was used for the comparison of monopoly and competitive output.[1] If the demand and supply curves are straight lines the monopolist will employ half the number of men employed under competition. And convexity of the demand curve for labour, and concavity of the supply curve of labour, will tend to increase the ratio of employment under monopoly to employment under competition, just as convexity of the demand curve and concavity of the supply curve for the commodity tend to increase the ratio of monopoly to competitive output. In every case the amount of employment under monopoly will be less than under competition.[2]

This will be true even though the competitive demand curve for labour may be perfectly elastic or may be rising.[3] For the supply curve of labour must be rising faster than the demand curve in order to secure equilibrium. The ratio of monopoly to competitive employment will be determined, as before, by the concavity of the demand and supply curves, but in this case

---

[1] No diagrams are provided for these comparisons, since the diagrams in Chapter 11 will serve to illustrate them. For β and a, the average and marginal cost curves including rent, read average and marginal cost of labour to the industry, for average revenue read average net productivity, and for marginal revenue read marginal net productivity. The required relationships will then be shown by those figures.

[2] Except when there is a kink in the demand curve or in the supply curve, in which case they will be equal: see Figs. 50 and 51, p. 148.

[3] See p. 263.

concavity of the demand curve will tend to increase the ratio, and convexity to diminish it.

3

We have so far assumed that the monopolist pays the rent of labour, but when the supply of labour to the industry is imperfectly elastic it is possible that he may discriminate in buying labour.[1] If he is in a position to discriminate perfectly, he will hire each unit of labour at its transfer wage and pay no rent for labour. The marginal cost of labour to the monopolist will then be equal to its average cost to the competitive industry and the amount of employment under monopoly will be regulated not by the marginal but by the average cost curve of labour to the competitive industry. In this case the monopolist will employ more than half the competitive number of men when the supply and demand curves are straight lines, and the relative amount of employment under monopoly will be greater the greater the elasticity of the competitive demand curve.

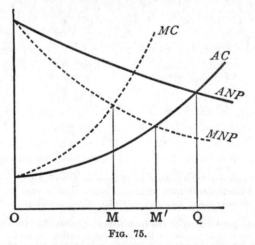

Fig. 75.

ANP is the competitive demand curve for labour.
MNP is the monopoly demand curve for labour.
AC is the supply curve of labour to the industry.
MC is the marginal cost curve of labour to the industry.

[1] See p. 150. We are here assuming that the transfer earnings of each unit of a scarce factor are independent of the amount of the factor employed.

The amount of labour employed under competition is OQ, and under monopoly, when rent is paid, OM.

When the monopolist does not pay rent, that is when he can discriminate perfectly in buying labour, the amount of labour employed is OM'.

If the competitive demand for labour is perfectly elastic, the amount of employment will be the same under monopoly and under competition, and if the competitive demand curve is rising the amount of employment will be greater under monopoly than under competition.[1]

Thus the amount of employment will be greater under monopoly than under competition if the monopolist pays no rent for labour when there are economies of large-scale industry sufficiently great to ensure that the competitive demand curve for labour is rising.

4

The foregoing comparisons are made upon the assumption that the monopolist pays rent for all factors other than labour. If capital is a scarce factor for which the monopolist does not pay rent, the cost of capital per man, with any given number of men, will be less under monopoly than under competition by the amount of the average rent. In this case, provided that the proportions of capital and labour cannot be altered, gross productivity is the same under monopoly and under competition, but average net productivity is greater under monopoly, since the cost of capital per man is less.[2] The marginal net pro-

---

[1] Thus we find once more, by another route, that output under monopoly can only be greater than under competition (as long as the proportions of the factors are fixed) when the economies of large-scale industry are so great that if the factor of production which actually is scarce (in this case labour) had been in perfectly elastic supply no equilibrium would have been possible. See p. 153, note.

[2] When the proportions of the factors are variable the fact that the monopolist pays no rent for capital will have a double effect upon the monopolist's demand for labour. He produces a larger output, but he employs fewer men for a given output. The rider to the proof given on p. 258 can be applied to this case if the terms are altered appropriately. The elasticity of the marginal revenue curve must take the place of elasticity of demand for the commodity, and the elasticity of substitution must be interpreted as the proportionate change in the ratio of the amounts of the factors employed divided by the proportionate change in the ratio of their marginal costs to the monopolist (see p. 330, note, below). Then it could be shown by means of the same proof that the monopolist's demand curve for labour is lowered or raised by the

ductivity curve of the monopolist (which gives his demand curve for labour) will therefore lie above the curve marginal to the competitive demand curve, and the amount of employment under monopoly will be greater than is shown by the comparisons set out above.[1]

non-payment of rent for capital according as this elasticity of substitution is greater or less than the elasticity of the marginal revenue curve. In the case considered in the text the elasticity of substitution is equal to zero, and the reduction in cost of capital must raise the demand curve for labour.

[1] It can be shown that, so long as there are no economies of large-scale industry, the monopolist's marginal net productivity curve must lie below the competitive average net productivity curve, and, consequently, employment under monopoly cannot exceed employment under competition. But if the economies of large-scale industry are sufficiently great, the monopolist's marginal net productivity curve for labour lies above the competitive demand curve, so that if the supply curve of labour is sufficiently elastic, or if the monopolist does not pay rent for labour, the amount of employment under monopoly will be greater than under competition.

CHAPTER 24

CORRECTION OF THE COMPARISONS

THE foregoing comparisons were made upon the assumption that the factors of production are used in the same proportions under monopoly and under competition.[1] As we saw in Chapter 14, the assumption that the proportions of the factors are fixed, that is to say, that there is only one way of producing any given output, is highly unplausible. Even if the proportions of land, labour, and capital can be imagined to be fixed in the long period, it is extremely improbable that the proportion of entrepreneurship to output should be fixed by technical considerations alone. We were able to find cases, however, in which the proportions of factors producing any given output would in fact be the same under monopoly and under competition, even when variation was technically possible. If the supply of all factors is perfectly elastic, or if the elasticities of all are equal, or if the monopolist pays no rent, and there are no economies of large scale, there is nothing to be gained in the production of any given output by altering the competitive proportions.

It may often happen that all factors are in perfectly elastic supply to an industry, and that there are no economies of large scale, so that the proportions of the factors are the same for any given output under monopoly and under competition. But our present task is to consider the productivity of a given number of men under monopoly and under competition. We must examine what would happen, not if such and such an output is being produced in both cases, but if such and such a number of men is being employed in both cases. To provide a basis for the first comparison we take all the supply curves of the factors as given,

[1] The more general objections to any comparison between monopoly and competition must be overcome by making assumptions similar to those suggested in Chapter 14.

* The analysis of this chapter is somewhat intricate and is not essential to the succeeding argument.

and suppose that the demand curve for the commodity is so adjusted that various outputs are produced. In arriving at the present comparison we take the demand curve for the commodity and the supply curves of factors other than labour as given, and suppose that the wage is so adjusted that various numbers of men are employed.

Now when there is a perfectly elastic supply of all factors (other than labour) and no economies, the proportions of the factors employed with a given amount of labour will not be the same under monopoly as under competition. The marginal productivity of capital to the monopolist (which regulates the amount of capital that he employs with a given number of men) will be less than the marginal productivity of capital to the individual firm (which regulates the amount of capital employed under competition with the given number of men). For there are no economies, so that marginal physical productivity is the same in either case, and marginal productivity to the monopolist is marginal physical productivity multiplied by marginal revenue, and to the competitive industry it is marginal physical productivity multiplied by the price of the commodity. The amount of capital employed by the monopolist with the given number of men will consequently be less than the amount employed under competition. Thus the most usual conditions in which the factors in a given output will be the same under monopoly and under competition will not provide a case in which the factors employed with a given number of men are the same. And, as we shall find in a moment, it is only in very peculiar conditions that the amount of the other factors employed with a given number of men will be the same under monopoly and under competition.

The manner in which the relative amounts of other factors employed with a given number of men are determined can be shown as follows: Suppose that capital is the only factor other than labour, and that capital is measured in efficiency units, so that all economies of large-scale industry are represented as a fall in the supply price of capital to the industry.[1] Now, supposing that any given number of men is being employed by the industry, draw a curve (MP_F) showing the relation between the marginal productivity of capital to the individual firm and the amount of

[1] See Appendix, p. 343.

capital employed by the industry with that number of men, and a curve (MP_I) showing the marginal productivity of capital to the industry. Marginal productivity to the firm is the marginal physical product of capital multiplied by the price of the commodity, and marginal productivity to the industry is the marginal physical product multiplied by marginal revenue.[1] Since the marginal physical product declines as the amount of capital increases, these two curves will not be marginal and average to each other, but for each amount of capital they stand in the same ratio to each other as marginal revenue to price. Next draw the marginal and average cost curves of capital to the industry (MC and AC). If capital is a scarce factor, these curves will be rising, and if there are economies of large-scale industry, they will be falling. The monopolist is assumed to be unable to discriminate in buying capital, so that he pays any rent that there may be. The curve MC therefore shows the marginal cost of capital to the monopolist.

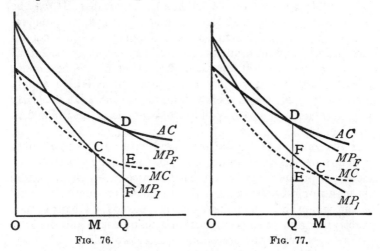

Fig. 76.   Fig. 77.

Then, in each diagram, the amount of capital employed with the given number of men by the monopolist (OM) is determined by the point of intersection (C) of the marginal cost curve (MC) and the curve of marginal productivity to the industry (MP_I). And the amount employed with this

[1] See p. 237.

same number of men under competition (OQ) is given by the point of intersection (D) of the average cost curve (AC) and the curve of marginal productivity to the firm (MP_F). Let DQ cut MP_I in F and MC in E. The two amounts of capital employed with the given number of men will be the same if MC cuts MP_I at F, that is, if F, C, and E coincide. Now DQ is in the same ratio to FQ as price to mar-. ginal revenue, so that $\dfrac{DQ}{DF}$ is the elasticity of demand for the commodity;[1] but $\dfrac{DQ}{DE}$ is the elasticity of supply of capital. Therefore E and F coincide, and the amount of capital employed under monopoly and under competition are equal, when the elasticity of demand for the commodity is equal to the elasticity of supply of capital both in numerical value and in sign.

This condition could only be fulfilled by an accident. It may be expressed by saying that the difference between marginal revenue and price, which inclines the monopolist to use less capital with a given number of men than would be employed with that number under competition, is exactly offset by the economies of large-scale industry (here represented by a falling supply curve of capital) which incline him to use more. It is clearly only by chance that this condition would ever be fulfilled in practice.

If the amount of capital employed with any given number of men were the same under monopoly and under competition, the gross productivity would be the same, the cost of capital per man would be the same, and average net productivity would be the same. The monopolist's demand curve for labour is then exactly marginal to the competitive demand curve, and the comparisons set out in the preceding chapter are valid.

When the amount of capital is greater under monopoly, the average gross productivity under monopoly of any given number of men is likely to be greater, and when the amount of capital is less the gross productivity is likely to be less, than it would be for the same number of men under competition. But it can be shown that whether the monopolist employs more or less capital

---

[1] See p. 36.

than is employed under competition the average net productivity under monopoly must be greater than under competition.
This can be proved as follows: The difference in the amount of
capital employed with the given number of men under monopoly and under competition is shown in Figs. 76 and 77 by the
distance MQ. The difference in gross productivity, due to the
difference in the amount of capital, is shown by the area MCFQ,
which lies under the curve of marginal productivity of capital to
the industry. The difference in cost of capital is shown by the
area MCEQ, which lies under the curve of marginal cost of capital
to the industry. The difference in net productivity is therefore shown by MCFQ *minus* MCEQ, that is, by the triangle
CEF. Thus when the monopolist employs less capital than is
employed under competition (as in Fig. 76) the excess of gross
productivity under competition, due to the additional capital
employed, is less than the excess of cost of capital. And when the
monopolist employs more capital than is employed under competition (as in Fig. 77), the additional gross productivity is greater
than the additional cost of capital. So that, in either case, the
net productivity of the given number of men is greater under
monopoly than under competition by the area CEF. Thus whenever the amount of capital under monopoly is different from the
amount under competition, net productivity under monopoly
will be greater than under competition. The difference in the
net productivities will be greater the greater is the elasticity
of substitution,[1] and the greater is the difference between the
elasticities of the demand curve for the commodity and the
supply curve of capital,[2] that is to say, the difference between
the net productivities under monopoly and under competition
will be greater the more easily do technical conditions permit
of variations in the proportions of capital and labour, and the
more there is to be gained by varying them. If the elasticity of
substitution is nil, it is not possible (for technical reasons) to
vary the proportions, and if the elasticity of demand for the
commodity is equal to the elasticity of supply of capital there is

---

[1] A low elasticity of substitution would be shown in the diagrams by a steep
slope of MP_I and MP_F. The greater the slope of these curves (other things being
equal) the smaller is the distance MQ.

[2] The elasticity of a rising supply curve of capital is reckoned as of opposite
sign to the elasticity of the demand curve, since the demand curve must be
falling.

no motive for varying them. This is analogous with the fact that the average cost of a given output under monopoly will be less than under competition by a greater amount the greater are the possibilities of substitution and the greater is the extent to which the elasticities of supply of the various factors of production diverge from one another.[1]

Since the monopolist's average net productivity curve will lie above the average net productivity curve of the competitive industry (which is the competitive demand curve for labour), it follows that the monopolist's demand curve for labour, which is marginal to his own average net productivity curve, must lie above the curve marginal to the competitive demand curve, just as his marginal cost curve will lie somewhat below the curve marginal to the competitive supply curve. The amount of labour employed under monopoly will therefore be a greater proportion of the amount employed under competition than it is when the proportions of labour to capital do not alter.[2] If the change in the proportions of factors made by the monopolist is sufficiently great, his demand curve for labour may actually lie above the competitive demand curve. Then, if the supply of labour is sufficiently elastic, the amount of employment will be greater under monopoly than under competition. The conditions in which this will occur are not, however, the same as the conditions in which output will be greater under monopoly than under competition. For if the output is the same under monopoly as under competition the amount of employment may be either greater or less, according as the monopolist employs a greater or smaller proportion of labour to other factors than is employed under competition.

---

[1] See p. 175.

[2] In order to make an exact comparison of the monopoly and competitive demands for labour when the proportions of the factors are variable, it is necessary to consider not the shape of the competitive demand curve for labour, but the shapes of the demand curve for the commodity and the supply curve of capital. For instance, if the supply curve of capital and the demand curve for the commodity are straight lines, the competitive demand curve for labour would be concave, and the crude comparison would lead us to suppose that the monopolist would employ less than half the competitive number of men if the supply curve of labour is a straight line. In fact he would employ somewhat more than this, and it can be shown that he would employ exactly half the competitive number of men (cf. p. 175, note).

BOOK IX
EXPLOITATION

CHAPTER 25

MONOPOLISTIC EXPLOITATION OF LABOUR

1

THE comparisons of monopoly and perfectly competitive demand for labour are not in themselves of much practical interest, but the analysis developed in order to make them may be useful. There are a group of problems connected with the "exploitation" of labour on which it may throw some light.

The problem of the exploitation of labour in general raises a group of questions which will be discussed in Chapter 27. At present we shall consider the case of a single industry and the effect of removing exploitation in one industry considered separately. It will thus be possible to assume that employment may be increased or diminished in the industry without having a significant effect upon other industries, and that the general level of prices is unaffected, so that a change in the money wages of the group of workers we are considering produces an equivalent change in their real wages.

It is commonly said that exploitation (the payment to labour of less than its proper wage) arises from the unequal bargaining strength of employers and employed, and that it can be remedied by the action of trade unions, or of the State, which places the workers upon an equality in bargaining with the employers. Bargaining strength, as we shall find, is important in many cases, but the fundamental cause of exploitation will be found to be the lack of perfect elasticity in the supply of labour or in the demand for commodities.

It is usually said that a factor of production is exploited if it is employed at a price which is less than its marginal net pro-

* Sections 4 and 6 of this chapter contain some intricacies which are no essential to the rest of the argument.

ductivity. Now it will be to the interest of each individual employer to use such an amount of each factor that its marginal cost to him is equal to its marginal net productivity to him. Thus if the market in a factor is perfect, so that its marginal cost to the individual employer is equal to its price, the self-interest of individual employers (provided they are not under the influence of a feeling of loyalty to their class) will ensure that the factor receives a reward equal to its marginal net productivity to the individual employer. Complete freedom on the part of individual workers to move from firm to firm would force employers to bid against each other for labour until the wage was equal to the marginal net productivity of the amount of labour employed, and the freedom of the market would serve in the place of labour organisations in securing to the workers their proper wage. If the market for labour is perfect, so that the marginal cost of employing an extra man is equal to the wage he receives, it is impossible for the wage in a competitive industry to be less than the marginal net productivity of labour to the firm, for if it were less it would pay employers to take on more men until the marginal net productivity of labour was reduced to equality with the wage. Exploitation on this definition is therefore impossible except when the supply of labour to the individual firm is less than perfectly elastic, so that the wage is less than the marginal cost of labour to the firm. Thus the function of a trade union or a minimum wage law in removing exploitation lies not so much in the fact that it improves the bargaining strength of the workers as in the fact that by means of a "common rule" it reproduces artificially the conditions of perfect elasticity of supply of labour to individual employers.

We find, therefore, that if exploitation is taken merely to mean that the wage is less than the marginal net productivity of labour to the individual employer, it can never occur as long as there is perfect competition in buying labour. But this definition is unnecessarily restricted. What is actually meant by exploitation is, usually, that the wage is less than the marginal physical product of labour valued at its selling price.[1] Upon this view, imperfection in the market for the commodity as well as imperfection in the market for labour may give rise to exploitation. When the selling market is imperfect the marginal net

---

[1] Cf. Pigou, *Economics of Welfare*, p. 549.

productivity of labour to the individual firm is the marginal physical product of labour multiplied by marginal revenue to the firm, and marginal revenue is less than price. Thus even if the wage were equal to marginal net productivity to the firm, there would still be exploitation.

The conflict between these two definitions of exploitation is merely a matter of words. A given situation remains the same whether we choose to call it exploitation or not. For our present purpose the wider definition is more convenient. We shall say that a group of workers are being exploited when their wage is less than the marginal physical product that they are producing, valued at the price at which it is being sold.

The removal of exploitation may alter both the marginal physical product of labour and the price of the commodity, and we shall find, paradoxical as it may seem, that the removal of exploitation is not always beneficial to the workers concerned.

2

The cases in which exploitation can arise may be divided into three classes: those which occur although the supply of labour to the individual employer is perfectly elastic: these are due to monopoly of the commodity; those which occur when the supply of labour is imperfectly elastic (although the commodity is sold in perfectly competitive conditions); and those which occur when the supply of labour is imperfectly elastic, and further, the employer has the power to discriminate in buying labour: these two classes are due to monopsony of labour. In the first two classes we will assume that all the men are alike in efficiency, and that all are paid the same wage. In the third class either individual men may differ in efficiency, or may be alike in efficiency but paid at different rates of wages. Further, a situation which is similar to exploitation, though excluded by our definition, may arise even though there is perfect competition, both in selling the product and in hiring labour, provided that there is not free entry of firms into the trade. In this case also it is convenient to assume that all men are alike in efficiency.

3

The simplest case of the type of exploitation which occurs when the supply of labour to the individual firm is perfectly elastic but there is not perfect competition in selling the commodity is the case of a single monopoly in isolation. Under monopoly that number of men is employed, as we have seen, whose marginal physical product multiplied by the marginal revenue of the monopolist is equal to the wage. The wage is therefore less than the marginal physical product multiplied by the price of the commodity, and, upon our definition, exploitation occurs. This cannot be cured by raising wages. A rise in wages would merely lead to unemployment, and exploitation at the higher wage would still continue. The only remedy for exploitation is to control prices in such a way as to obtain the competitive output from the monopolist.[1]

4

When instead of an isolated monopolist there are a number of firms selling in an imperfect market, exploitation will again occur, even though the supply of labour to each firm is perfectly elastic. If there is freedom of entry into the trade, so that profits are normal, each firm will be of less than optimum size.[2] The wage will be equal to the average net product of labour (if this were not the case the average cost of the commodity would be less than the price and there would be more than normal profits), and to marginal net productivity to the individual firm; but marginal net productivity to the firm will be less than the marginal physical product of labour valued at the price of the commodity (since the demand for the product of the firm is not perfectly elastic). Exploitation of this type cannot be removed by raising wages, but it would disappear if the market became perfect. This type of exploitation is probably very common, and it is worth while to examine at some length the effect upon labour of the removal of market imperfection.

When the market becomes perfect the firms will expand, and

---

[1] See Chapter 13. Competitive output is here used to mean the output at which price is equal to average cost.
[2] See p. 97.

in the new position of equilibrium, when profits are once more normal, the firms will be of optimum size, costs will be lower, and the price of the commodity will have fallen.

The removal of the imperfection of the market must therefore lower the price of the commodity. It is likely also to alter the marginal physical productivity of the number of men formerly employed in the industry, since the workers are now organised in optimum firms instead of sub-optimum firms. In the old position they were receiving less than what was then the value of their marginal physical product, and in the new position they will receive the value of their marginal physical product, but it does not follow that they will be better off in the new position than in the old, since the value of the marginal physical product may have diminished: the marginal physical product may have diminished, and the price of the commodity must have fallen.

In order to elucidate the problem it is convenient to consider the effect upon the average physical productivity of labour of a growth in the size of the firm. It is more natural to expect that average physical productivity per man (the total physical product of the firm divided by the number of men employed) should increase when the firm grows to its optimum size.[1] It may, however, happen that average physical productivity is reduced by the growth in the size of the firm. But this could only occur if the increase in the number of men employed by the firm leads to no economies of large-scale production, or if any economies are offset by the diseconomies which arise from employing some fixed element (for instance of plant or management) beyond its optimum capacity. It is therefore unlikely to be a common case.

The cost of other factors employed per man may either increase or diminish when the firm grows to its optimum size.[2]

So far we have proceeded upon the assumption that the number of men employed in the industry is kept unchanged, and that the wage is appropriately altered by the removal of exploitation. It is also possible to assume that the wage remains unchanged and that the amount of employment is altered appropriately. For our present purpose the second method will be more convenient. The results obtained by either method must be the same; for if employment at the old wage would increase, it follows that it would be possible to raise the wage without reducing employment, so that the wage at which a fixed number of men would be employed would be raised by the removal of exploitation; and if, at the old wage, employment would have been reduced, the removal of exploitation would lead to a reduction of the wage obtained by a fixed number of men.

For the sake of simplicity let us suppose that the cost curves and demand curves of all the firms in the imperfect market are alike, so that the same output is produced by each, and sold by each at the same price.[1] Now when the market becomes perfect the cost of production will fall and there will be an increase of output, assuming that the wage is unchanged. But this increase of output need not necessarily lead to an increase of employment at the given wage. If physical productivity per man (the total physical product divided by the number of men employed) is reduced when the firms reach their optimum size employment must be increased. But we have just seen that physical productivity per man is more likely to increase. There will then be a double effect. The fall in costs, by leading to an increase in output, will tend to increase employment, but the rise in physical productivity per man must mean that the number of men required to produce a given output is reduced. It remains to inquire, therefore, which effect predominates.

In so far as the fall in cost per unit of output is due entirely to the increase in physical productivity per man it will only tend to increase employment if the elasticity of the total demand for the commodity which the industry produces is greater than unity. This can easily be seen. The cost per man of the other factors employed is in this case the same when the firms are of optimum size as when they were of less than optimum size. Since the wage is unchanged, it follows that the total cost per man is unchanged. Hence cost per unit of output (which is equal to the total cost per man divided by physical productivity per man) falls in the same proportion as the physical productivity increases, and the price of the commodity falls in the same proportion. Then, if the elasticity of demand for the commodity is

---

[1] The following analysis is based upon the assumptions that the supply of all factors to the industry is perfectly elastic, and that there are no economies of large-scale industry. When these assumptions are not fulfilled the necessary complications can be introduced into the framework of the argument without any fundamental alteration in its structure.

equal to unity, output increases in the same proportion as physical productivity per man, and there will be no change in employment. There will be an increase or decrease in employment according as the elasticity of demand is greater or less than one.

On the other hand, in so far as the fall in the cost of the commodity is accompanied by a fall in cost of the other factors employed per man, without any change in physical productivity, it must lead to an increase in employment (at the given wage) unless the demand for the commodity is completely inelastic. If there is both an increase in physical productivity per man and a fall in cost per man, then employment would increase if the elasticity of demand for the commodity was equal to unity, and would diminish only if the elasticity of demand fell short of some value less than unity. Such a fall in the cost of other factors employed per man might occur if there were some fixed element in the productive equipment (for instance the entrepreneur himself, or some large indivisible unit of plant, such as a railway line) which requires a certain fixed reward, so that its cost per man falls as the number of men increases. On the other hand it is probable that in most types of production the degree of mechanisation increases as the firm grows to its optimum size. The cost per man of the other factors employed is therefore in general likely to increase. The cost of the commodity then falls in a smaller proportion than the physical productivity per man increases and employment is reduced if the elasticity of demand for the commodity is equal to unity. Only if elasticity exceeds some value greater than unity will employment in this case be increased.

Thus in each case there is a certain critical elasticity of the total demand for the industry's product at which employment remains unchanged. If the cost per man of the other factors employed is the same in the optimum firm as in the sub-optimum firm the critical elasticity is unity, and if the elasticity is less than unity labour will suffer by the removal of market imperfection. If cost per man is greater for the optimum firm than for the sub-optimum firm the critical elasticity is greater than unity. And if cost per man is less for the optimum firm the critical elasticity is less than unity. By means of this formula we can discover in each case whether the removal of market imperfection is likely to be a benefit to labour or the reverse.

It may appear strange that the removal of exploitation should ever be disadvantageous to labour. But the explanation can be found in two facts. First, when the demand for the commodity is inelastic anything which raises the cost of the commodity increases the total receipts of the industry. Consequently an increase in physical output per head can be of no advantage to labour when the demand for the commodity is inelastic, and labour may gain, at the expense of the consumer, from the fact that the firms are of less than optimum size. Second, when the market is imperfect it may not be profitable for the individual firm to undertake a degree of mechanisation which becomes profitable when the market becomes perfect. Thus labour may gain, at the expense of capital, from the fact that the firms are of less than optimum size.

In every case, whether the imperfection of the market is of benefit to labour or not, it must cause the price of the commodity to be higher than it would be if there were perfect competition. Therefore, in so far as labour gains from the imperfection of the market at the expense of the consumer it is only a sectional advantage. There is a loss to the consumers of the commodity (who must pay a higher price) and to the community in general (since less real wealth is being produced). It does not follow that because the labour attached to the industry gains by the imperfection of the market that it is therefore not desirable to remove it.   Moreover, if all industries were in this case labour would not gain from the existence of imperfection, since their loss as consumers would more than offset their gain as wage earners.

But even when exploitation is universal, so that firms in all industries are of less than optimum size, it is possible that if firms of less than optimum size tend to employ less capital per man than optimum firms, the imperfection of the market may benefit labour at the expense of capital. If all markets became perfect capital would tend to gain at the expense of labour, and it is possible, though not likely, that labour would lose, on balance, by the removal of exploitation.

5

We have so far been concerned with positions of long-period equilibrium. It is also necessary to consider the quasi-long period,[1] in which the number of firms does not increase in response to a rise in profits. The firms may then be of any size. If the market became perfect the output of each firm would increase and the price of the commodity would fall. If the firms were already so large that no technical economies were to be gained from an increase in output, the physical productivity of labour would be likely to decline as the firms grew in size. The removal of the market imperfection must then be of advantage to labour, whatever the elasticity of the total demand for the commodity.

6

It remains to consider a perfectly competitive industry into which new firms do not enter in response to abnormal profits. We shall here find a situation similar to exploitation. But it does not conform to our definition of exploitation; for if the market for the commodity and the market for labour are both perfect, the amount of employment given by each firm will be such that the marginal net productivity to the firm will be equal to the wage, and marginal net productivity to the firm will be equal to the value of the marginal physical product of labour. There will not, therefore, be exploitation upon our definition. But so long as new firms do not enter the trade the existing firms may be of more than optimum size, and may be earning more than normal profits.[2] The wage will then be less than the average net productivity of labour, to which wages are equal in a perfectly competitive industry in full equilibrium. The situation is therefore akin to exploitation, and it can be analysed by the technique developed in the analysis of exploitation upon which we are engaged.

Quasi-exploitation of this type would be removed as new firms entered the trade, so that long-period full equilibrium was established. The effect of the entry of new firms into the industry would be to lower the price of the commodity. Existing firms would be reduced to the optimum size, corresponding to a normal level of profits, and at the same time the output of the commodity (unless the demand for it was absolutely inelastic) would increase.

[1] See p. 47.
[2] The situation of the individual firm in such a case is illustrated in Fig. 36 on p. 96.

U

As before, we will assume that the wage is constant and we will examine, by the same method as before, whether employment at the given wage will increase or diminish when full equilibrium is established. If the physical productivity per man declines when the firms are reduced to optimum size employment must increase. The physical productivity of labour is likely, however, to be increased by the reduction of firms to their optimum size. But the abnormal profits earned by the firm of more than optimum size must be added to the cost of other factors per man, and this cost, including profits, is almost certain to be less when the firm is of optimum size and profits are reduced to normal. Now we found that when there is both a rise in physical productivity and a fall in the cost per man of the other factors, the critical elasticity of demand, at which employment is unchanged at the given wage, is less than unity. Since the fall in other costs (including profits) is likely to be considerable, we may say in general that unless the elasticity of demand is very small the return to full equilibrium and normal profits will be likely to increase employment in the industry.

7

We found that monopolistic exploitation cannot be removed by raising wages. But the quasi-exploitation which we have just been considering would be removed, so far as the particular industry was concerned, if wages were raised until the abnormal profits disappeared, so that conditions of full equilibrium were produced.

And it seems probable that in such a case wages would in fact alter more quickly than firms could enter the trade. If labour is organised the trade union might discover that profits are more than normal and press for higher wages. If they were successful, and if the wage rose just sufficiently to reduce the profits to normal, no new firms would enter the trade, the existing firms would be reduced in size, and employment would be diminished. A rise in wages of this sort would remove abnormal profits, and looking merely at this industry, without comparing the wages which it was paying with wages elsewhere, it would be impossible to tell that anything was amiss.

But to remove the quasi-exploitation in this way is not necessarily a desirable course. If the return to normal profits is brought about by a rise in wages, the price of the commodity is higher and the amount of employment in the industry less than would have been the case if the readjustment were brought about by an expansion of the industry. As a result there may be unemployment or a reduction of wages in other industries. Moreover the high demand for the commodity which caused abnormal profits in the first place will fail to lead to an increase in its supply. Under the perfectly *laissez-faire* conditions of the economic text-books the direction of resources into different types of manufacture is brought about by the fluctuation of profits above and below normal. When profits are more than normal the industry is supposed to expand, and when they fall below normal, to contract. By this means the changing demands of the consumer are implemented. If profits are kept at the normal level by changes in wages (an assumption probably far more realistic than the assumption of the text-books), the mechanism by which resources are directed from one use to another breaks down. There is a moral here, both for those who seek to patch up our present economic system by introducing profit-sharing schemes in particular industries and for those who complain, when losses are being made, that wages in a particular trade are too high. The system of the text-books perhaps never existed, and perhaps if it did it would not have been a very admirable one. But it has some merits. A system of un-controlled private enterprise in which wages are more plastic than profits must entail the misdirection of resources and the waste of potential wealth on an extensive scale.

CHAPTER 26

1

WE must now examine the type of exploitation which arises because the supply of labour is imperfectly elastic to the unit of control. The supply to an industry may be less than perfectly elastic for any of the reasons discussed in Chapter 8. The nature of the limitation upon the supply of labour is not relevant to our inquiry, for our analysis can be applied to limitations of any type, but for the sake of simplicity we will first deal only with one case: that in which all the workers employed are alike in their efficiency in the industry in question, and yet progressively higher wages have to be paid to all in order to attract fresh supplies of labour. This might occur because it was necessary to tempt labour away from better paid occupations, to overcome the cost of movement from more distant regions, or to overcome a preference for other occupations.

The notion of an imperfectly elastic supply of labour presents some difficulties, because the elasticity of supply will vary greatly according to the period of time under consideration. It is likely to be more elastic the longer the period under consideration. And a supply of labour once attracted to a certain area or a certain industry by a rise in wages may not immediately (or indeed ever) cease to be available when wages fall back to their former level. But for the purposes of our formal analysis it is only necessary to postulate that there is a rising supply curve of labour over a period long enough to allow normal equilibrium to be established. In this, as in all the problems with which this book attempts to deal, a very artificial degree of simplification

---

* *Sections 3 and 4 of this chapter contain an argument similar to that of Sections 4 and 6 of the last chapter, and are of the same degree of complexity.*

is necessary to the formal analysis. The most that can be hoped from it is to indicate some of the considerations that have to be taken into account in dealing with actual problems.

2

When the supply of labour is less than perfectly elastic to any employing agency, that amount of labour will be employed whose marginal cost is equal to its marginal net productivity, and the wage will be equal to the supply price of the amount of labour employed. The demand curve for labour of the employing agency may be of various forms. If it is an isolated monopoly the demand curve for labour must be drawn up on the principles discussed in Chapter 21. But if the employing agency is an industry composed of a number of independent firms they may act in concert in regulating wages although they compete in selling the commodity which they produce. In practice agreements to regulate wages are usually worked in a very rough and ready way, but it is worth while to consider the exact analysis of an agreement which follows some definite principle. It is possible to distinguish two principles upon which the demand curve for labour may be drawn up. First, if there is merely a "gentleman's agreement" not to spoil the market by bidding up wages, the individual firms composing the industry may be conceived to be in perfect competition in every respect except in hiring labour. Then the amount of capital employed with a given number of men will be such that the marginal productivity of capital to the firm is equal to its price, that is to say, the competitive amount of capital will be employed with any given number of men. And each firm will wish to employ that amount of labour whose marginal productivity to the firm is equal to the marginal cost of labour to the whole group, ignoring the effect upon the price of the commodity of an increase in output. The industry's demand curve for labour [1] will then be shown, for any given number of men, by the value of the marginal physical product of labour. Second, a more far-reaching type of agreement amongst the firms, which still falls short of complete monopoly, will be found if the competitive amount of capital is employed with each number of men, but the organised group of

---

[1] In the sense discussed on p. 235.

firms take into account the fall in the price of the commodity
due to an increase of output, and so employ that amount of
labour whose marginal net productivity to the whole group is
equal to its marginal cost. In any actual case neither of these
principles is likely to be followed exactly, but this fact is not
relevant to the analysis, for, however the demand curve for
labour is drawn up, the analysis follows the same course once
the demand curve for labour is given.

On whatever principle the demand curve is constructed it is
necessary to assume that there are a fixed number of firms, that
is to say, that the profits due to monopsony do not draw new

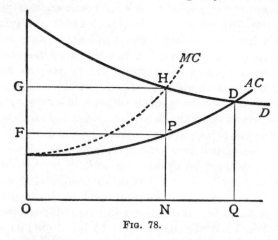

Fig. 78.

firms into the industry; for the amount of the monopsony profit
depends upon the conditions of supply of labour, and cannot be
represented in the demand curve. If the existence of a monopsony profit, or its removal, are conceived to alter the number of
firms in the industry, a new monopsony demand curve must be
drawn up for each number of firms.[1]

The amount of employment given by the monopsonist organisation will be restricted to the amount at which the marginal
cost of labour to the whole group is equal to its demand price
for each particular type of organisation. The wage will be equal

[1] This was first pointed out to me by Mr. P. M. Forrester, who was then
reading for the Economics Tripos. The case of a competitive industry in long-
period equilibrium, in which profits are always normal, is discussed below
(p. 296).

to the supply price of labour, and this, in each case, will be less than the value of the marginal physical product of labour. Thus exploitation will occur.

Monopsonistic exploitation of this type can be removed by the imposition of a minimum wage.

(Fig. 78.) Let D be the demand curve for labour of the monopsonist organisation, upon whatever principle it may be drawn up. Then the amount of labour employed (ON) will be that at which MC (the marginal cost curve of labour) cuts the demand curve, D.

Now, suppose that a trade union or a trade board imposes a minimum wage upon the industry; then the supply of labour to the industry becomes perfectly elastic at the imposed wage, up to that number of men whose supply price to the industry is in any case equal to that wage. Beyond this number the new supply curve of labour must coincide with the old. If the authority imposing the minimum wage is sufficiently strong to be able to choose freely what wage to impose, there are several alternatives before it. If, at the lower limit, the existing wage (NP) is imposed as a minimum everything remains as before. If the wage (NH) is chosen, which is equal to the demand price for the number of men employed in the exploited position, employment will remain unchanged and the wage will be raised. For any higher wage employment will be reduced, and for any wage between NP and NH employment will increase. The maximum increase in employment will occur at the wage (QD) at which the old supply curve of labour cuts the demand curve of the monopsonist organisation.[1] Thus the rise in wages which reduces exploitation and transfers a part or the whole of the monopsony profit to labour will actually result in an increase of employment.

Even when the wage QD, or some higher wage, is imposed, exploitation does not wholly disappear except in the case where D, the demand curve for labour of the group of firms, represents the value of the marginal physical product of labour.[2] The element in exploitation due to monopoly cannot be eliminated

[1] I am indebted to Mr. Shove for this analysis, but my presentation of it is slightly different from his.

[2] This will be the case when a number of independent firms, acting in concert for the regulation of wages, arrange their employment of labour on the first of the principles described on p. 293.

merely by removing the inelasticity of the supply curve of labour.

3

Monopsonistic exploitation can also arise where firms are not acting in concert, but where the supply of labour to each firm is less than perfectly elastic, just as monopolistic exploitation arises where the market for selling the commodity is imperfect. We have seen in what circumstances the supply of a factor to an industry may be less than perfectly elastic. The supply of labour to an individual firm might be limited for the same sort of reasons. For instance, there may be a certain number of workers in the immediate neighbourhood and to attract those from further afield it may be necessary to pay a wage equal to

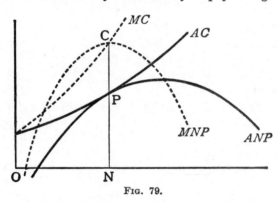

Fig. 79.

what they can earn near home *plus* their fares to and fro; or there may be workers attached to the firm by preference or custom and to attract others it may be necessary to pay a higher wage. Or ignorance may prevent workers from moving from one firm to another in response to differences in the wages offered by the different firms.

If the supply of labour to individual firms is less than perfectly elastic and if profits are normal the firms will be of less than optimum size,[1] even though the selling market is perfect. Profits will be normal and the industry in full equilibrium when

---

[1] The average cost of each firm is, of course, a minimum in the situation in which it finds itself. The term "optimum firm" is to be interpreted as referring to a situation when the supply of labour to each firm is perfectly elastic.

the wage is equal to average net productivity, and each firm will employ that number of men whose marginal net productivity to the firm is equal to their marginal cost to the firm.[1] With this analysis we are already familiar.[2]

Fig. 79.) AC and MC are the average and marginal cost curves of labour.

ANP and MNP are the average and marginal net productivity curves of labour.

ON men will be employed by each firm at the wage PN when the industry is in equilibrium.

CN is the marginal cost and marginal productivity of ON men to the individual firm.

Exploitation of this type would be removed if the labour market became perfect.

In studying exploitation due to imperfection of the market for the commodity we assumed that the wage remained unchanged and considered the effect on employment of making the market perfect.[3] But in this case it will be more convenient to make use of the other device and to study what would happen to the wage if the same number of men were employed as had been employed when exploitation existed. Both methods of making the comparison must, as we saw, yield the same result, but when we are dealing with an imperfect market for labour, and not for the commodity, the second method is easier to handle.[4]

Suppose that the labour market is made perfect (for instance by breaking down the ignorance and inertia which led to imperfection or by the provision of cheaper transport) and that a new position of equilibrium is attained with normal profits and the same fixed amount of employment as before. The firms will now be of optimum size, and the wage must be given by the

---

[1] In this case it is impossible to draw up a demand curve for labour of the industry upon the principle employed when the market for labour is perfect, since the number of firms will be influenced by the monopsony profit, which depends upon the conditions of supply of labour (cf. p. 294).

[2] See p. 250. Fig. 79 is a replica of Fig. 74.

[3] See p. 285.

[4] We will again assume that there are no economies of large-scale industry and that the supply to the industry of factors other than labour is perfectly elastic. When these assumptions are not fulfilled the necessary modifications can easily be introduced into the analysis.

maximum on the curve of average net productivity of labour to the individual firm.[1]

If the physical productivity per man is less when the firms are of optimum size, the total output of the given number of men in the new position is less, and the price of the commodity must rise. The curve of average net productivity to the individual firm will therefore be raised, and the wage must necessarily rise. This is analogous to the case where the removal of monopolistic exploitation necessarily leads to an increase of employment at a given wage (even though the demand for the commodity is perfectly inelastic) if average physical productivity per man falls when the firms become of optimum size.[2]

But, as we saw, physical productivity per man is likely to increase when the firms grow to optimum size. The output of the given number of men will then increase, and the price of the commodity must fall. The average net productivity curve will be lowered, and it is then possible that the new wage, given by the maximum value on the new curve, may be below the wage (PN in Fig. 79) which obtained when the firms were of less than optimum size. As in the analogous case of monopolistic exploitation, the result will depend upon the elasticity of demand for the commodity. If the cost of other factors per man is the same in the new position as in the old, then (since we are studying the fate of a given number of men) the aggregate of other costs will be the same as before. The aggregate of wages will be equal to aggregate receipts *minus* aggregate other costs. Therefore if the elasticity of demand for the commodity is less than unity (so that total receipts are reduced by the fall in price) the total of wages (and the rate per man) will be less in the new position than in the old. If the demand is elastic, wages will be greater. If the elasticity of demand is equal to unity, wages will remain the same. This is on the assumption that the cost of other factors per man remains the same. If the cost of other factors per man is greater when the firms are of optimum size, the critical elasticity, at which wages remain the same, is greater than unity. If the cost of other factors is less, the critical elasticity is less than unity.

[1] See p. 249.　　　　　　[2] See p. 286.

4

It is possible to remove exploitation which is due to imperfection of the labour market by imposing a minimum wage, instead of by making the market for labour perfect. But this method is less likely to lead to results favourable to labour. If a minimum wage is imposed at any level higher than that which prevails in the imperfect labour market the average cost curve of labour to each firm (*AC* in Fig. 79) will be raised. Therefore if normal profits are to prevail, the average net productivity curve of labour to the individual firm must also be raised, so that the two curves remain tangential to each other. That is to say, the price of the commodity must rise and its output be reduced (by the elimination of firms unable to survive when the wage is raised). It follows that, unless the physical productivity of labour is much reduced, the amount of employment at the higher wage will be less than at the lower wage. It is therefore only in the unlikely case where physical productivity falls to a sufficient extent to compensate for the reduction in output that it is possible to impose a minimum wage without causing unemployment; while the removal of market imperfection will, as we have seen, raise wages without causing unemployment in a large range of cases.

The difference between the result obtained by imposing a minimum wage in this case and in the case of an isolated monopsonistic organisation (considered in Section 2) arises from the fact that in this case profits are assumed to be normal; that is to say, the existence of a monopsony profit has led to an increase in the number of firms and in the output of the commodity up to the point at which the earnings of the entrepreneurs (including the monopsonistic element in their profits) are reduced to the normal level; so that the rise in wages, by robbing the firms of part of their profits, must reduce the number of firms and the output of the industry in the long period.

5

We must now examine cases in which discrimination in buying labour is possible. In the following analysis we shall only deal with the case of an isolated monopoly, but the possibility of discrimination may be, as it were, superimposed upon any of the cases in which exploitation occurs as a result of imperfection in the supply of labour.

We have so far assumed, for the sake of simplicity, that all workers are alike in efficiency in the industry in which they are employed. It is now necessary to consider cases in which this assumption is not fulfilled. One type of discrimination then occurs even though the same wage is paid to each man. Suppose that the transfer wage is the same for all workers but that individual workers differ in efficiency from the point of view of the industry; then the supply of labour to the monopsonist organisation, measured in efficiency units, is not perfectly elastic, although the supply of men is perfectly elastic. The amount of employment will be so regulated that the marginal net productivity of the least efficient man is equal to the uniform wage. Discrimination will then be perfect,[1] since each man receives his transfer wage and the whole rent of labour is retained by the monopsonist. Different men represent different amounts of efficiency, and though each man is paid the same wage different efficiency units of labour are paid for at different rates. For instance, taking the efficiency of the least efficient man to represent one unit, suppose the wage to be ten shillings. Then a man twice as efficient is providing two efficiency units at five shillings per efficiency unit; a man three times as efficient is providing three units at three and fourpence per efficiency unit, and so forth. This kind of discrimination cannot be remedied by raising the wage, since this would merely raise the whole supply schedule of efficiency units of labour, and would lead to the dismissal of the least efficient men. In the new position once more the least efficient men employed would be receiving a wage equal to the marginal net productivity of an efficiency unit of labour, and more efficient men would still be paid at various lower rates per efficiency unit. Discrimination of this type could only be removed if each grade of labour was paid in proportion to its efficiency, so that men of different efficiency received different wages per day, but each unit of labour was paid at the same rate.[2]

[1] See p. 225.
[2] This apalysis may throw light on the dispute between Marshall and Mr.

6

A different type of discrimination may arise when men of the same efficiency are paid at different rates. This will occur if a separate bargain is made with each man, or with different groups of workers, and if the various men or groups differ in the minimum wage they are prepared to accept.

Let us once more assume that all men are alike in efficiency and that the supply curve of labour to the monopsonist is imperfectly elastic because it is necessary to pay higher wages to some men than to others in order to attract them to the industry. If perfect discrimination obtains, so that each individual man is paid a wage equal to his minimum transfer earnings, the curve of marginal cost of labour to the employer coincides with the supply curve of labour.[1] Employment is then adjusted so that the wage of the most expensive man is equal to the marginal net productivity of the group, but the whole rent of labour is retained by the employer. If, by the introduction of a common rule, the wages of all are raised to equal the wage of the most expensive man, the marginal and average cost of labour become equal to this wage, employment is unaltered (provided that the profit due to monopsony was a surplus above the normal profits necessary to maintain the employer in production), and the rent is transferred from the employer to the workers. If, however, it is merely stipulated that there must be a common rule, without enforcing a minimum wage, the effect is merely to remove discrimination, and employment is reduced. The marginal cost of labour is now shown by the curve marginal to the supply curve of labour to the monopsonist, and the case becomes one of simple exploitation such as we have already examined.

If the supply of labour to the individual employer is imperfectly elastic both because individual men are unlike in efficiency and because they are unlike in the minimum wage which they will accept, the amount of employment will be such that the marginal cost of an efficiency unit of labour is equal to its

and Mrs. Webb upon the "marginal productivity theory" of wages (see *Principles*, p. 705). It seems to have arisen because Mr. and Mrs. Webb failed to realise the implications of the assumptions of perfect competition, while Marshall failed to recognise the extreme unreality of those assumptions.

[1] See p. 226.

marginal net productivity to the monopsonist. In such a case it would be necessary, if exploitation is to be completely removed, both to grade workers according to their efficiency and to impose a minimum wage for each grade of efficiency.

7

Perfect discrimination is probably rare in buying labour, but imperfect discrimination may often be found. For instance there may be two types of workers (for example, men and women, or men and boys) whose efficiencies are equal,[1] but

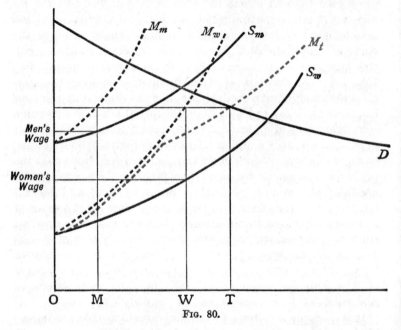

FIG. 80.

whose conditions of supply are different. It may be necessary to pay the same wage within each group, but the wages of the two groups (say of men and of women) may differ. The amount of labour employed will then be such that the marginal cost of the total amount of labour is equal to its demand price, and is equal

---

[1] This assumption is made merely for simplicity. If the efficiency of one group is less than the other in a smaller proportion than their wages, discrimination exists just as much as it does when the efficiency of each group is the same.

to the marginal cost of each type of labour; and the wage of each type will be equal to the supply price of the amount employed.[1]

Fig. 80, D is the demand curve for labour.

S_m is the supply curve of men's labour.

M_m is the marginal cost curve of men's labour.

S_w is the supply curve of women's labour.

M_w is the marginal cost curve of women's labour.

M_t is the marginal cost curve of total supply of labour obtained by summing $(M_m + M_w)$ laterally.

OT (total amount of labour employed) = OM (number of men employed) + OW (number of women employed).

A special case of discrimination arises when the men are organised in a trade union which enforces a minimum wage, and the women are not. Then the supply of men is perfectly elastic, and the supply of women is less than perfectly elastic. The amount of employment will be such that the demand price for labour is equal to the wage of the men. The marginal cost of each type of labour must be equal; [2] (see Fig. 81).

Thus the number of women employed (OW) will be such that their marginal cost is equal to the minimum wage of the men; and the number of men (WT) will make up the difference between the number of women employed and the total amount of labour employed (OT). Any rise or fall in the demand curve for labour would be met by fluctuations in the employment of men; the employment of women would remain constant (at OW) until the demand curve for labour fell so low that no men were employed at all.

This analysis of exploitation is highly simplified, but a cursory view of existing conditions seems to suggest that it may have some bearing upon actual cases. In order to analyse any actual case many refinements and complications would have to be introduced into our simple analysis, and at best it can only indicate a first approximation which may be a useful though inadequate guide to the intricacies of the real conditions of the labour market.

---

[1] See p. 224. The analysis of this and the following case is analogous with the analysis of price discrimination under monopoly, discussed in Chapter 15. Various problems, for instance, the effect upon total employment of instituting a common rule as between men and women, can be solved by the methods there developed.   [2] Cf. p. 184.

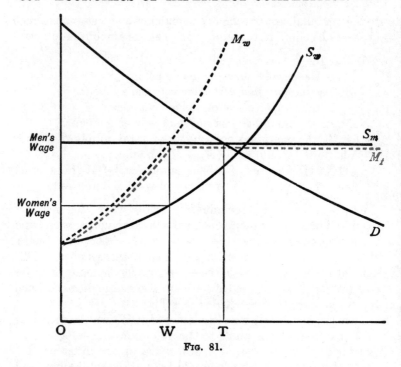

FIG. 81.

D is the demand curve for labour.

S_m is the supply curve and marginal cost curve of men's labour.

S_w is the supply curve of women's labour.

M_w is the marginal cost curve of women's labour.

M_t is the marginal cost curve of total supply of labour.

OT = total amount of labour employed.

OW = number of women employed.

WT = number of men employed.

BOOK X

A WORLD OF MONOPOLIES

CHAPTER 27

A WORLD OF MONOPOLIES

1

IT is customary, in setting out the principles of economic theory, to open with the analysis of a perfectly competitive world, and to treat monopoly as a special case. It has been the purpose of the foregoing argument to show that this process can with advantage be reversed and that it is more proper to set out the analysis of monopoly, treating perfect competition as a special case. We have been concerned, however, only with the problem of price and output for a single industry considered in isolation, and it must be conceded that for problems connected with the distribution of resources between different uses, and the distribution of the proceeds of industry between the factors of production, the assumption of competition forms a more useful starting point. For instance, we have already found it necessary to appeal to perfect competition in order to find a criterion of exploitation. But if our theory of value is to be based upon the conception of monopoly it is obviously necessary to discover what becomes of the theory of distribution upon the basis of monopoly. It is therefore necessary to attempt the analysis of a world in which every commodity is produced under monopoly. Moreover, this problem obviously has some practical relevance in the present age. We see on every side a drift towards monopolisation under the names of restriction schemes, quota systems, rationalisation, and the growth of giant companies.

Our question can only be answered precisely if it is precisely stated and the assumptions underlying it clearly set out, but

---

* *This chapter represents an excursion into the field of analysis covered by the* Economics of Welfare. *But a reader unacquainted with the work of Professor Pigou will be able to catch the drift of the argument without completely understanding its structure.*

when we have answered it upon the most abstract terms, some moral may be drawn from it which may be applicable to the actual situation.

2

In order to solve the theoretical problem in its simplest form a number of assumptions must be made which will be removed as we examine various aspects of the problem.

The most convenient assumptions at the first stage are these:

(1) There are n industries producing n commodities for each of which the conditions of demand and supply are exactly similar. Each commodity will be to some extent a substitute for every other, but none will be a perfect substitute. Thus, if a certain volume of incomes is being spent on commodities, so that the elasticity of demand for all taken together is equal to unity, the elasticity of demand for each considered separately will be greater than unity.

(2) There is a fixed total amount of each factor of production. This entails that there are a given number of workers of given efficiency, who always work equally hard for the same number of hours throughout the story; and that there is no net addition to capital throughout the story. The existing stock of capital is kept intact by replacement but can be changed in form if it is profitable to do so.[1]

(3) The supply of each factor to every industry considered separately is perfectly elastic, and there are no economies of large-scale industry. Thus each of our n commodities is produced under constant returns, and the proportions of the factors employed do not alter with changes in output. The supply of each commodity taken separately is perfectly elastic, and of all taken together perfectly inelastic.

(4) We take as the basis for the comparison a world in which there is perfect competition in every way.

---

[1] The problem of measuring the stock of capital presented no difficulty as long as we were concerned only with a single industry, for then it was possible to measure capital in money value (assuming the general rate of interest to be constant), but when we have to deal with the total stock of capital the problem presents difficulties which no attempt is here made to solve.

(5) The community which we are considering is a closed system.

(6) We treat only of positions of full equilibrium, that is to say, of positions in which there is no spontaneous tendency towards any alteration in the existing state of affairs.

(7) The monopolists who come into the story have no function except the control of output. Each consists of a controlling agency which has negligible running costs and is capable of an indefinitely large output. When such an agency comes into command of an industry the general structure of the industry in separate firms is maintained, though the constitution and outputs of the firms may be altered if it is profitable to do so. The head of the firm is retained as a manager, and is paid as a salary whatever sum would have constituted his transfer profit to a competitive industry.[1] The profits of the monopoly may be divided up in any sort of way we please to imagine, after they have been secured. Management, in the sense of the managers of the firms, must be treated on the same footing as the other factors, but it may be the same individuals who were the entrepreneurs under competition who share in the spoils of the monopolists. This assumption about the nature of the monopolists will not be removed throughout the argument.

(8) There is no collusion between monopolists. Each tries to maximise his own profits without regard to the interests of the others.

3

Now, starting from the position of perfect competition, suppose that each of these n commodities comes into the hand of a monopolist, everything else remaining the same. At first sight we might be inclined to suppose that the monopolists would reduce the output of everything; for instance, that if all the demand curves were straight lines half of the former output of each commodity would be produced. But this is obviously absurd. Half of the supply of each factor of production would be unemployed, and there would not be equilibrium—there

---

[1] Cf. p. 171.

would be a tendency for the rewards of the factors to be reduced. But the supposition that all outputs would be restricted is absurd for another reason. When we are considering one industry in isolation, we can find the monopoly output with the existing demand curve, but if output is restricted in all industries all demand curves will alter. The method which applies to one industry separately cannot be applied to all taken together.

It is not to our present purpose to discuss how equilibrium would be attained. There is no natural tendency even under competition to maintain full employment, which depends upon the levels of saving and of investment. We are here only concerned to discuss an economic system in equilibrium, and we must suppose that both under competition and under monopoly the conditions necessary to full employment are maintained.[1]

If all the factors of production are in full employment under the monopolists, it follows from our assumptions that the national dividend will be the same as before, since there is a fixed amount of each factor of production and all commodities are alike in respect of their conditions of demand and supply. Further, since we have assumed that the supply of each factor to each industry is perfectly elastic, it follows that the proportions in which the factors are employed is the same as before, so that their relative rewards are unaltered. But the distribution of the national dividend will have been altered, and the factors of production will be exploited.

We have defined exploitation as a state of affairs in which the

---

[1] We have assumed that the stock of capital is not increasing (assumption 2). It is therefore necessary to equilibrium that the gross amount of saving should be just sufficient to provide for the depreciation of the existing stock. If investment and net saving are both assumed to be equal to zero in equilibrium, it is only necessary to suppose that the owners of the factors of production continue to spend some money when they become unemployed (so that net saving becomes negative) in order to see how equilibrium would be attained. The total money cost of the output of all goods would be equal to the total earnings of the employed factors *plus* the incomes of the monopolists. But the total money expenditure on all goods would be the earnings of the employed factors *plus* the incomes of the monopolists *plus* the expenditure of any factors which were unemployed. As soon as unemployment occurred, therefore, there would be a tendency for prices to rise and output to increase, until the unemployment disappeared and equilibrium was restored. If net savings are not equal to zero, the level of investment must be assumed to be so adjusted that equilibrium is ensured. Then if there was full employment under competition, in equilibrium conditions, there will be full employment under the monopolists.

wage of a factor is less than the value of its marginal physical product,[1] and we have distinguished two types of exploitation, monopolistic exploitation which arises when the demand curve for the commodity is not perfectly elastic, and monopsonistic exploitation which arises when the supply curve of the factor is not perfectly elastic to the individual employer. We are at present assuming that the supply curves of the factors are perfectly elastic to the separate industries, that is to say, to each monopolist; thus it is only with monopolistic exploitation that we are for the moment concerned.

Under perfect competition the factors received their marginal physical product multiplied by the price of the commodity they produce. Thus if we take the price of the commodity in each industry as an index number of all prices, the factors received in real wages their marginal physical product. Under the régime of the monopolists their money wages are equal to their marginal physical product multiplied by marginal revenue.[2] Thus their real wages may be represented as marginal physical product multiplied by $\dfrac{\text{marginal revenue}}{\text{price}}$ in each industry. Under the conditions that we are at present assuming, the marginal physical productivity will be unchanged by the advent of the monopolists. Thus the earnings of the factors have been reduced in the ratio of marginal revenue to price. For instance, suppose that the money wages of all factors of production remain the same when the monopolies are set up. The costs of all commodities will then be unaltered, and in order to ensure full employment the prices of all commodities must rise until the new marginal revenue from each commodity is equal to its old price,[3] so that the output of each commodity under monopoly (at which marginal revenue is equal to cost) is equal to its former output under competition (at which price is equal to cost). The price level will then have risen in the ratio of price to marginal revenue in the new position, and the real earnings of the factors will be reduced in the same ratio, since their money earnings remain unchanged.

[1] See p. 283.   [2] See p. 237.
[3] We must suppose that the quantity of money can be freely increased in order to support the new price level. In equilibrium the total money value of the national dividend (which is unchanged in physical magnitude) will be greater than before by the amount of the total incomes of the monopolists.

The extent to which the factors are exploited will depend upon the elasticity of demand for the commodities. The ratio of marginal revenue to price is equal to $\dfrac{\epsilon - 1}{\epsilon}$ where ϵ is the elasticity of demand.[1] It follows that the smaller the elasticity of demand for the separate commodities the greater will be the degree of exploitation. Thus, if the elasticity of demand is, say, 20, the factors receive as real wages $\dfrac{19}{20}$ of their marginal products, but if the elasticity of demand is equal to 2 they receive only half of their marginal physical products.

4

Already from this highly abstract case, we can draw a moral for the real world. First, it is worth while to notice that in the position just described each monopolist would be earning normal profits, for the normal profit in each industry is the profit which can be earned elsewhere, and the reward of enterprise would be no higher in any one industry than in any other. The wages of labour would be fair in the sense that work of equal skill would receive the same reward in all industries.[2] If we looked at each industry separately, we should see that the wages of the factors were equal to average as well as to marginal net productivity, for in calculating average net productivity we should be obliged to subtract from the gross product the normal profits of the entrepreneur, which are now everywhere swollen by monopoly gains. Any arbitrary rise of wages in a single trade would lead to unemployment. The wage would then be "uneconomically high", and it would be generally considered desirable to lower it again. No ordinary touchstone would be able to tell us that anything was amiss. Yet the factors of production would all be exploited, and the monopolists would be keeping the spoil.

Secondly, our abstract case has shown that the factors of production are more likely to be exploited the larger is the unit of control which employs them. As we have seen, the degree of

---

[1] See p. 36.

[2] *Economics of Welfare*, p. 549. Professor Pigou's definition of *fair* wages includes the absence of exploitation, for he envisages a world of perfect competition.

exploitation is greater the smaller the elasticity of demand for the commodities. And the elasticity of demand is likely to be less the greater is the unit of control in industry. When the unit of control is one firm selling in competition with others the elasticity of demand for its particular output is likely to be very high, even if the market is not so perfect that the elasticity is infinite. The output of each firm in the same line of business will be a close substitute for the output of every other, and the elasticity of demand for each of them will be great. But if the unit of control consists of a combination of all the firms producing some well-defined commodity for which the substitutes are different articles rather than different brands of the same article, the elasticity of demand must be considerably less. Moreover, the smaller the number of firms producing any one commodity the smaller will be the elasticity of demand for the output of any one of them.[1]

Our abstract analysis must therefore lead to the reflection that the prevalence of imperfect competition in the real world sets up a tendency to exploitation, and that this tendency must be greatly strengthened by the formation of large combines absorbing a large number of formerly competing firms. As we have seen, the degree of exploitation due to imperfect competition may be very great. Even with an elasticity of demand as great as two, the factors receive only half the perfectly competitive real wage.

5

We must next examine the effect of removing the third assumption, that the supply of the factors is perfectly elastic to each industry, while retaining the assumption that there are no economies of large-scale industry.

We found in Chapter 14 that when the elasticities of supply of various factors to a particular industry are not all alike a monopolist will alter the competitive proportions of the factors

---

[1] Further, the elasticity of demand for the output of any one firm is likely to be less the smaller is the total number of firms in all industries. If the unit of control is everywhere large, so that the total number of firms is small, then a rise in price by any one firm will cause an appreciable rise in the prices charged by all other firms. And if a rise in the price of the commodity produced by one firm raises the price of rival commodities the elasticity of demand for the commodity whose price is raised will be less than it would be if the prices of other commodities were unaltered.

and produce a given output at lower average cost. It might at first sight appear, therefore, even if we start from a position of perfect competition, that when the industries are working under rising costs our monopolists will be able to improve upon the competitive method of production and that the national dividend would be increased. This, however, would be a false inference. We cannot deduce results applicable to all industries taken together from results applicable to one industry in isolation by a simple process of multiplication.

Let us suppose that the industries are all alike, but that the supply of some factors is less elastic, and of some more elastic, to every industry. Then, looking at the matter from the point of view of one industry, we can see that the monopolist will restrict his use of the factors which are in less elastic supply. The effect will be to lower the price of these factors and to cause part of them to become unemployed. But this will lower the transfer cost of these factors to all other industries, and their reward will be reduced in each industry, until they are absorbed into employment. The proportions of the factors, in each industry, will be the same as before, and the same national dividend as before will be produced. The only effect will be that the relative rewards of the factors will be altered. Those which are in less elastic supply will be worse off than those which are in more elastic supply. In short, by postulating an imperfectly elastic supply of factors to an industry, we have admitted the possibility of monopsonistic exploitation.

The marginal cost of each factor will be equal to its marginal physical productivity multiplied by marginal revenue. Since the proportions are unaltered, marginal physical productivity is the same as before, and the real wage is reduced (below the competitive wage) first in the ratio of marginal revenue to price, and secondly in the ratio of average to marginal cost of the factor to each industry.[1] Now the average cost of the factor (the money wage) can be expressed as $M\dfrac{E}{E+1}$ where M is marginal cost and E is the numerical value of the elasticity of supply.[2] Thus the real wage of each factor under the

---

[1] See p. 294.
[2] See p. 36. The formula is modified in this way because the elasticity of a rising curve is treated as negative.

monopolists will be equal to the competitive wage multiplied by $\left(\dfrac{\epsilon-1}{\epsilon}\right)\left(\dfrac{E}{E+1}\right)$, where ϵ is the elasticity of demand and E is the numerical value of the elasticity of supply of the factor. Thus those factors whose supply is relatively less elastic will be most exploited.[1]

Moreover if the supply of a factor is less than perfectly elastic to a particular industry, it is possible that the monopolist may discriminate in buying it,[2] so that the factors of production may be deprived of the rents which they earned under competition.

Thus we may add to the moral which we draw from the abstract analysis that perfect competition not only in selling commodities, but in buying the factors of production, is advantageous to the factors, and that any increase in the size of the unit of control, by reducing the elasticity of supply of the factors to the employing agency, will increase the degree of exploitation.

6

So far we have been concerned with the effect of monopoly upon the distribution of the national dividend. In order to isolate this problem we have assumed that all industries are alike. We must now examine the effect of monopoly upon the distribution of resources between various uses, and to do so we must remove our simplifying assumption. This can be done most conveniently in three stages. We shall first retain the assumption that the elasticities of demand are all equal and examine the case in which there are no economies of large-scale industry, but in which the elasticity of supply of each factor is different to different industries. Then, supposing that there are no scarce factors (from the point of view of an individual industry) we shall examine the effect of economies of large scale. And finally we shall remove the assumption that the elasticities of demand are all alike,

First, suppose that to some industries the supply of any one

---

[1] The existence of economies of large-scale industry would have the same effect as an increase in the elasticity of supply of the factors, and would reduce the degree of exploitation.

[2] See p. 301.

factor is more elastic than it is to others. Then (assuming that the monopolists pay some rent for the factor) the use of it will be restricted in those industries to which its supply is least elastic. Its reward will therefore fall, and its use in those industries to which its supply is more elastic will increase. There will thus be a change in the composition of the national dividend. The factors will be diverted from those uses to which their supply is relatively less elastic to those where it is relatively more elastic. Now, it can be shown that the optimum distribution of resources between industries is achieved under conditions of perfect competition,[1] for, under perfect competition, the value of the marginal physical product of resources is equal in all uses, so long as there are no economies of large-scale industry. Therefore (so long as we retain the assumption of no economies) the distribution brought about by monopoly will be different from the optimum, and the national dividend will be reduced.

But when there are economies of large-scale industry the optimum distribution of resources is not achieved under competition, since the value of the marginal physical product of resources is greater (under competition) in those industries which are subject to economies than in those which are not.[2] Suppose that there are no scarce factors, and that different industries are subject to economies of large scale to varying degrees. Then, under the monopolists, the output of commodities most subject to economies will be increased, and the output of commodities subject to less degree of economies will be contracted until the marginal productivity of resources is everywhere the same,[3] and the optimum distribution of resources will be brought about by the

---

[1] The argument of the *Economics of Welfare* is the basis of the above analysis. But it is clearly necessary to ignore Professor Pigou's references to an "archetypal industry" which need not exist in fact (*op. cit.* p. 215), and to interpret his analysis as applying to a world in which the generality of industries are conducted under perfect competition. The optimum distribution of resources will be attained provided that the marginal cost to the individual employer is equal to the marginal cost to society (*loc. cit.* p. 802) and this will, in general, be attained (in the absence of economies of large scale) under perfect competition. Exceptions occur (even when there are no economies of large scale) in the case of costs (such as the smoke nuisance or industrial disease) which are not borne by the employer. See also p. 318 below.

[2] Pigou, *op. cit.*

[3] The assumption that all elasticities of demand are equal is necessary to this conclusion, for it is only then that the equality of marginal productivities entails the equality of the values of marginal physical productivities.

monopolists. Thus we find that in respect of rising costs the monopolists do harm and in respect of falling costs they do good. When both are present together the net effect of monopolisation may be either to improve upon the competitive distribution of resources or the reverse, and on balance the national dividend may be either increased or diminished.

7

We have so far retained the assumption that the elasticities of demand are all equal. The effect of removing this assumption can be isolated by reverting to the assumption that all commodities are produced under constant cost. We may now suppose that though the elasticity of demand for each commodity is the same before and after the advent of the monopolists,[1] the elasticities of demand of different commodities are different.

Now in a world of absolutely perfect competition without economies of large-scale industry, the marginal cost to society of every commodity is equal to its price.[2] And the price of each commodity is equal to its marginal utility to the individual buyer. Thus we may say (leaping a dangerous chasm into which we must peer in a moment) that under perfectly competitive conditions the marginal utility of every commodity is equal to its marginal cost to society. Resources are thus distributed so that a unit of resources will yield the same marginal utility[3] in every direction, and the maximum of satisfaction is obtained from a given supply of resources. But under conditions of monopoly it is not price but marginal revenue which is equal to marginal cost. Under the monopolists resources will be distributed so that the marginal revenue obtained by employing

---

[1] The advent of the monopolists alters the distribution of incomes and so would be likely to change the elasticity of demand of many commodities. And this would have some further repercussions. If the things consumed by the monopolists are mainly produced under increasing cost, and the things consumed by the exploited factors under decreasing cost, the position of the factors will be still worse. If the things consumed by the monopolists are produced under decreasing cost they will gain a further advantage, but there will be no offset to the exploited factors. We can abstract from this effect either by supposing that the monopolists consume all commodities in the same proportions as the rest of the community, or by supposing that the profits of the monopolists are taxed away from them and distributed as a bonus to the rest of the community.

[2] Pigou, *op. cit.* p. 802.

[3] See p. 214 for the difficulties involved in this conception.

a unit of resources is everywhere the same, and marginal revenue is not equal to marginal utility. If the elasticities of demand of the commodities are not all equal, the ratio of marginal utility (measured by price) to marginal revenue will be different in different industries and the marginal utilities (from an increment of resources) will not be everywhere equal. The output of commodities for which the demand curves are relatively more elastic will be expanded, and there will be a further reason to expect that the composition of the national dividend will be changed. If the national dividend in the first position under perfect competition yields the maximum satisfaction from the given resources, the national dividend under monopoly will yield less than the maximum.

But is this picture of the ideal distribution of resources under competition really justified? We leapt over a very doubtful step in the argument when we supposed that it was. To a strictly logical mind any discussion of utility to more than one individual is repugnant. It is not really justifiable to talk about maximum satisfaction to a whole population. But common sense protests that if we treat all individuals as being exactly alike it is then permissible to sum their satisfactions, and that human beings, in their economic needs, are sufficiently alike to make the discussion of aggregate satisfaction interesting. Upon this basis we may say that if any two individuals have the same real income they derive the same satisfaction from it. We may further say that if one individual has a larger real income than another the marginal utility of income to him is less. Now in the world of perfect competition, with constant cost for each commodity, all marginal costs are equal to prices, and prices are equal to marginal utilities, measured in terms of money. If income is perfectly equally distributed its marginal utility is equal for every individual. Therefore the distribution of resources is then such that satisfaction is at a maximum. Thus to represent the competitive world as an ideal state we have had to introduce the highly unreal assumption that wealth is equally distributed. If it is not equally distributed, there is no reason to suppose that the satisfaction obtained from given resources is at a maximum in a perfectly competitive world.

Our world of monopolists therefore has not after all such a very high standard with which to compete. But even when we

A WORLD OF MONOPOLIES

abstract from the change in distribution of wealth brought about by the monopolists, it seems on the whole justifiable to say that the composition of the national dividend under monopoly will be even further from the ideal than it was under competition, since both will be subject to the maldistribution of resources due to unequal wealth, and the dividend under monopoly will be subject to a further maldistribution due to the different divergences of marginal revenue from price.

The monopolists would be freed from this charge, and might even improve upon the competitive distribution of resources, if it were the case that the demand for commodities consumed by richer classes of consumers was generally less elastic than for commodities consumed by poorer classes. The production of goods consumed by the poorer owners of the factors would then be expanded, and their prices lowered, relatively to those of goods consumed by richer owners of the factors. There may be some reason to suppose that this is the case. But it is probable that demands tend to be more elastic when the market is made up of a larger number of income groups, and to be less elastic both when the market is composed entirely of rich individuals and when it is composed entirely of poor individuals. If there are two equally homogeneous markets the demand in the poorer market is likely to be the more elastic, but if the poorer markets are the more homogeneous the elasticity of demand for goods consumed by poorer individuals may be less than for goods consumed by richer individuals. The change in the composition of the national dividend brought about by the monopolists would then enhance and not mitigate the maldistribution of wealth.

One further point remains to be considered. We have seen that some factors will be exploited more than others. The individuals who provide the factors for which the supply to individual industries is relatively less elastic and which are therefore most exploited may be richer than those which provide the less exploited factors. This would tend to mitigate the maldistribution of wealth. For instance, if land is relatively more exploited than labour, and if landlords are richer than workmen, there will be a tendency in this direction. In so far as labour is strongly organised in trade unions while the supply of land to a particular industry is often imperfectly elastic, it is

probable that land is more exploitable than labour. But the
factor of production which is at once the poorest and the most
exploitable is unorganised unskilled labour. It is therefore unlikely that monopolists can claim much credit for a beneficial
redistribution of wealth between the factors of production.

8

In comparing the world of monopolies with a world of perfect
competition we have found that monopoly may have an unfavourable effect upon the distribution of resources between
different uses and must have an unfavourable effect upon the
distribution of wealth between individuals. But we cannot conclude that the spread of monopolistic combinations in the real
world must be harmful until we have compared monopoly with
imperfect competition, for in the real world competition is not
perfect. Let us suppose, once more, that the demand curves and
cost curves for each of the n commodities are alike, but let us
suppose that, before the arrival of the monopolists, the market
within each of the n industries is imperfect.

There are then n groups of firms; the individual demand curve
of each firm will be more elastic than the demand curve for the
commodity, but not perfectly elastic, and if profits are normal
for each group, the firms are all of less than optimum size.[1]
When the group of firms comes into the hand of a monopolist
he will be able to organise the industry more efficiently. If, as
we have supposed, the supply of each factor to the industry is
perfectly elastic, the monopolist will reproduce exactly the
methods of production that would obtain in a perfect market,
efficiency will be increased, and costs of production will fall.[2]

The reorganisation of the industries may bring about the
specialisation of firms by the process of lateral and vertical disintegration, and there may be a very great increase in efficiency.
But even if there are no possibilities of reorganisation of this
sort there may be an increase in efficiency. If each firm in the
world of imperfect competition was producing a homogeneous
commodity (so that there is no possibility of lateral disinte-

[1] See p. 97.
[2] Cf. p. 169. The manner in which perfect competition ensures the maximum
efficiency of industry is further discussed in the Appendix on Increasing and
Diminishing Returns.

gration) by a single process (so that there is no possibility of vertical disintegration), then there may still be economies for the monopolists to introduce, for in the world of imperfect competition the firms would be of less than optimum size. If technical economies could be gained from growth in the size of the firms the monopolists would reorganise industries in fewer and larger productive units and the average physical productivity of the factors would be increased.[1]

But even if the average physical productivity of the factors is raised it does not necessarily follow that their marginal physical productivity will be raised, since marginal physical productivity must begin to fall (as the output of firm increases) before average physical productivity.[2] It is only if the firms, under imperfect competition, were so small that marginal physical productivity was rising that there is any possibility of a gain to the factors of production from a mere growth in the size of the firms.[3]

Thus a growth in the size of the firms may increase the marginal physical productivities if the firms were sufficiently small under imperfect competition, and the reorganisation of the industries by vertical and lateral disintegration is likely to increase them. There may thus be some offset against the additional exploitation, and, on balance, the factors may

---

[1] The saving in cost brought about by a growth in the size of the firms may be divided into two parts: technical economies due to the larger scale of production, and the economy of spreading the fixed cost of the entrepreneur over a larger output. Thus even if the firms in the world of imperfect competition were of such a size that there were no technical economies to be gained from growth, they would still be of less than optimum size. There would be a tendency for the monopolist to increase the size of the productive units in order to reduce cost by spreading the reward of the entrepreneur (who takes service under the monopolist as a manager) over a larger output. But we have supposed that the supply of entrepreneurs is perfectly inelastic to industry as a whole. The attempt of the monopolists to increase the size of firms and dismiss some entrepreneurs would therefore be countered by a reduction in the reward of the entrepreneurs. This would reduce the optimum size of the firms, and if all the entrepreneurs are employed by the monopolists their reward will be reduced to the point at which the new optimum size of the firms is equal to their former actual size. Thus the size of the firms will be unaltered.

But if there are technical economies to be gained from a growth in the size of firms the monopolists would not employ the full number of entrepreneurs even if their reward was reduced to zero. The firms would then be larger in size and some of the entrepreneurs would be permanently unemployed or would be obliged to seek some other occupation, such as unskilled labour.

[2] Cf. Fig. 71, p. 246.

[3] The relative positions of the factors may be altered by a growth in the size of the firms. Cf. p. 288.

Y

even gain from the advent of the monopolists. In both positions the factors receive as real wages their marginal physical product $\times \dfrac{\text{marginal revenue}}{\text{price}}$. In the new position the ratio of marginal revenue to price is less than before, since the demand curve for the commodity is less elastic than the demand curve for the output of the individual firm, but it is possible that. marginal physical productivity will have increased (because of the increase in efficiency) to an extent sufficient to balance or overbalance this loss. The absolute real income of the factors may therefore be increased, and they may have cause after all to be grateful to the monopolists.

But there is a strong presumption that the factors will not gain. Marginal physical productivity will only be increased by the mere growth of the firms if competition was very imperfect, and the firms very small, before the monopolists reorganised the industries. And though it is probable that the disintegration of firms will increase marginal physical productivity it is only when marginal physical productivity increases by more than the increase in the ratio of price to marginal revenue that the factors can gain from the advent of the monopolists.

By removing the assumption that the market in each commodity was perfect in the first position we have put fresh powers into the hands of the monopolists. If the conditions which made the markets imperfect persist, the monopolists will be able to discriminate in selling each commodity, in a way which was impossible in the first case when we took perfect competition as the basis of the comparison, since the same causes which make the market imperfect make discrimination possible.[1]

If the monopolists can discriminate their profits will be larger, and they will gain at the expense of the factors of production not only in paying them a lower wage but also in allowing them a smaller consumer's surplus on their purchases.[2] At the

---

[1] See p. 180.

[2] We found when we were considering a single monopoly in isolation that the power to discriminate in selling will sometimes lead to a larger output, sometimes to a smaller output, and sometimes to the same output as would occur if the monopolist could only sell at a single price (see Chapter 15, Section 5). If our n industries in the monopolised world conform to the conditions of those cases where the output for one industry tends to increase, the difference between marginal revenue and price to the monopolists will be

same time, although taken as a whole consumers are worse off, some members of the community will be better off than under a system of simple monopoly. It is impossible to set the damage to those individuals who have to pay higher prices against the gains of those who pay lower prices. But since there is a presumption that those to whom higher prices are charged will be on the whole richer than the rest, the monopolists, in playing the part of Robin Hood, may once more be conceded to have some redeeming features.

9

If we remove our second assumption that no capital accumulation occurs, the other factors of production will enjoy a further offset against the damage done to them by the monopolists. It may be assumed that the class sharing in the monopoly gains consists of fewer individuals than the owners of the factors of production, and since their earnings will be increased by all that the other factors are forced to forgo, the distribution of wealth will have become more unequal than it was before. If capital accumulation is to be allowed into our scheme, it is therefore on the whole probable that it will go on faster than before, although the lower rate of interest may reduce the volume of saving coming from those who were providing new capital under the competitive régime. The lower return to capital will be a disadvantage to former capital owners, but the increase in the amount of capital will increase the national dividend, and it will tend to increase the real wages of labour progressively through time. The fact that an unequal distribution of wealth promotes saving is not, of course, a justification for inequality (if saving can be secured in any other way), but it is a redeeming feature of inequality, and to this extent our monopolists may be given credit for it.

10

It may appear rash to draw any conclusion applicable to the real world from the highly abstract analysis which we have

less than under simple monopoly. The degree of exploitation will therefore be less, but it will not be sufficiently less to offset the loss of consumers' surplus, since the monopoly profit must in any case be larger under discrimination than under simple monopoly.

made. But one general result appears to emerge from it. We find in comparing a world of monopolised industries with a world of imperfect competition that there may be very considerable improvements in the technique of production when the unit of control in industry increases in size. But we find that an increase in the size of the unit of control will lead to an increase in the inequality of the distribution of wealth. The problem of the world of monopolists thus resolves itself into the familiar dilemma between efficiency and justice. In order to form a judgment upon the present-day movement towards monopoly we must decide whether it is worth while to put power into the hands of large concerns for the sake of the increase in productivity which they promise to bring about. This is a problem which no amount of abstract analysis can help us to solve. It resolves itself into two questions. The first is a question of fact. How great will the economies of monopolisation actually be— how great is the improvement in the organisation of industry that we may expect from an enlargement of the unit of control? It is clearly of the utmost importance to evaluate the gains which may be expected from monopolisation, before we can decide whether it is worth while to submit to the possible dangers which it entails. The second question is one of judgment. What gain in the efficiency of production would be sufficient to make us consider that monopolisation was desirable?

The first question is outside the scope of a theoretical treatise. A great and detailed knowledge of the exact technical situation in many industries would be necessary before any estimate could be formed of the economies to be expected from monopolisation. But it is legitimate, even for the theorist, to suggest that different types of monopoly hold out very different hopes of technical reorganisation. When a scheme takes the form of machine-wrecking pure and simple, as in the case of the National Shipbuilders' Security, Limited, or of restriction of output by quotas without any concentration, as under the Coal Mines Act of 1930, there seems little reason to expect any increase in efficiency; whereas an organisation which exercises a detailed control over a large number of productive concerns may have very great possibilities of technical improvement.

The second question involves a matter of personal judgment upon which everyone must have his own opinion. But it is im-

portant to remember that a question does arise, the question
of balancing the possible efficiency of monopoly against the
dangers of an increased maldistribution of wealth. It is not
sufficient to show that monopolisation will increase efficiency in
order to show that it is desirable.

11

Three of the assumptions necessary to the most abstract case
remain to be discussed.

First, there remains the assumption that the world of monopolies consists of a closed system within which the supply of
factors is perfectly inelastic, each taken as a whole. If this
assumption is removed it becomes probable that the advent of
the monopolists will reduce the national dividend. If labour, for
instance, is strongly organised in trade unions which stand out
for a certain real wage the advent of the monopolists, by reducing real wages, will cause unemployment. And if capital can be
invested abroad in countries where it can earn a higher reward
there will be (in the long period) a reduction in the amount of
capital available for the monopolised industries. In either case
the national dividend will be reduced when the real reward of
the factor in question is lowered by the introduction of the
monopolies.

Secondly, we have not discussed the assumption that full
equilibrium is maintained with full employment of the factors
of production. An examination of this subject would carry us
outside the sphere of this book. But the study of a world of
monopolies cannot be completed until we know, first, whether
the introduction of monopolies is likely in itself to upset
equilibrium, and secondly, whether there would be at least as
good a chance of maintaining equilibrium under a system of
monopolies, once they have been established, as there is in the
actual world. It may be that a sudden and widespread introduction of restriction schemes will lead to very prolonged and
perhaps permanent unemployment. And it may be that the
very imperfect mechanisms by which full employment can be
re-established under competitive conditions would be even less
effective under a régime of monopoly. In either case a very
important item would have to be added to the list of the disad-

vantages of monopolies which must be set against the possible improvements in technique that they may introduce.

Finally, there remains our last assumption, that there is no collusion amongst the monopolists. If they were to make common cause the wages of the factors might sink to almost any level, since the supply of each factor, taken as a whole, is highly inelastic. The powers of the monopolists would then be so great that they would only be restrained from exercising them by the fear of provoking a revolution on the part of the owners of the factors of production, and no precise analysis is possible of what would occur.

CONCLUSION

THE purpose of this book has been to provide a box of tools for the analytical economist. The area within which these tools can work is very narrowly bounded. A number of unsolved problems lie behind and before the problems with which they are adapted to deal. Behind lie the fundamental problems on whose solution depends the validity of the whole supply-and-demand-curve analysis. To these general questions the tools, in the nature of the case, can have no contribution to make. But even within their own sphere the tools can do no work unless they are given some materials to work on. The imaginary examples of the shapes and movements of demand curves and costs curves, constructed in order to display the apparatus, serve to show the kind of results that the tools could produce if they were given some realistic matter on which to exercise their ingenuity. Ahead lie a number of problems for which fresh tools may be required, but which are soluble at the same level of abstraction as the problems here discussed. Beyond them again lie the problems which require some more complicated technique, such as could survive at a lower level of abstraction.

The level of abstraction maintained in this book is distressingly high. The technique can only survive in an atmosphere rarefied by the adoption of very severe simplifying assumptions. The reader who is interested in results immediately applicable to the real world has every right to complain that these tools are of little use to him. The knives are of bone and the hammers of wood, only capable of cutting paper and driving pins into cardboard. But the analytical economist who is prepared to work stage by stage towards the still far-distant ideal of constructing an analysis which will be capable of solving the problems presented by the real world may perhaps find in this tool-box some implements which will serve his turn.

APPENDIX

1

In the foregoing analysis we have made use of the supply curves of particular commodities and of the supply curves of factors of production to particular industries. But these conceptions involve some fundamental questions which we have not discussed. It is possible to make use of a large part of the technical apparatus set out in this book whatever view on these fundamental questions may be adopted, and the attempt to solve them in the following pages is only a provisional one.

2

A rising cost curve of a commodity is sometimes described as *diminishing returns*, and a falling cost curve as *increasing returns*. This leads to confusion.[1] Increasing and diminishing returns are more usefully regarded as general principles which may be brought into operation by influences applying to a factor of production, considered separately. The cost of a commodity is built up of the costs of the productive units employed in making it. A rise or a fall in cost (with increases of output) can only come about because the cost, per unit of product, of some item—labour, land, capital, or enterprise—has increased or diminished. As output increases, some of the factors may be found to fulfil the conditions which bring the Law of Increasing Returns into operation, and some the Law of Diminishing Returns. The net result may be a state of affairs in which all the cost curves distinguished in Chapter 10 are rising, or all falling, or some rising and some falling.

[1] Professor Pigou recommends the use of the phrases "increasing supply price" and "decreasing supply price" on the ground that the word "cost" is ambiguous, since it sometimes occurs that average cost is falling, while marginal cost is rising, or average cost rising while marginal cost is falling (*Economics of Welfare*, p. 217). "Supply price," however, is open to the more fundamental objection that it has no meaning for a single firm. It is impossible to speak of the supply price of a monopolist. The best course appears to be to speak of increasing and decreasing cost, and to specify where necessary which cost curve is in question. In the above passage, average long-period cost is the relevant cost.

It is one purpose of this appendix to argue that for a single industry increasing and diminishing returns can be represented in a perfectly symmetrical manner in terms of the supply curves of the factors of production, drawn up in efficiency units appropriately chosen, and they have been treated in this way in the foregoing chapters. But in their nature increasing and diminishing returns are not symmetrical, and we must now examine how they arise.

3

The Law of Diminishing Returns, as it is usually formulated, states that with a fixed amount of any one factor of production [1] successive increases in the amount of other factors will after a point yield a diminishing increment of the product. Looking at the matter from the point of view of cost of production, if one factor is fixed in amount and increased amounts of the other factors are used with it, and if no improvement in the efficiency or reduction in the price of these other factors is introduced by the increase in the amount used, after a point the cost of production per unit of output will rise.

At first sight this law appears so obvious as to require no further explanation, but it is possible to restate it in a manner which throws more light on its real meaning. A moment's reflection will show that what the Law of Diminishing Returns really states is that there is a limit to the extent to which one factor of production çan be substituted for another, or, in other words, that the elasticity of substitution between factors is not infinite. [2] If this were not true it would be possible, when one factor of production is fixed in amount and the rest are in perfectly elastic supply, to produce part of the output with the aid of the fixed factor, and then, when the optimum proportion between this and other factors was attained, to substitute some other factor for it and to increase output at constant cost.

Thus the Law of Diminishing Returns entails that the various elements required for the production of any commodity should be divided into groups, each group being a factor of production, in such a way that the elasticity of substitution between one factor and another is less than infinite. The Law of Diminishing Returns

---

[1] The association of the Law of Diminishing Returns with the factor land only arose because land, from the point of view of society as a whole, is by definition fixed in amount. When we are studying the supply curve of a single commodity, there is no reason to expect that land, rather than any other factor, will be scarce. All that the law tells us is that where there is a scarce factor there will be diminishing returns, and labour, capital, and enterprise are just as much subject to it as land.

[2] Elasticity of substitution is defined on p. 256. But for our present purpose it is more convenient to adopt the equivalent but more fundamental definition : the proportionate change in the ratio of the amounts of the factors divided by the proportionate change in the ratio of their marginal physical productivities.

then follows from the definition of a factor of production, and requires no further proof.

Increasing cost for a particular commodity will arise whenever one of the factors of production, defined in this way, is not in perfectly elastic supply to the industry producing that commodity. In the limiting case the supply of a factor may be perfectly inelastic.

Given the elasticity of supply of the scarce factor, the extent to which the cost of the commodity will rise, as output increases, will depend upon the elasticity of substitution. If, in the extreme case, there is no elasticity of substitution, so that the production of the commodity requires constant proportions of the factors, the cost curve of the commodity will rise as steeply as the supply curve of the scarce factor. If the scarce factor is rigidly fixed in amount, the supply of the commodity will be perfectly inelastic, and no increase in its output will be possible.

In more usual cases some substitution will be possible and the proportions of the factors will be altered. The cost curve of the commodity will then rise less steeply than the supply curve of the scarce factor, and some increase in output would be possible even though the scarce factor was rigidly fixed in amount. The rise in the cost of the commodity, as output increases, will be less the greater the elasticity of substitution.[1]

An example will make these propositions clear. Suppose that there is a single site available for building a house. Then, if capital and builders' labour were perfect substitutes for land, an infinitely high sky-scraper could be erected on this site at constant cost, and there would be no Law of Diminishing Returns. At the other extreme, if no substitution was possible, only a bungalow could be built on the site, and no increase in the demand for house-room, however great, could lead to an increase in its output. In any ordinary case the proportions of the factors can be altered, but not without limit, and the construction of house-room on a given site is carried out at increasing cost.

Because the proportions of the factors are usually altered (as output increases) when one of them is scarce, the Law of Diminishing Returns is associated with changes in the proportions of the factors. But it is clear that diminishing returns are not due fundamentally to changes in the proportions of the factors, but to the fact that there is a limit to the extent to which the proportions can change.

4

We must now consider the supply curve of a factor of production to an industry. For the moment we will assume that there are no economies of large-scale industry.

[1] See p. 123, note.

If the factor which we are considering is perfectly homogeneous in respect to its efficiency in this industry, there is no difficulty in drawing its supply curve. Each unit of the factor (say an acre, or a man) is like every other from the point of view of this industry, and the elasticity of substitution between one portion of the factor and another is infinite. But the supply of the factor to the industry may be less than perfectly elastic, and its cost to the industry may rise as more of it is employed.[1] Here there is no difficulty.

But one of the commonest reasons why the supply of a factor is less than perfectly elastic to an industry is because the factor is not homogeneous in efficiency from the point of view of that industry. It is then necessary to draw up the supply curve of the factor not in its natural units, acres, men, or money capital, but in efficiency units. This can be done as follows: When a given amount of a factor, say land, is being employed by an industry, take any natural unit of the factor, for instance a certain acre, and imagine it to be replaced by other portions of the factor, everything else remaining the same. When another piece of land, working with the same amount of other factors as this standard acre, yields the same product, its efficiency is equal to that of the standard acre. The original acre, arbitrarily chosen, will thus serve as a standard unit, and other areas of land can be reduced to terms of the standard unit, so that the whole supply of land employed in the industry can be expressed in terms of this standard unit of efficiency. It is convenient to call this unit the *corrected natural unit*. It represents natural units of the factors corrected for their idiosyncrasies.[2] The elasticity of substitution, measured in terms of corrected units, will be perfect between one portion of the factor and another. That is to say, if by chance a certain piece of land or a certain number of workers, representing one corrected unit of the factor, were to demand a higher price than the rest they would be dismissed from the industry or be forced to accept the same price as the rest.

If the factor is homogeneous in regard to its efficiency, the corrected units are the same as the natural units, for instance men, acres, or a given amount of money capital, and no correction is necessary. But

---

[1] See Chapter 8 for the conditions which may produce this effect.

[2] This method of correction is not perfectly satisfactory. The relative efficiencies of different natural units may alter with the amount of other factors employed. The difference between the efficiency of a rich acre and a stony acre may be smaller when wages are low and a high proportion of labour is employed with a given amount of land than when wages are higher and fewer men are employed per acre. It is impossible to say *a priori* in which direction the difference is likely to lie, and our correction would have to be corrected in each case according to the technical conditions of the industry in question and the costs of other factors. This difficulty appears to be insuperable in some cases, but for most of the uses for which we require the conception of the supply curve of a factor to a single industry it can be overcome (see p. 344, note, below).

even if the factors are not homogeneous, so long as there are no economies of large-scale industry, when each factor is increased by, say, ten per cent. in terms of corrected natural units, physical output will also be increased by ten per cent. That is to say, there are constant physical returns. Of course if the price of one of the factors (in these units) is rising it would not in fact be increased by ten per cent. when the others were increased by ten per cent. ; an increase of ten per cent. of the physical output would in fact be produced by increasing this factor by less than ten per cent., and the others by more. But if each *were* increased in the same ratio then output *would* be increased in that ratio. It follows that the marginal physical productivity of every amount of a factor, measured in terms of the corrected units, combined in constant proportions with the other factors (again measured in corrected units), is the same, and depends merely upon the proportions of the factors.

Now supposing there are no economies of large-scale industry, so that constant physical returns obtain, draw up a supply curve in terms of corrected natural units. If the factor is heterogeneous in respect of efficiency, but the difference in efficiency between one natural unit and another is the same in this industry and in a number of other industries, the transfer costs of different units will be in the same ratio as their efficiencies,[1] and the supply curve of the factor in corrected natural units will be perfectly elastic. If the factor is scarce from the point of view of this industry, its price per corrected natural unit will increase as more is employed, and the factor will tend to give rise to increasing cost for the commodity.

5

We must now consider economies of large-scale industry, and examine the Law of Increasing Returns. The Law of Increasing Returns differs from the Law of Diminishing Returns in that it cannot be reduced to a tautology. The Law of Diminishing Returns, when the factors of production are defined in a certain way, is merely a matter of logical necessity. But the Law of Increasing Returns is a matter of empirical fact. It may be formulated thus: When an increased amount of any factor of production is devoted to a certain use, it is often the case that improvements in organisation can be introduced which will make natural units of the factor (men, acres, or money capital) more efficient, so that an increase in output does not require a proportionate increase in the physical amount of the factors. This law, or rather tendency, like the Law of Diminishing Returns, may apply equally to all the factors of production, but unlike the Law of Diminishing Returns, it does not apply in every

[1] See p. 112.

case. Sometimes an increase of the factors will lead to improvements in efficiency, and sometimes it will not.

It remains to inquire how increases in efficiency can arise. They arise because the factors of production, in the world as we know it, consist of indivisible units, each of which is not equally well adapted to performing all the tasks required in production. If all the factors of production were finely divisible, like sand, it would be possible to produce the smallest output of any commodity with all the advantages of large-scale industry. But actually the factors consist of men (providing labour and entrepreneurship); money capital, which is finely divisible, like sand, but must be turned into instruments of production each of which, for technical reasons, must be of a certain size; and land, which is usually divisible, but which sometimes, for technical reasons, cannot be divided without limit. It is therefore impossible for an industry to equip itself to produce one unit of a commodity without immediately providing capacity to produce more than one unit.

How does this fact account for a fall in cost of production as output increases? The point can be illustrated as follows: Suppose that there is one indivisible unit of a certain factor of production, and that the rest can be increased by small increments, and at constant prices. Then if the cost of the fixed factor is left out of account, the cost per unit of the product up to a certain point will be constant. At first only a part of the fixed amount of the indivisible factor will be used, and as output increases more of this factor will be brought into use. As soon as the whole of the scarce factor is in use, diminishing returns will set in, and the cost of output in terms of the other factors will rise. But meanwhile, if this indivisible factor has a certain cost which must be incurred whether it is fully utilised or not, the average share of each unit of product in this fixed cost will have been falling. Thus at first the average cost of the whole will be falling until the point is reached at which the increase in the cost of the other factors per unit of output outweighs the reduction in cost per unit of the indivisible factor.

The curve representing the average cost per unit of output of the indivisible factor is a rectangular hyperbola, subtending a rectangle equal in area to the cost of the factor, and falling continuously as output increases. The average cost of the other factors is constant up to the output OS, at which diminishing returns begin, and then rises. The curve of average total cost, which is the sum of these two curves, falls up to the output OT and then rises. The curve of marginal cost will be constant up to OS and then begin to rise, cutting the curve of average total cost at its lowest point, for the output OT. When the rise in cost has reached a certain point it will become profitable to use a second unit of the indivisible factor, and the whole process will begin again.

We are already familiar with this effect, for we have used it in the analysis of cost to the individual firm. The indivisible unit is there the entrepreneur, and the other factors are variable. But the same process is at work wherever there is an indivisible unit of a factor which requires a certain price irrespective of its output—a man, who commands a certain wage, or a machine which has a certain cost—and it is this fact which accounts for the technical economies which a firm can introduce when its output increases, over and above the economy of spreading the fixed cost of the entrepreneur over a larger output.

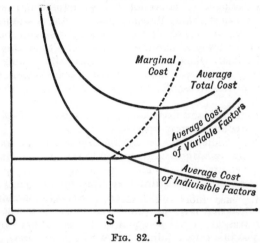

Fig. 82.

The possibility of increasing returns is widened by the fact that various units of the factors are adapted to performing different tasks. Men differ in their natural abilities, and can acquire skill when they concentrate on a single task;[1] acres vary in their natural capacities, and machines can be designed for special tasks. For any kind of production there will be a hierarchy of possible technical methods, each using more highly specialised units of the factors than the last, and production is carried out most efficiently when each separate action in the productive process is performed by a unit of a factor of production specially adapted (by nature, by practice, or by human ingenuity) to that particular task. But since the units of the factors are indivisible, the most specialised method of production will involve the largest outlay, and it is not profitable to make use of the

[1] The increase in efficiency which arises from the fact that "practice makes perfect" is itself a result of the indivisibility of the units of the factors. If labour could be finely divided, like sand, each grain of labour could be occupied constantly at a single task and could acquire the maximum amount of practice.

full equipment of highly specialised factors for a very small output. As output increases a method higher in the hierarchy of specialisation can be adopted, and for this reason cost falls as the output of a commodity increases.

The units of the factors are very often imperfectly specialised, and when output is small a single indivisible unit of a factor, for instance a man, may perform a number of different tasks. The Law of Increasing Returns is often associated with the fact that, as output increases, the number of tasks performed by indivisible units of the factors is reduced. For instance Adam Smith speaks of "the advantage which is gained by saving the time commonly lost in passing from one sort of work to another",[1] and Marshall refers to the waste involved in employing a skilled worker on tasks equally well performed by an unskilled worker, when the output is too small to occupy him constantly at a task which requires his skill.[2] But, fundamentally, the economy of large scale does not arise because particular units of the factors are versatile, but because they are not perfectly versatile.

The maximum rate of decreasing cost would occur if each unit of the factors was completely specialised and capable of performing only one task. If, in Adam Smith's pin factory, each of the workers had been bound by a rigid caste system to a single occupation, then to produce even one pin it would be necessary to employ the whole number of workers—one to draw out the wire, another to straight it, a third to cut it, and so forth. Then, if the wage per man were independent of his output,[3] the total cost of the capacity output of the team of workers would be equal to the cost of one pin, and the maximum possible rate of falling cost would be obtained. When the capacity output of one team was reached a fresh team would have to be employed and there would be no further possibilities of specialisation.

In more usual cases the units of the factors are capable of performing various tasks. Thus small outputs will be less costly than they would be if the maximum possible degree of specialisation had to be introduced at the outset. Each increase in output will require some increase in the amounts of the factors employed, but the increase in output will be more than in proportion to the increase in the factors, because more specialised indivisible units of the factors can be employed as output increases.

---

[1] *Wealth of Nations*, Book I. chap. i.

[2] *Principles*, pp. 264-65.

[3] The device of paying a unit of a factor according to its output produces the same effect as though the unit were perfectly divisible. If Adam Smith's pin makers were paid at the same rate per pin when each worked separately as when they co-operated the cost of pins would not alter as their output increased.

6

We have found that increasing returns are due to the indivisibility of particular units of the factors. In order to account for falling costs for a particular commodity it is therefore necessary to find, at some point in the productive process, a single indivisible unit of some factor of production. So long as there are a number of units of the same kind engaged in any process we know that for the existing output the possibilities of increasing returns are exhausted. There may be some higher degree of specialisation which it is not profitable to introduce unless output is increased. The single unit which will give rise to increasing returns is then, as it were, still over the horizon, but in every case where increasing returns are found there must be some point in the process of production at which a single unit of a factor is engaged.[1]

It is therefore easy to account for falling costs of production so long as only one firm is engaged upon a particular commodity. The firm may be of less than the size at which average cost is a minimum because some part of its productive equipment, a piece of plant, a salaried employee, or the entrepreneur himself, is capable of co-operating in an increase of output without any increase in cost of that part of the equipment of the firm. When competition is not perfect, firms will be in equilibrium when they are of less than optimum size (if profits are normal), and an increase in the output of a single firm would lead to a fall in average cost.

The question of whether falling cost can occur in a perfectly competitive industry is more complicated. To isolate the effect of increasing returns let us suppose that there is a perfectly elastic supply to the industry in question of all factors measured in corrected units.[2] The industry in equilibrium will be composed of a number of firms, each of optimum size. But the capacity of a single unit of entrepreneurship is limited, and it may be that when the firm is of optimum size there are still technical economies to be gained, in some departments, by a further utilisation of indivisible units of

---

[1] Cf. Robinson, *Structure of Competitive Industry*, p. 25.

[2] If we say that the supply of the factor is perfectly elastic to a certain industry, we mean that when more labour, capital, land, or enterprise is devoted to one industry, it is attracted by the same payment as before, but once it finds its way into the industry, its efficiency may be increased by specialisation, so that its efficiency price to this industry falls, not because it has become cheaper in general, but because a given portion of it can be turned to better use when a greater total is being employed. When we are studying the question of increasing returns, not in one industry but in industry in general, it is impossible to assume a price for the factor in general, and the inquiry becomes mysterious and difficult in the extreme. As long as we are studying one industry in isolation it can be imagined as drawing upon a general pool of the factor in question, and the cost of a natural unit of the factor can be measured in terms of money price.

z

the factors or by a higher degree of specialisation of the factors, which are not realised because they are outweighed by diseconomies of large-scale management.[1]

We are tempted to conclude that increasing returns could then occur through the specialisation of firms. Each firm may relieve the strain upon management by abandoning some processes of manu-facture to other firms, and so be enabled to carry out the production which it retains upon a larger scale, making use of those indivisible units of the factors which were not fully occupied before. More technical economies can thus be realised, and at the same time it is possible that there will be an additional gain from the fact that individual entrepreneurs, concentrating upon a smaller part of the productive process, may acquire specialised knowledge and skill. But we must examine the matter more closely before we can be satisfied that the specialisation of firms can lead to decreasing cost under the conditions of perfect competition.

The specialisation of firms may be of two types, lateral disin-tegration [2] and vertical disintegration. Lateral disintegration is the process by which firms, each formerly producing a number of different commodities or types of a commodity, gradually specialise upon a narrower and narrower range of products until (at the last resort) each is only producing a single type of a single commodity. Pro-fessor Pigou finds in this process a sufficient explanation for the existence of decreasing supply price, and he quotes as an example the contrast between the British and German cotton industries. The British industry is larger and more highly specialised than the German industry. "The range of work undertaken by the typical factory in Germany is far greater than that undertaken by the typical factory in England. Hence naturally the skill of the operatives is far less in Germany; more time is wasted and factory organisation is less perfect."[3] This principle of lateral disintegration is of the greatest importance in the real world, but will it serve to explain the existence of decreasing costs under conditions of perfect com-petition? If an industry grows up from the first in a perfect market, we should expect it to develop from the beginning the maximum possible degree of specialisation. If there is anything to be gained by concentrating upon a few counts of cotton we should expect a perfectly competitive spinning industry, while it was still upon a relatively small scale, to consist of a number of firms each producing different counts. It would consist, in short, of a number of industries,

---

[1] Cf. Robinson, *Structure of Competitive Industry*, chap. vii.

[2] It would be more natural to speak of horizontal disintegration, but "hori-zontal integration" is commonly used to mean the combination of firms making the same article, and "horizontal disintegration" had best be preserved to mean the contrary process.

[3] Sir Sydney Chapman, quoted by Professor Pigou, *Economics of Welfare*, p. 221.

each in the hands of a monopolist. At first, as the industry grew, there would be some decrease of costs, for as the market in each count increased, the firms could specialise each upon fewer counts ; but as soon as the market was large enough to support several firms each producing the same count, the decrease of costs would come to an end, since there would be no further possibility of gaining economies by specialisation. This criticism upon Professor Pigou's argument serves to show one of the absurdities latent in the assumption of a perfect market. It is very unlikely that the saving in cost upon a consignment of yarn, due to extreme specialisation between firms, would be large enough to offset the inconvenience and expense to the purchaser due to ordering each count from a separate producer. If a manufacturer requires a number of different types of yarn at the same time he will prefer to order them all from the same house, unless the prices quoted by a firm which can supply him with all of them are considerably higher than the prices quoted by firms which each specialise upon one or two. But we are now engaged in discussing a perfectly competitive industry, selling in a perfect market. In a perfect market, the customer must be assumed to prefer the goods of the firm that can sell them at the cheapest price, however small the difference in price, and however great the other advantages offered by a firm whose price is slightly greater. Thus in a perfect market the maximum degree of specialisation between firms would come about from the beginning, and the only type of decreasing cost which we should expect to find is that which occurs in a one-firm industry, when the firm is of less than optimum size.

Lateral disintegration, upon our definition of an industry, is the separation of a single industry into a number of parallel industries. Vertical disintegration [1] is the separation of an industry into a series of processes each carried on by separate firms. The cotton industry will again provide an example. In England the cotton industry is divided into sections consisting of firms each devoted to a single process, spinning, weaving, bleaching, dyeing, and so forth. The business of dealing in raw cotton and of selling in foreign markets is also disintegrated and is in the hands of brokers and merchants separated from the producing firms. In Japan, on the other hand, single firms carry out the whole process from buying cotton to selling piece-goods. In the cotton industry the maximum possible degree of vertical disintegration is rapidly attained. When spinning is separated from weaving, neither process can be subdivided any further, but in the case of a complicated object like a motor car, the possibilities of disintegration are almost endless. If a motor firm begins to feel the pressure of diminishing returns from entrepreneurship, as it grows in size, it can abandon the manufacture of some

[1] See Robinson, *Structure of Competitive Industry*, p. 110.

part of the car, the radiator or the body for instance, to a specialist firm, and continue to increase its output of cars without increasing its staff. Meanwhile the specialist firm, as the scale of its output increases, will gain from those technical economies which could not be achieved by the car-producing firms because each individually produced too few of this particular part to allow their full development.[1]

In vertical disintegration as much as in lateral disintegration the degree of specialisation depends upon the size of the market, and again we should expect under perfect competition to find the maximum degree of specialisation at each stage in the growth of the industry. As soon as two or three firms were engaged on each process, we should expect to find that the possibilities of further decreasing cost had come to an end.[2]

Thus we find that when we follow out strictly all the implications of the assumption of perfect competition the grounds for expecting decreasing cost due to the specialisation of firms are very much narrowed, and it is only when there is at some point in the productive process a single indivisible unit of a factor at work (in this case a single specialist firm) that decreasing costs can occur.

If there are no economies from disintegration, either because all the technical economies of large-scale production were already exhausted before the firms grew to the optimum size, or because for technical reasons vertical disintegration is impossible, or because all the economies of disintegration have already been brought about and no further specialisation is possible, then an increase in the output of the industry can only come about by the addition of optimum firms, each like the rest, or of groups of firms carrying out between them the whole productive process.

Even then it is possible that there may be falling costs, for there may be *external economies*. When a new firm enters the industry it may enable all the firms to produce more cheaply so that, while each produces at its minimum average cost, the cost at the minimum is

---

[1] The vertical disintegration of the British motor industry is continuing every year, and Mr. Ford, whose aim was formerly to control the whole process of manufacture from growing raw rubber for his tyres, has now begun to proclaim its benefits; see *Moving Forward*, pp. 153-54.

[2] We should expect, however, that vertical disintegration would take place less rapidly, as output increases, than lateral disintegration. There will be certain costs of co-ordinating the disintegrated processes which will be reflected in the cost of the commodity. If a commodity is manufactured by a number of processes, each carried on by a different firm, there must be some costs of transport, including the costs of ordering and invoicing, involved in assembling the parts of the finished product. These costs are likely to decline as output increases, for there will be economies in handling goods on a large scale. Thus a degree of disintegration may become profitable for a large output which would not be profitable for a smaller output even though some technical economies could already be gained when the output was small.

reduced. The simplest example of this type of external economies is the case where machinery can be bought more cheaply when the industry presents a larger market to the machine-making industry.[1] But this is properly to be regarded as an example of vertical disintegration. The machine-making industry represents a part of the productive process, already disintegrated from the main industry, which is working under falling costs. We must, then, inquire how the machine-making industry came to have falling costs, and so we pursue the whole inquiry afresh, and find the falling costs to be due either to the existence of a single sub-optimum firm,[2] or to increasing returns due to the progressive specialisation of firms, or to external economies. If they are due to external economies, we must again pursue them until they are finally run to earth.

But there is another type of external economy which does not arise from the scale of a subsidiary industry. If a large labour force is accustomed to work at a certain trade, it may be that a traditional skill is developed, and each individual worker is more competent than he would have been in a smaller industry. Economies of this type, however, which can be found to depend on the size of the industry whose supply curve we are considering, rather than upon the general development of industry, are likely to be rare and unimportant, unless the industry is growing from a very small initial size.

7

External economies and the economies of specialisation of firms may be grouped together under the title of economies of large-scale industry, as opposed to the economies of individual expansion, or internal economies, which depend upon the size of the firm. Economies of large-scale industry are likely to have the effect of altering the optimum size of the firm, and the reorganisation of the firm to adapt

---

[1] In order to study the principle of increasing returns or of diminishing returns in any one particular industry it is necessary to suppose that a change in the amount of any factor employed in this industry has a negligible effect upon the price and efficiency of the factor in general. If this condition is not fulfilled, any change in one industry will alter all costs of production and therefore will have a reaction upon the demand curve for the commodity produced by the industry in question. In practice this condition will often fail to be fulfilled. For instance any increase in the scale of any one industry in a certain district is likely to reduce the costs of all industries in respect of transport, banking, and other facilities enjoyed in common by all the local industries. All the commodities produced in the district will therefore become cheaper, and the demand curve for the commodity produced by the expanding industry will be likely to alter. In such a case it is impossible to treat the demand curve for the commodity as independent of the amount produced. See Sraffa, *Economic Journal*, December 1926.

[2] The fact that the sub-optimum firm must be a monopoly complicates the position. Not every increase in demand will lead to lower prices, though it will lead to lower average cost.

itself to the new optimum size may lead to further economies. These have been described by Mr. Robertson as internal-external economies.[1] They are internal economies, because they depend upon the size of the firm, and external economies because they depend upon the size of the industry. It is easier, *a priori*, to think of reasons why the optimum firm should grow smaller as the result of external economies[2] than of the reasons why it should grow larger. The cheapening of machinery, for instance, will reduce one of the advantages which large firms have over small. If a specialised machine becomes cheaper, the loss due to working it at less than its full capacity becomes smaller, and one of the influences tending towards a large optimum technical size for the firm becomes less strong. On the other hand, any influence tending to reduce the costs of other factors relatively to the cost of entrepreneurship will increase the optimum size of the firm. Professor Pigou, following Marshall,[3] asserts that in general firms tend to grow with the growth of the industry, but the fact that this occurs in the real world can be accounted for by the fact that in an imperfect market the equilibrium size of firms is likely to increase as the industry expands.[4] In the real world there is no reason to expect that firms are at their optimum size, and the fact that firms are growing does not prove that the optimum is becoming larger. Moreover, in the real world inventions have to be taken into account, and a historical movement toward the growth of firms may be due to the introduction of new methods of production suitable to large-scale use. However this may be, the internal-external economies are not likely to be of much importance compared with the economies of large-scale industry which give rise to them.

We may summarise the results of the foregoing analysis as follows. Decreasing costs may occur for the output of a firm of less than optimum size; and for a perfectly competitive industry they may occur when the optimum size of the individual firm is not sufficiently large to allow the full development of all the possible technical economies of large-scale production in every process, so that increasing returns arise from the specialisation of firms, and even when

---

[1] "Symposium", *Economic Journal*, March 1930, p. 86.

[2] The effect of specialisation upon the size of firms is difficult to discuss, because of the difficulty of defining size. Ordinarily we should measure the size of a firm by its output, but this becomes impossible when the output is changing in nature as the result of specialisation. Measurement by men employed is too crude, and by men *plus* equipment too complicated to be of use. Since the point has not much relevance to the present discussion, it does not seem worth while to attempt to devise an index for the measurement of the size of the firm; cf. Shove, *Economic Journal*, March 1930, p. 115.

[3] *Economics of Welfare*, p. 221; *Principles*, p. 318.

[4] See p. 101. Marshall, who never followed out in the text of the *Principles* the rigid view of perfect competition implicit in his diagrams, may have had this effect in mind.

all the possibilities of specialisation have been exhausted decreasing cost may be due to external economies.

8

In every case increasing returns arise from improvements in productive technique. As output increases the efficiency of the factors can be increased by the fuller utilisation of indivisible units of the factors, or by the adoption of more specialised methods of production. Thus increasing returns are fundamentally different from diminishing returns, which are brought into play, not by a change in the efficiency of the factors, but by an alteration in their price. It is possible, however, to devise a method by which the economies of large-scale industry can be represented in terms of the prices of the factors, so that increasing returns from the point of view of a single industry can be treated in a manner symmetrical with diminishing returns.

We will first consider the simplest type of economies of large-scale industry. Suppose that the same kind of machines are used when the industry expands and the machines become cheaper. Then if we add, say, ten per cent. to the other factors (in terms of corrected natural units) and ten per cent. to the number of machines, we shall have added ten per cent. to output. Thus the machine can be regarded as an efficiency unit of capital, and increasing returns of this simple type could be regarded as arising from a fall in the price of these efficiency units of capital when more are employed.

More complicated types of increasing returns can be treated in the same way, but when the technique of production changes as output is increased it ceases to be possible to see immediately in what the efficiency unit consists. An efficiency unit, however, can be devised as follows: First increase each factor except one by ten per cent. in terms of corrected natural units; now increase the remaining factor, say capital, until ten per cent. is added to the output. If there were no economies it would need an increase of ten per cent. in units of money capital;[1] if there are economies, it will need an increase of less than ten per cent. We shall then say that we have increased capital by ten per cent. in units of efficiency. We are thus provided with an efficiency unit of capital in which to draw up the supply curve of capital to the industry. If it requires less than ten per cent. increase in money value of capital to increase output by ten per cent. (when all other factors are increased ten per cent.), and if the supply of capital in money units is perfectly elastic, the cost of capital will have been increased by less than ten per cent., and the supply price

---

[1] Since we measure capital in units of money for long-period problems, no correction for non-homogeneity will be needed in this case, and the corrected natural units will be the same as the natural units.

of capital in terms of these efficiency units will be falling.[1] Thus economies of large-scale industry can be represented by a falling supply curve (in efficiency units) of one of the factors to the industry. In the same way, when we were considering the simple case of machines which become cheaper without altering their form, the machine is the efficiency unit, and since the corrected unit of capital

[1] When the technique of production alters as output increases, a difficulty arises similar to that which was discussed in the note to p. 332. The change in efficiency due to a given increase in corrected units of capital (that is to say, money) will depend not only on the amount of capital employed in the first position, but also on the amount of other factors employed in the first position. The amount of other factors will depend on their costs; thus the supply curve of capital in terms of efficiency units is not independent of the supply curves of the other factors. In the simplest possible case, when the factors are uniform in nature, but falling in supply price, like the machines which become cheaper when more are employed, this difficulty does not arise, but in order to use this device for more complicated cases it is necessary to have a base line from which to start—some point at which the combination of the factors is known. For increases of output beyond this point the device will work accurately, but if the base line changes, all the separate supply curves of the factors have to be redrawn.

In some of the cases in which we have made use of this device there can actually be no base line. For instance, when we are comparing monopoly with competition, the proportions of the factors under monopoly (either producing a given output or working with a given number of men) may be different at every point from the proportions under competition. We introduced the separate supply curves of the factors in order to deal with the fact that the average cost curve of the commodity and the average net productivity curve of labour are not always the same under monopoly and competition. We now find that even the separate supply curves are not always the same under monopoly and competition. It was for this reason that, in the foregoing chapters, when we discussed economies of large-scale industry (shown by a falling supply curve of capital), we took as an example the case of machines becoming cheaper but unchanged in form, when more are employed by an industry, for in that case the supply curve of the factor is independent of the proportions in which it is used. It need not cause us much distress to discover that even the corrected comparisons between monopoly and competition are often inaccurate. There are so many general common-sense reasons why these comparisons should not be made (see Chapter 14) that we have not lost much when we discover this somewhat refined analytical reason why they cannot be made.

In the other cases where we have made use of this device it will not betray us. When we discuss the competitive demand curve for labour, we take as data the demand curve of the commodity and the supply curves (in natural units) of the other factors. We can then start at any point with the proportion of other factors (in natural units) to a given number of men, and then, taking this as the base line, construct the supply curves of the other factors in efficiency units for greater or smaller amounts. When we discuss the composition of the competitive supply curve, we must take as data the supply curves in natural units of all the factors. Then, starting from any output of the commodity, with the proportions of the factors that would be used in making it, we can draw up the supply curves of the separate factors in efficiency units for greater or smaller outputs.

Thus it is only in the comparisons between monopoly and competition, and then only in certain cases, that the above objection to our analytical device impairs its validity.

is a certain amount of money, this unit becomes more efficient when more is employed, because it can buy more machines as the machines become cheaper, and the supply price in efficiency units is falling. In more complicated types of economies of large-scale industry it cannot so easily be seen to which factor the economies can be attributed, but by means of this device they can be represented in the supply curve of any one of the factors, arbitrarily chosen.

When the amounts of the factors are measured in terms of efficiency units, constant physical returns will prevail. That is to say that when the amount of each factor in efficiency units is increased in the same proportion, output will also be increased in that proportion and the marginal physical productivity of each factor (measured in efficiency units) will be the same as before. Thus by means of this device conditions of constant physical returns are established, and any change can be imputed to the prices of efficiency units of the factors. This device for drawing up the supply curves of the factors throws no fresh light on the nature of increasing and diminishing returns, and can tell us nothing that we do not know already about the cost curve of a commodity. It is merely a piece of analytical apparatus which makes it possible to treat every type of increasing and diminishing returns in the terms appropriate to the simplest possible type, the type in which a uniform factor of production, composed of exactly similar men, acres, or machines, has a rising or falling supply price to an industry.

9

In the course of the argument in the foregoing chapters, we have made use of this device. When we drew up the demand curve for labour of a competitive industry we reckoned labour in natural units (men) and allowed economies to show themselves in a falling supply curve (in efficiency units) of the other factor (capital). If we wished to draw up a demand curve for capital, we should reverse the process and reckon capital in units of money and labour in units of efficiency, so that if there were economies of large-scale industry they would be shown in a falling supply curve of labour.

When we were dealing with the demand for labour of an individual firm, we found it unnecessary to make use of this device. We reckoned both labour and capital in physical units (men and money capital) and allowed the economies of large scale of the firm to show themselves merely in the increase of the physical productivity of labour and capital as the amount employed by the firm increases.

In comparing the demand for labour under monopoly and competition, we had to consider the relationships of the marginal productivity of a factor to the firm with its marginal productivity to the industry. One is the marginal physical productivity of the factor to the firm multiplied by the price of the commodity; the other is marginal physical productivity to the industry multiplied by marginal revenue. It remains to show that we were justified in treating marginal physical productivity to the firm and to the industry as identical, so that the ratio of the marginal productivity of a factor to the firm to its marginal productivity to the industry is the same as the ratio of price to marginal revenue. If we were to reckon any factor not in efficiency units but in natural units, this would not be true. To take, once more, the simplest case in which capital consists of a certain type of machines which become cheaper (without any other alteration) when more are employed: then if we measure capital in money (which is the corrected natural unit), when one firm increases the amount of capital which it employs by one unit of money capital, machines become cheaper for all the firms, and if the amount of capital employed by the other firms measured in money remains constant, they are using more machines and producing a larger output. Thus marginal physical productivity to the industry would be greater than to the firm. But if we measure capital in efficiency units (in this case the machines, which are all alike) and if the only economy consists in the fall in the price of machines, then when one firm increases its employment of capital by one efficiency unit, a machine, and the other firms keep constant the amount of capital in efficiency units (that is, the number of machines), their output does not increase, and the whole benefit to them is shown in the fall in the price of machines. The marginal physical productivity of capital, measured in efficiency units, is then the same to the firm and the industry.

More complicated cases can be treated in the same way. If the number of efficiency units of capital employed by the other firms remains constant when the amount employed by one firm increases, then (by the definition of an efficiency unit) their output remains constant, and marginal physical productivity to the firm and to the industry are identical. The benefit to the industry due to the increase in capital is shown entirely in the cheapening of the efficiency unit of capital, that is to say, it is shown in the supply curve of capital to the industry, and not in the physical productivity of capital. Thus, when the whole of the economies are represented in the supply curve of the factor whose marginal productivity we are measuring, the marginal physical productivity of that factor is the same to the firm and to the industry. If the economies are shown in the supply curve of some other factor, this will not be the case. If economies are shown in the supply curve of capital, the marginal physical productivity of labour to the industry will be greater than to the firm.

10

We find that it is possible to represent both increasing returns and diminishing returns in the supply curves of the factors to an industry and from the point of view of a single industry they are perfectly symmetrical. Diminishing returns arise from a rise in the efficiency cost of a factor when more is employed, and increasing returns arise from a fall in the efficiency cost of a factor when more is employed.

But in their nature, as we have seen, increasing and diminishing returns are not symmetrical. Increasing returns arise when the employment of more of a factor has a favourable reaction upon the efficiency of the units already employed, and diminishing returns arise when the employment of more of a factor has an unfavourable reaction upon the price of the units already employed.

A type of increasing return symmetrical with diminishing returns would arise if a factor became cheaper (its efficiency remaining the same) when more was employed. This is very unlikely to occur in practice.[1] A type of diminishing returns symmetrical with increasing returns would arise if a factor became less efficient (its price remaining the same) when more was employed. This may sometimes occur. We found that increasing returns to an industry would arise in three ways. Firstly, it can arise from specialisation of firms. It is impossible to find a type of decreasing returns symmetrical with this. Secondly, it can arise from external economies which are independent of the size of any subsidiary industry, for instance from an improvement in the natural gifts of the labour force when a larger number of men are employed in one industry. If it were the case that when a large labour force was devoted to a single industry the labour deteriorated, so that each man became less competent when more were employed, we should have an external diseconomy symmetrical with this type of external economy. Thirdly, external economies can arise when a subsidiary industry becomes more efficient as it grows in size. External diseconomies symmetrical with this type of external economies are more likely to occur. If a machine-making industry were working under increasing cost, the supply price of machines would rise, and the same amount of capital, supplied at the same rate of interest, would buy fewer or worse machines. This would have the same effect from the point of view of the industry as if the supply price of capital rose when more was employed. But we must not

---

[1] A reduction in piece-rates may sometimes lead to an increase in the supply of labour, since each man may produce more pieces when he is paid less per piece. But this does not provide a true example of a falling supply curve of labour, since here it is the fall in the price of labour which is the cause of the increase in supply, and not the increase in supply which is the cause of a fall in price.

leave the matter until we have inquired why the machine-making industry is working under increasing cost,[1] and this must be due to a scarce factor of production somewhere, or else to the somewhat improbable cause of an actual deterioration of factors, supplied at the same price, as in the case where we imagined that workers became less competent when more were employed. Thus we find that the common types of increasing and diminishing returns are not symmetrical, but that it is possible to imagine cases in which the common type of diminishing return (due to a scarce factor) would be symmetrical with a rare type of increasing return (when the factor becomes cheaper as more is employed), and in which the common type of increasing return (due to improvements in the efficiency of the factor) is symmetrical with a rare type of diminishing return (when the factor deteriorates as more is employed). In any case from the point of view of an industry increasing and diminishing returns are perfectly symmetrical.[2]

Although from the point of view of an industry the various types of diminishing returns and of increasing returns can be regarded as symmetrical, the distinctions between them are of fundamental importance to society as a whole. A change in efficiency represents a net gain or loss to society as a whole, while a change in price does not. Thus changes in cost which are due to the rare type of diminishing returns and the common type of increasing returns (changes in the efficiency of the factors) are increasing or decreasing cost both from the point of view of the industry and from the point of view of society; while changes in cost due to the rare type of increasing returns and the common type of diminishing returns (changes in the price of the factors) are decreasing or increasing cost only from the point of view of the industry, and not from the point of view of society.[3]

---

[1] If the subsidiary industry is in a foreign country the chase may be conceived to end at the frontiers of the home country. Professor Pigou regards a rise in the price of imported raw materials (when the home industry expands) as an example of diseconomies of large scale to the home industry rather than as the result of the existence of a scarce factor of production. (*Economics of Welfare*, p. 222.)

[2] In the analysis set out in this book no account has been taken of decreasing cost due to a change in the price of the factors, or of increasing cost due to a change in the efficiency of the factors (measured in each case in terms of corrected natural units). But the analysis can easily be adapted to deal with these rare types of decreasing and increasing cost.

[3] See *Economics of Welfare*, pp. 219-27.

INDEX

Note.—References to Professor Pigou's *Economics of Welfare* are to the Third Edition, and to Marshall's *Principles of Economics* are to the Seventh Edition, which is identical with the Eighth Edition.

THE END